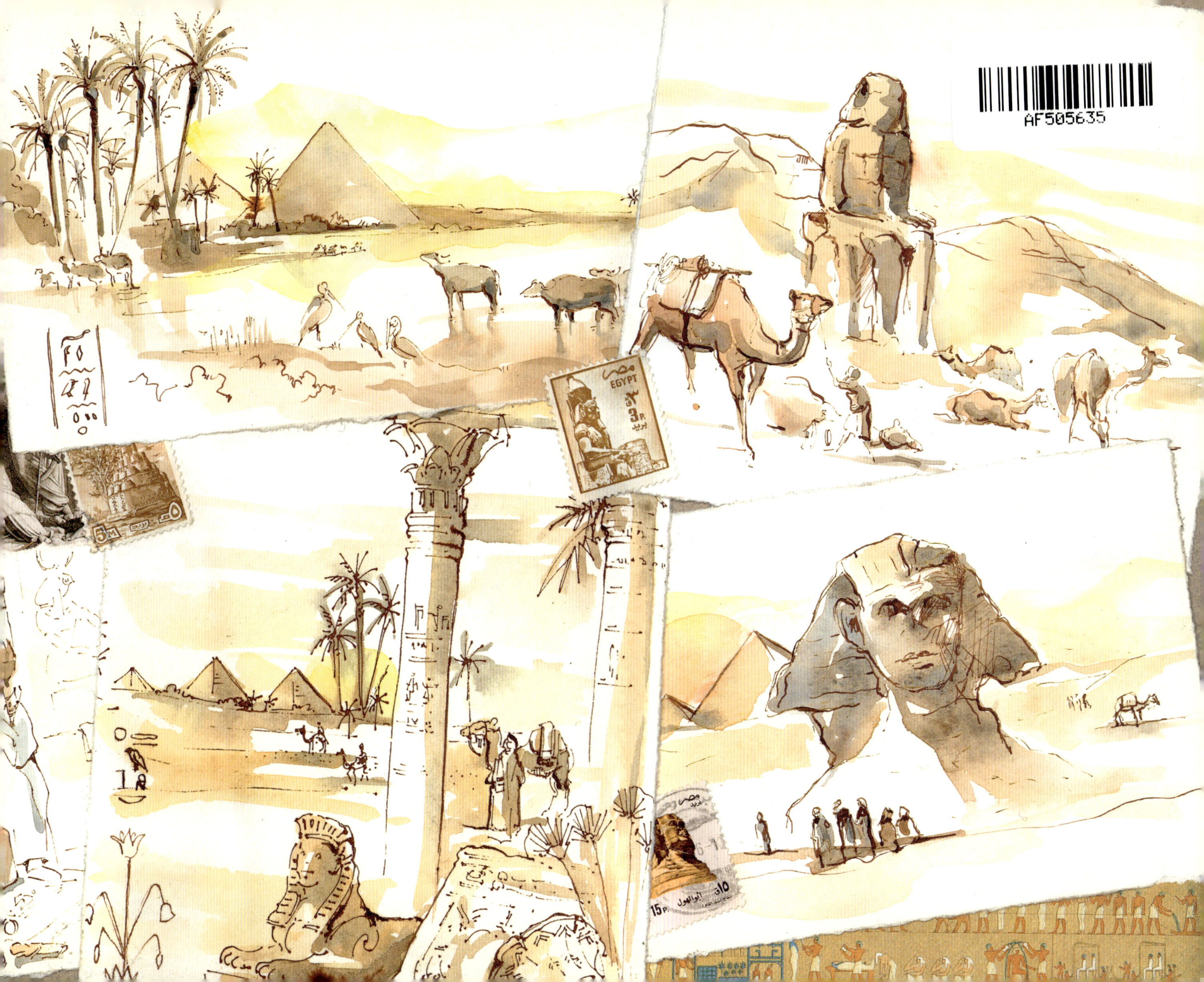

AF505635
EGYPT
3 P.
5 M
15 P.
أبو الهول

FLORINE ASCH

My Egyptian Sketchbook

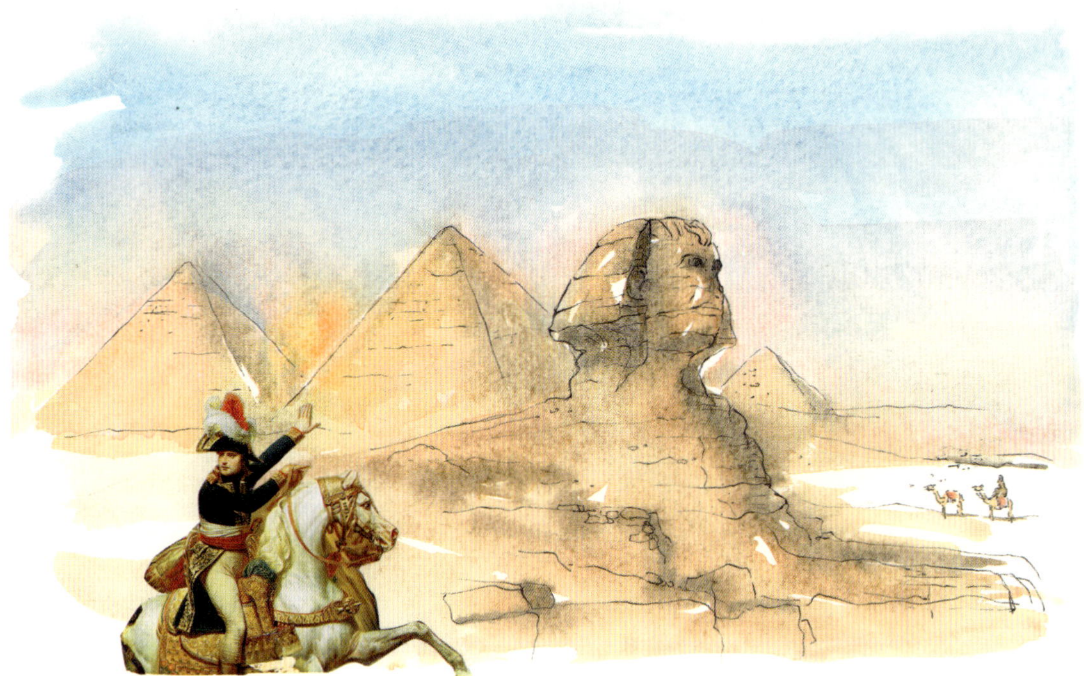

Flammarion

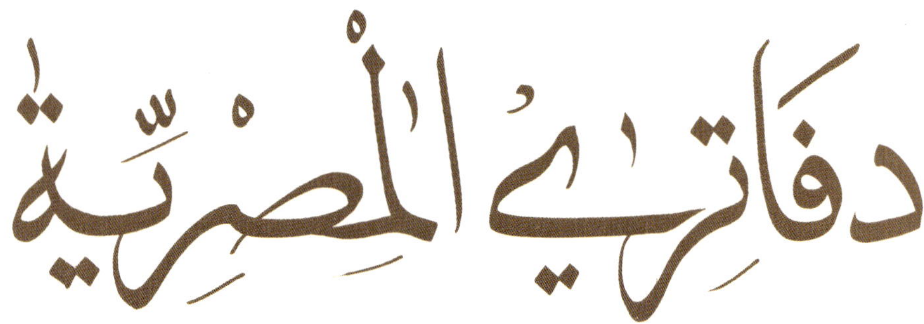

Translated from the French by Fui Lee Luk
Copyediting: Chrisoula Petridis
Typesetting: Thomas Gravemaker
Proofreading: Linda Gardiner
Color Separation: Eurésys

Previously published in French
as *Mes Carnets d'Egypte*
© Éditions Flammarion, 2003
English-language edition
© Éditions Flammarion, 2004

Images © Florine Asch

Quotations
© 1996, *Flaubert in Egypt*, Penguin Classics
© 1999, *Selected Writings*, Penguin Classics
© 2001, *Dictionnaire amoureux de l'Égypte*,
Éditions Plon

All rights reserved. No part of this publication
may be reproduced in any form or by any
means, electronic, photocopy, information
retrieval system, or otherwise, without
written permission from Éditions Flammarion.

26, rue Racine
75006 Paris
www.editions.flammarion.com

04 05 06 4 3 2 1
FC0439-04-III
ISBN: 2-0803-0439-9
Dépôt légal: 03/2004

Printed in Spain by JCG

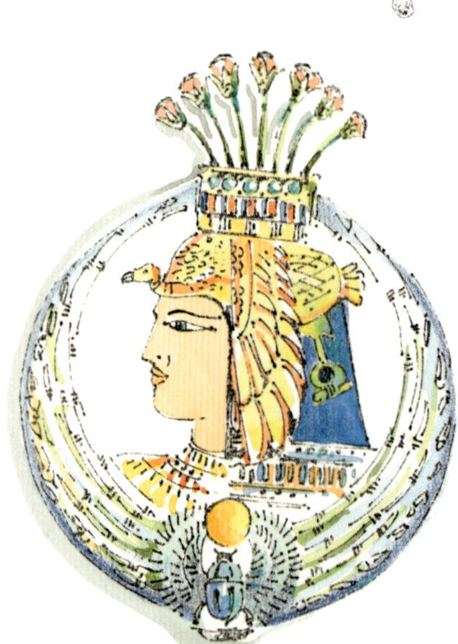

"My Egyptian sketchbook" was published
with the help of Banque Misr.

WATERCOLORS BY FLORINE ASCH

Preface by Christiane Desroches Noblecourt

My Egyptian Sketchbook

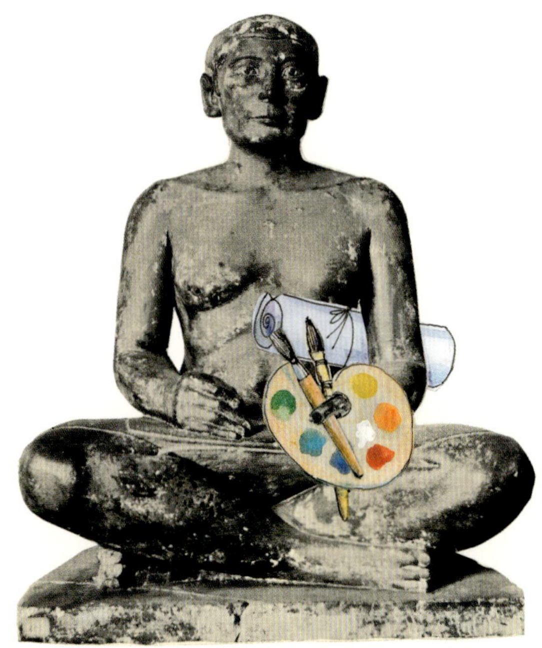

To my uncle, Paul Barba Negra

Flammarion

Egypt through Florine's eyes   by Christiane Desroches Noblecourt

Florine phoned me, and then came to visit, a portfolio tucked under one arm. With a smile, she spread out on my table several of her luminous watercolors, which reflected the light of Egypt. Her editor had already sent me one of her recent books, which featured her witty impressions of Italy. So how could I resist wanting to get to know the Egypt she had captured over a number of short trips?

This is Egypt as Florine experienced it. Throughout, her soft colors are a treat for the eyes. Her curiosity and original way of looking at things led her to stray from the well-beaten tourist track. She visited the most renowned archaeological sites and had to portray the imposing pyramids, but to bring them closer to us, she has the diminutive yet spirited Napoleon introduce them—on horseback, of course. Turning her attention to less familiar sights, Florine discovered the surprising gentleness of the Egyptian countryside where the timeless and hospitable fellahin divide their time between crops, animals, and their families and friends. Her curiosity also led her to Nubia, where she paid homage to the colossi of the great Ramses. She also discreetly portrays the somewhat old-fashioned yet still welcoming ambience of a grand hotel, the Old Cataract at Aswan, once home to lords, ladies, and maharajahs. Saving the oases of the Western Desert for future trips, she discovered new scenery and new colors further north, at Siwa, near the Libyan border, where the oracle of Ammon crowned Alexander the Great. From there she entered the inner chambers of the dwellings of the pashas, where the furniture expresses the opulence of the French Second Empire—a style adopted in Egypt after France's Empress Eugénie visited the Suez Canal. Florine's watercolors also record her fleeting visit to the museum of pharaonic antiquities in Cairo—at the very moment when the man on duty was slowly but surely carrying out his dusting chores. At the *souks*, she observes vendors of spices, fabrics, fruit, leather, lamps, and gold—and even the last tarboosh maker.

She takes us to the famous El-Fishawy café where men play never-ending games of backgammon. The presence of a regular, wrapped from head to toe and calmly smoking her narghile, is not lost to Florine's paintbrush. It is clear that the charming artist

Nefertiti

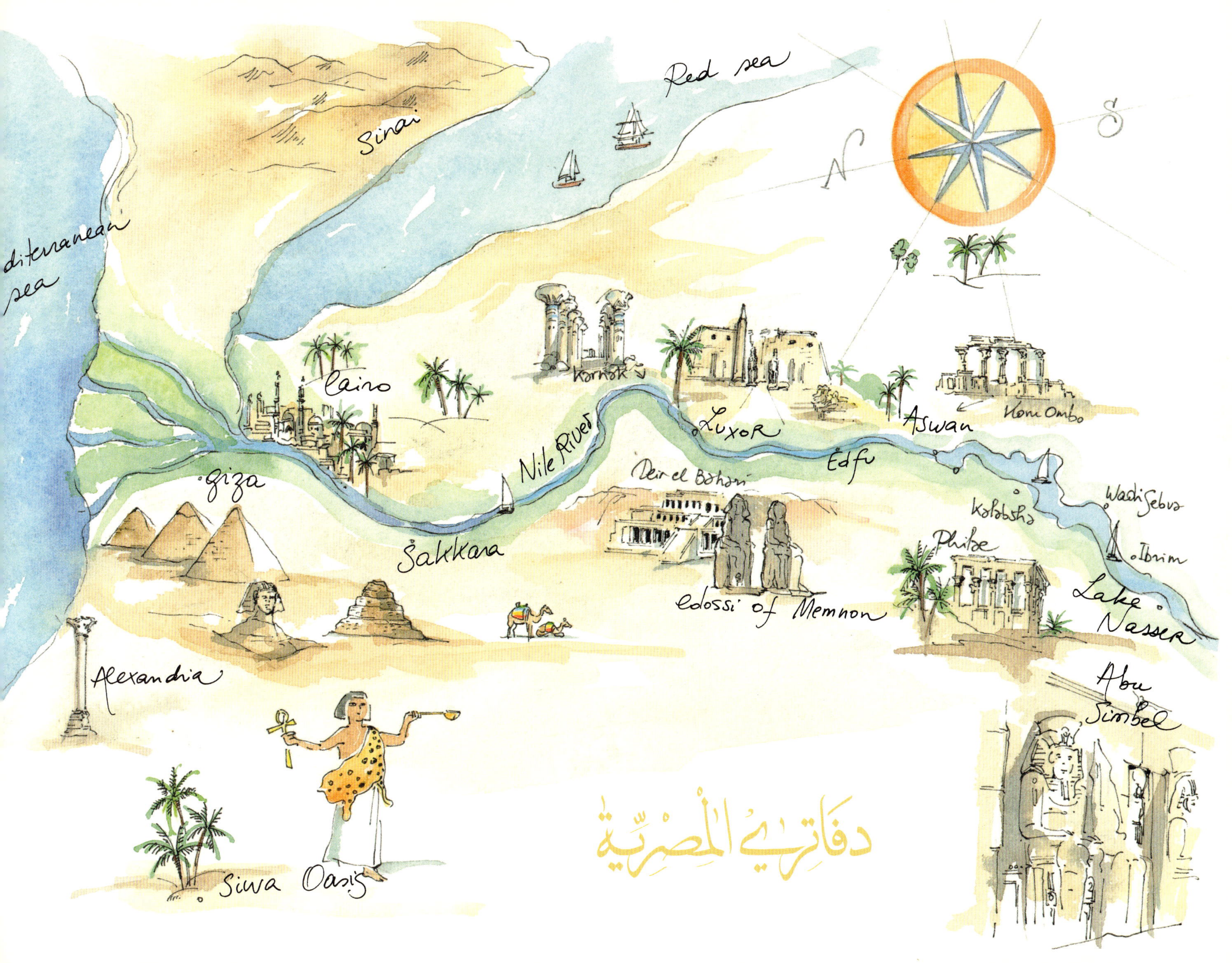
Red sea
Sinai
diteranean sea
N
S
Cairo
Karnak
Luxor
Kom Ombo
Aswan
Nile River
Edfu
Giza
Deir el Bahari
Wadi Sebua
Kolabsha
Sakkara
Ibrim
Philae
Colossi of Memnon
Lake Nasser
Alexandria
Abu Simbel
Siwa Oasis
دفاتري المصرية

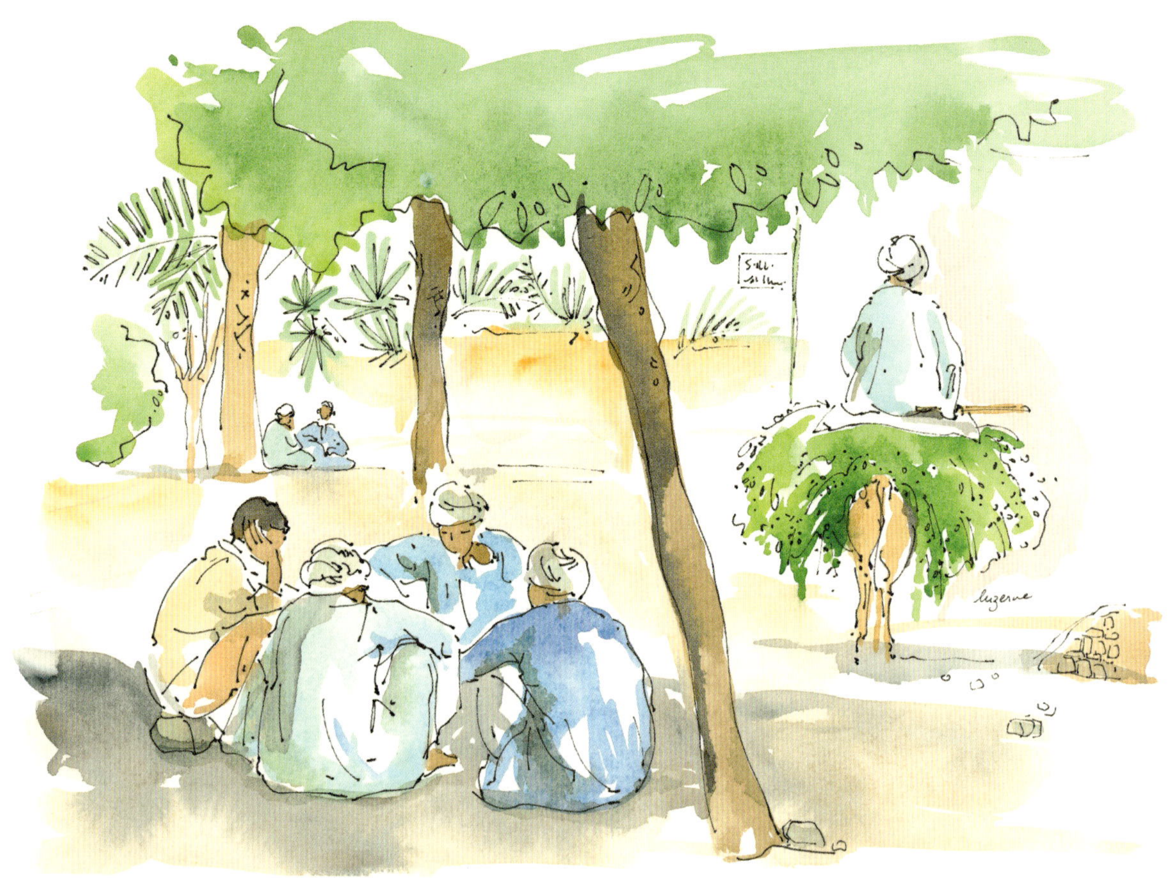

has succeeded in capturing the Egyptian sense of humor, which seems to have accompanied her throughout her stay on the banks of the Nile. Thus, she allows us to delight in the sight of a fellah family, dressed in galabias—long, loose traditional robes—visiting the tomb of a distant ancestor. The chapel wall is decorated with a still shimmering painting of delectable young barely-dressed Theban women. The fellahin can hardly believe their eyes.

Christiane Desroches Noblecourt is an Egyptologist and the Honorary General Curator of the Museums of France. She helped introduce Egypt to a wide public through her numerous works, including Tutankhamen: Life and Death of a Pharaoh *(Bulfinch Press, 1976) and* The Great Pharaoh Ramses and His Time *(Hacker Art Books, 1988).*

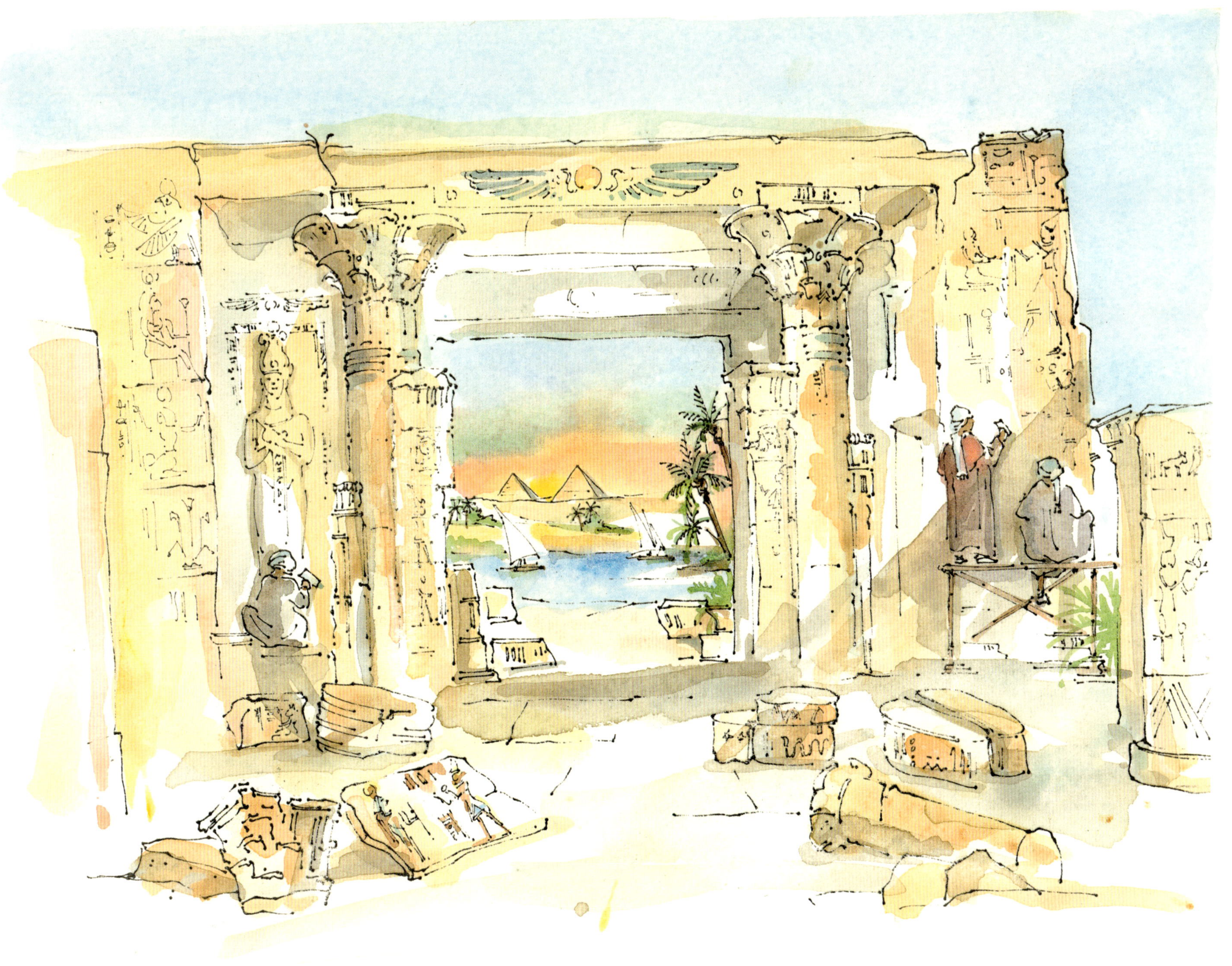

We first saw Florine Asch at work at what for us is a microcosm of ancient Egypt: the sphinx temple of Wadi el-Sebuah. Lost in the wilderness of desert and water that is central to the vast landscape of Nubia, it was (like so many sites in that area) saved from inundation by the High Dam at Aswan, whose construction allowed the preservation of part of Egypt's heritage—a heritage of infinite value to us all. So it was a good place to see Florine's use of the eyes and the imagination, and her infusion of both with happiness and artistry, all harnessed in tribute to Egypt. The watching sphinxes doubtless approved of what they saw—though, being inscrutable, they would not admit it.

Egyptology is a very exact—and exacting—science. One of the remarkable features of our knowledge of ancient Egypt is the precision of that science. We see the scientific method at work from the nineteenth century when Napoleon's team of savants drew up the great *La Description de l'Égypte*, a precise and objective account of the Egypt they discovered. Egypt certainly deserves this attention. This country has a modern personality and culture of enormous significance, but also an ancient past, which spanned three of the last five thousand years. What Florine offers, looking at Egypt through the artist's imaginative eye, blessed with free hand and free spirit, is a picture which does not conflict with the precise and exacting nature of Egyptology, but complements it—even though she is the first to admit that she is not concerned with producing a scientific record of what she has seen, but a notebook of her travels.

It is therefore worth bearing in mind that even *La Description* starts with an appeal to the imagination. The frontispiece of the first tome depicts a capricious Nile winding through a summary of all the wonders recorded in succeeding volumes. In truth, a journey through Egypt raises the same question for the Egyptologist as for those of us with a non-scientific approach to the Egyptian past. What is it that causes Egypt to inspire so many with a vital resonance? Why does it have such power over the receptive eye?

Is it, for example, that ancient Egyptian art was fashioned and developed from such early times, and over so long a period, that it came to embody some deeper truths about things to which the human mind is particularly ready to respond? Not for nothing do symbols such as obelisks and sphinxes seem

Bakelite candlestick

familiar parts of modern landscapes far from the banks of the Nile. Not for nothing does the Hymn to the Sun contain well-recognized echoes of the language in the Psalms.

Or is it that throughout the centuries, Egypt and the Egyptians have shown a greater pull towards the compass points of peace and happiness than pain and war? Not for nothing do the carefully crafted images of the ancient world, portraying funeral bearers, or crews of ships under sail, to take two random examples, show gently smiling faces. Not for nothing do the reliefs in tombs show that the idea of happiness in the afterlife was simply an extension of those good things with which the artist was familiar on earth.

Is it the fact that the Nile valley was home to a society in which nature and the gods worked together to offer prosperity? How enviable a world in which the annual truth of the inundation, accepted as a sign that human life is subject to irresistible forces beyond our control, was not so much a threat as the promise of food for the year to come. How enviable a world in which the hostile desert gave way to a ribbon of fertility offering not just the sense of self-sufficiency, but also the sense that clear lines can be drawn between the familiar and the alien.

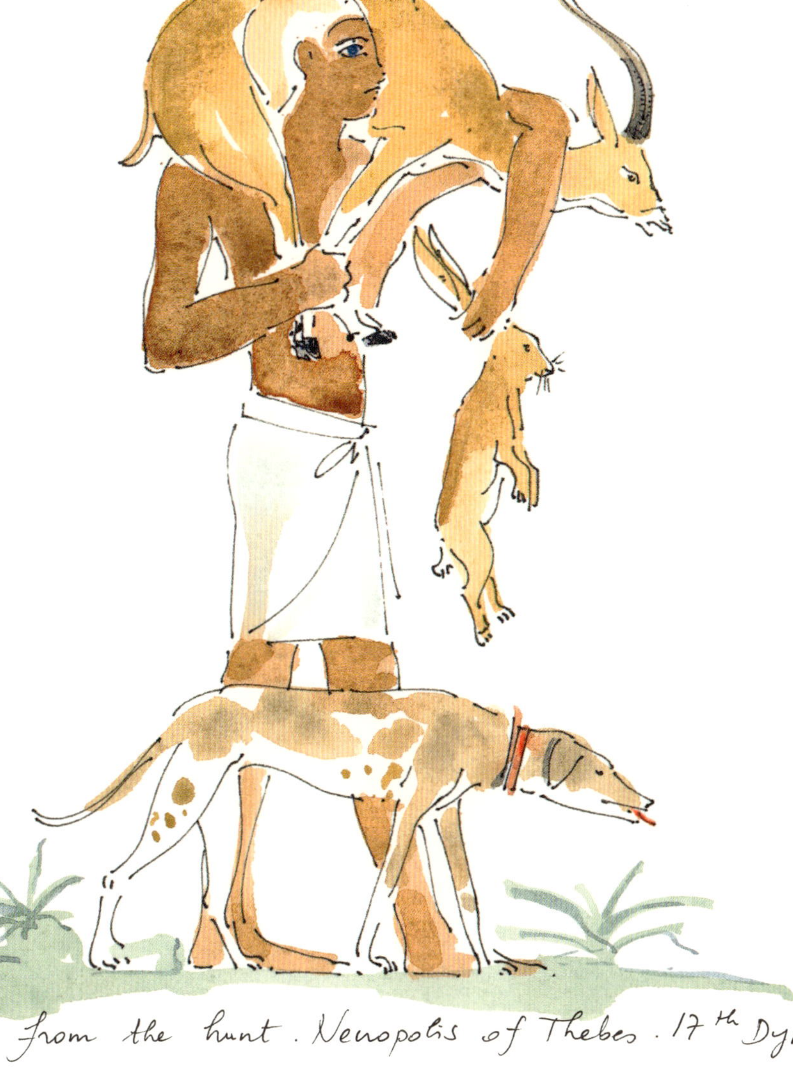

Return from the hunt. Necropolis of Thebes . 17ᵗʰ Dynasty

So it is not hard to find reasons why those who are new to Egypt so often react with sheer delight at their first encounter. It was, and indeed it is, a generous land to those who have the imagination to see its promise. It may be said that the worst thing for an ancient Egyptian was to have to go abroad, whether for the purposes of war or peace. Heaven was to be at home in the valley of the Nile, in the midst of the family, with familiar gods at hand. The repeated misconception that slave labor built the Pyramids shows how hard it is for the modern mind to conceive of a civilization that was not constructed by compulsion, but by the persuasion of commitment and beliefs.

Of course, wars were not unknown in Egypt. Nevertheless, violence was still shocking to the Egyptian who, in his heart, expected the gods to be kind. Not for nothing do the shoulders of pair statues so often show the husband's hand reaching out from behind, in a gesture that makes clear to the eye, five thousand years later, the undying comforts of intimacy and affection.

To this day, the visitor to Egypt finds himself in a land where the instinct of his host is to welcome the stranger, a reception which is a shock above all else because it is a reminder that so many of us have lost the art of disinterested and spontaneous friendship. The visitor finds himself in a culture that has retained the most ancient traditions.

He discovers a society where art and architecture, prayer and beliefs, mingle to create a setting for everyday life. So to record the features of daily life in modern Egypt is no less a crucial part of the task of recording the country than to testify to the inheritance from the past. One without the other is less than half the whole. To do the whole justice, the eye and the imagination must have their free rein.

The eye was one of the greatest symbols of ancient Egypt. The ancient Egyptians used their imagination to make sense of the wonders of daily life that sustained them from day to day, from year to year—the sun that set in the mountains on one side of the river only to rise again next day on the other side, the annual blessing of the floods that spelled a fruitful harvest ahead. They saw wonders, and they interpreted them. In awe at what they had understood they created art and architecture, giving thanks for their lives, and paying homage to the happiness of their society. We also give thanks to them, and respond to their world with a deep sense of their generosity. How else indeed to explain the willingness with which the very young take on board the basics of ancient Egypt, or the readiness of modern artists to encompass Egyptian thought and motifs?

And so a notebook of a journey through Egypt should make us feel happier as we turn the pages. It should make us grateful to all those who have interpreted the subject for us, both the Egyptologists who have translated the past on the strength of their scientific discipline, and the artists and writers—from Herodotus to the present day—whose imagination has allowed us to see Egypt, present and past, with something of the sense that made the ancient Egyptians think that it was heaven to live on the banks of the Nile. Florine's work is part of a good tradition, and a happy one.

Henrietta and Christopher MacCall, London, March 2003. Henrietta is an Egyptologist, Christopher an Egypt enthusiast. Both are fascinated by the Sphinx.

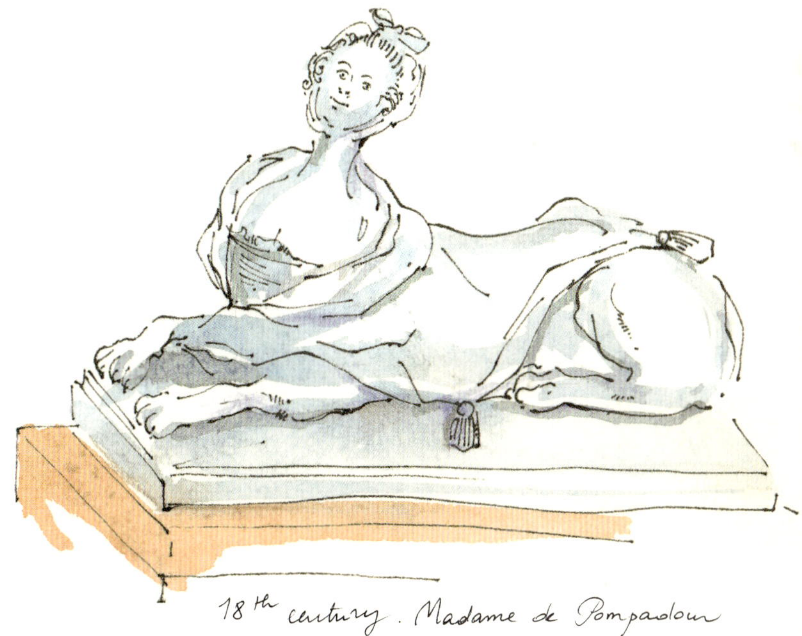

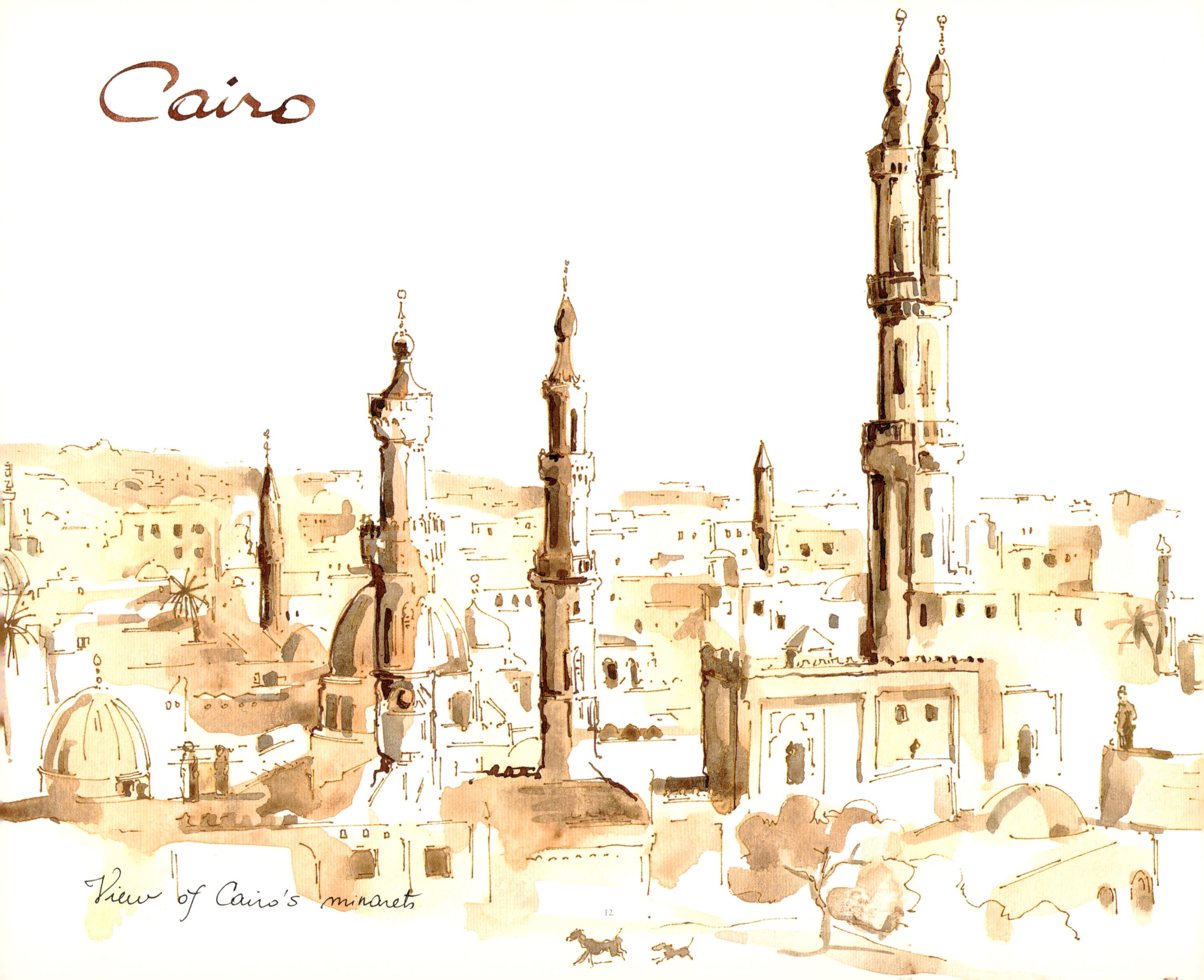

Cairo
View of Cairo's minarets

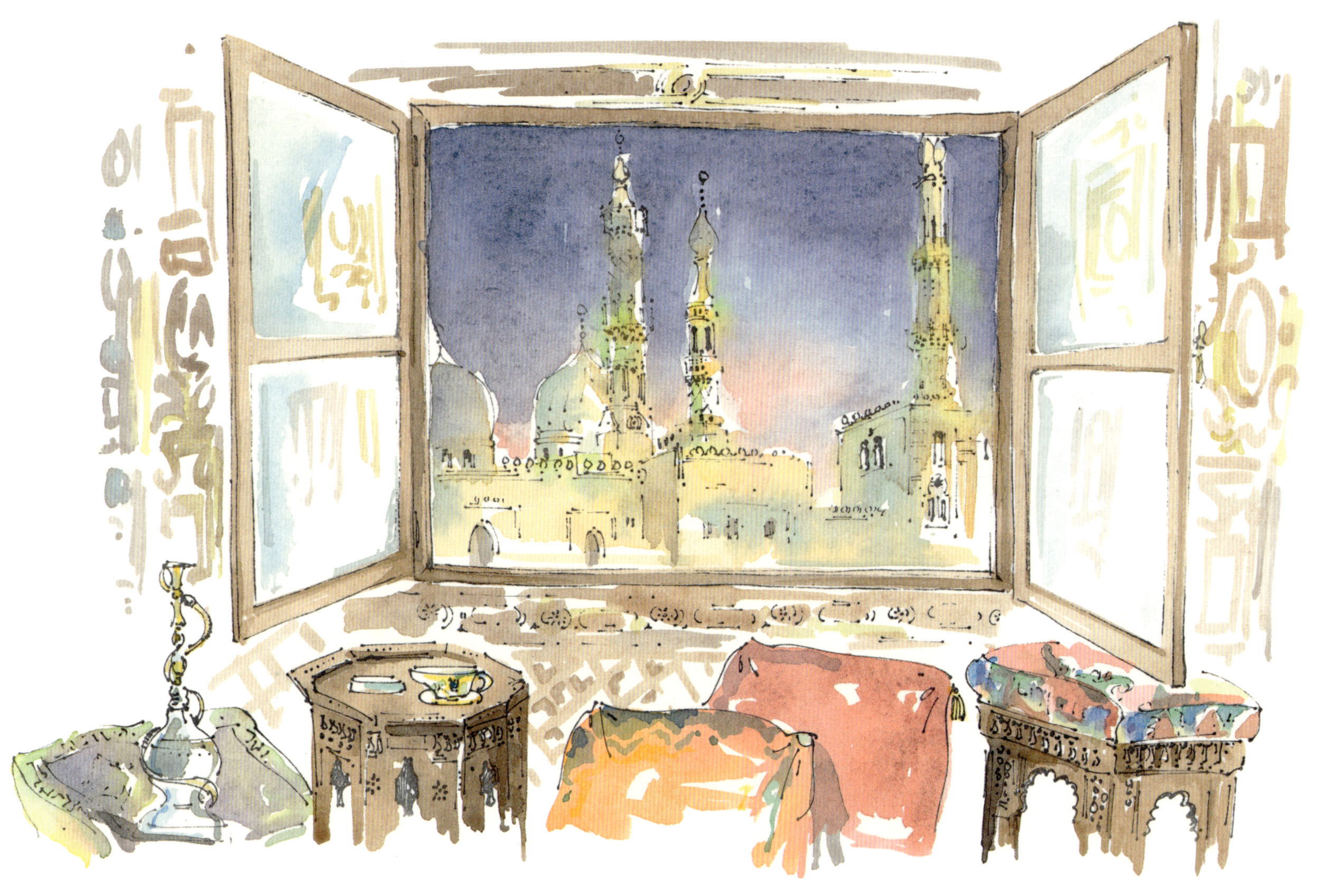

"Keep your secret, confide in no one, for
he who tells a secret has already lost it"
A Thousand and One Nights

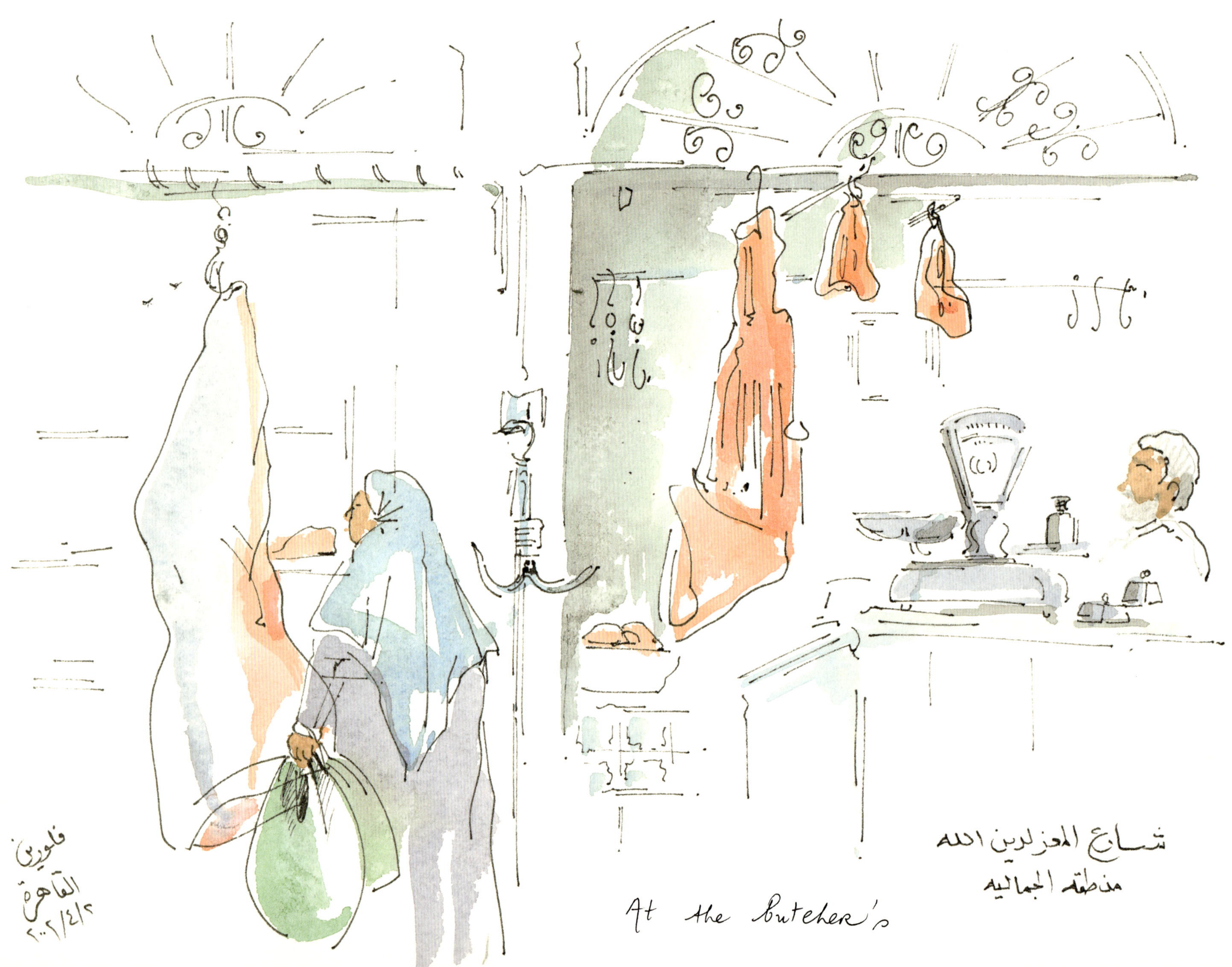

شــارع المعز لدين الله
منطقة الجماليه

فلورين
القاهرة
٢٠٠٦/٤/٢

At the Butcher's

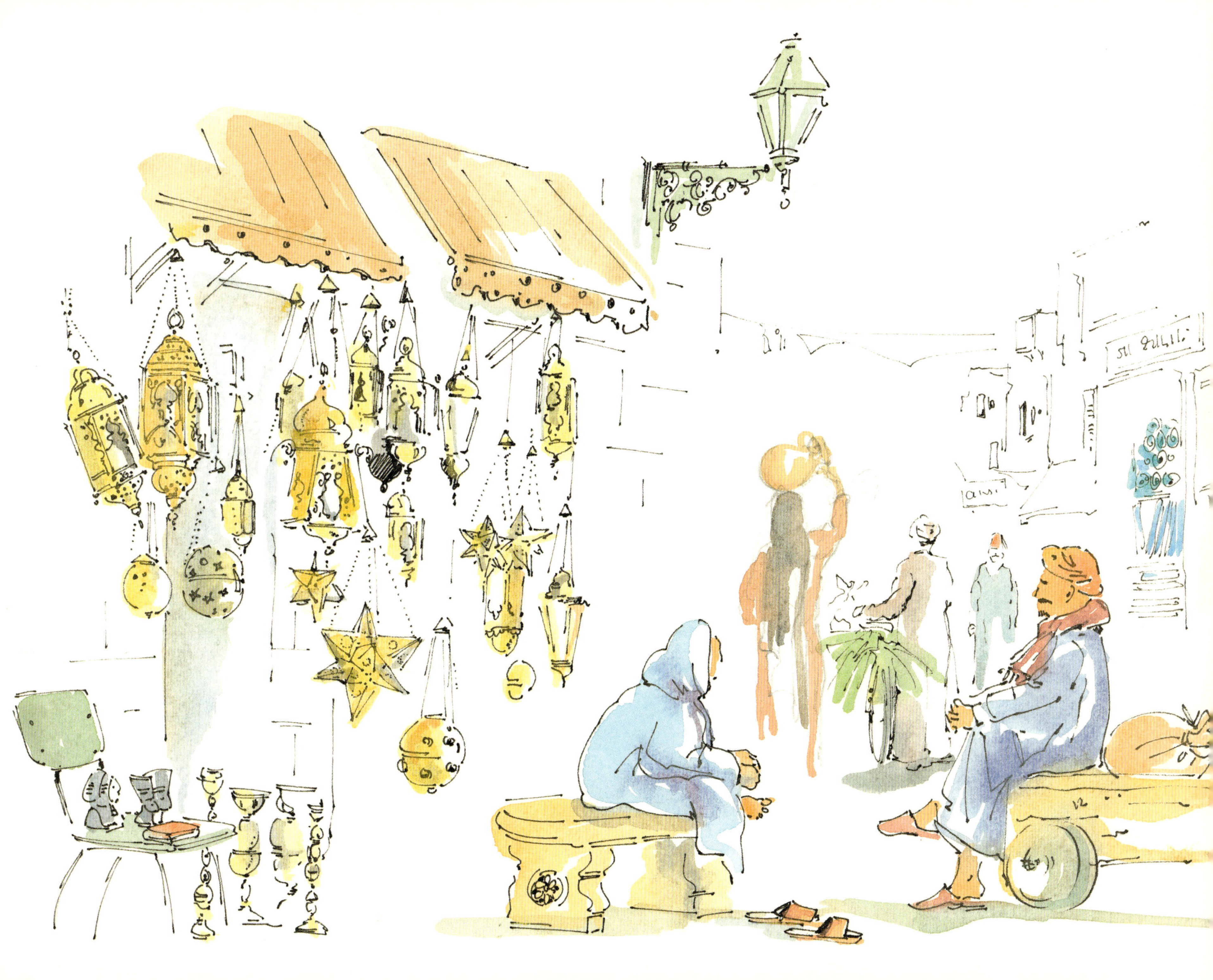

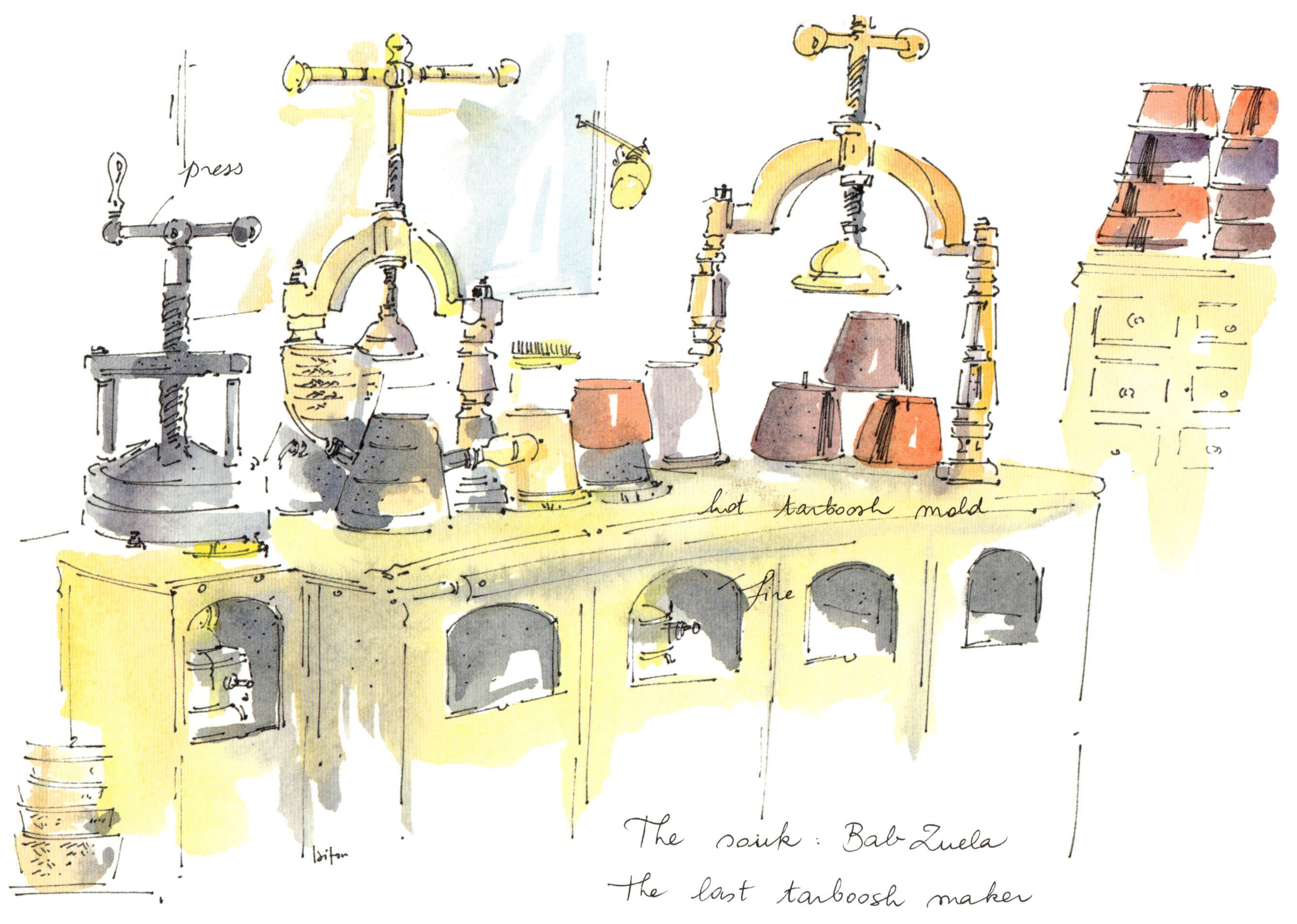

press
hot tarboosh mold
fire
briton
The souk : Bab Zuela
the last tarboosh maker

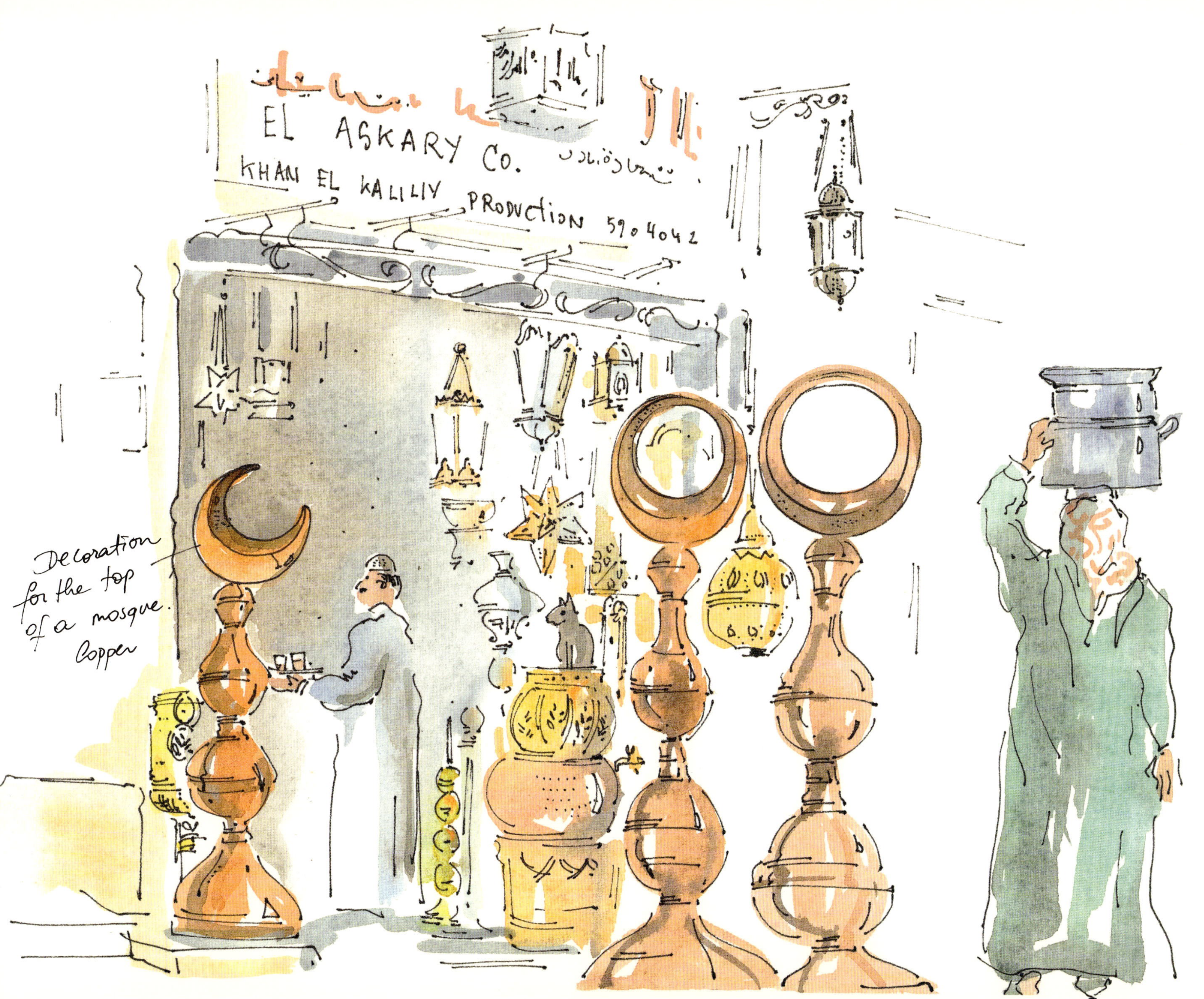

EL ASKARY CO.
KHAN EL KALILIY
PRODUCTION 590 4042
Decoration
for the top
of a mosque.
Copper

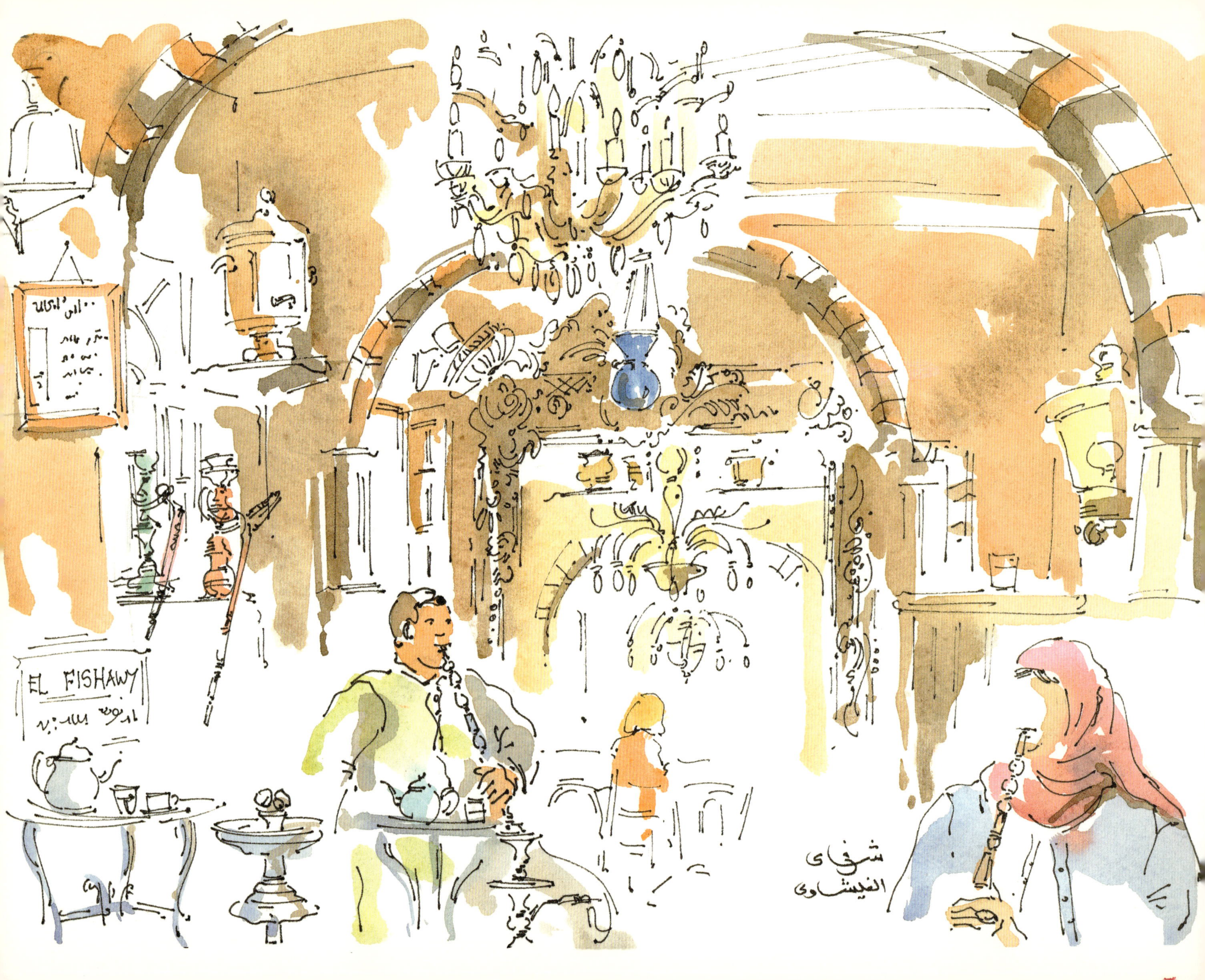

EL FISHAWY
شاى الفيشاوى

We ate with our fingers, the food was brought one dish at a time on a silver tray—about thirty different dishes
made their appearance in this way. We were on divans in a wooden pavilion, windows open on the water.

Gustave Flaubert (French writer, 1821–1880),
Flaubert in Egypt, translated by Francis Steegmuller, Penguin Classics.

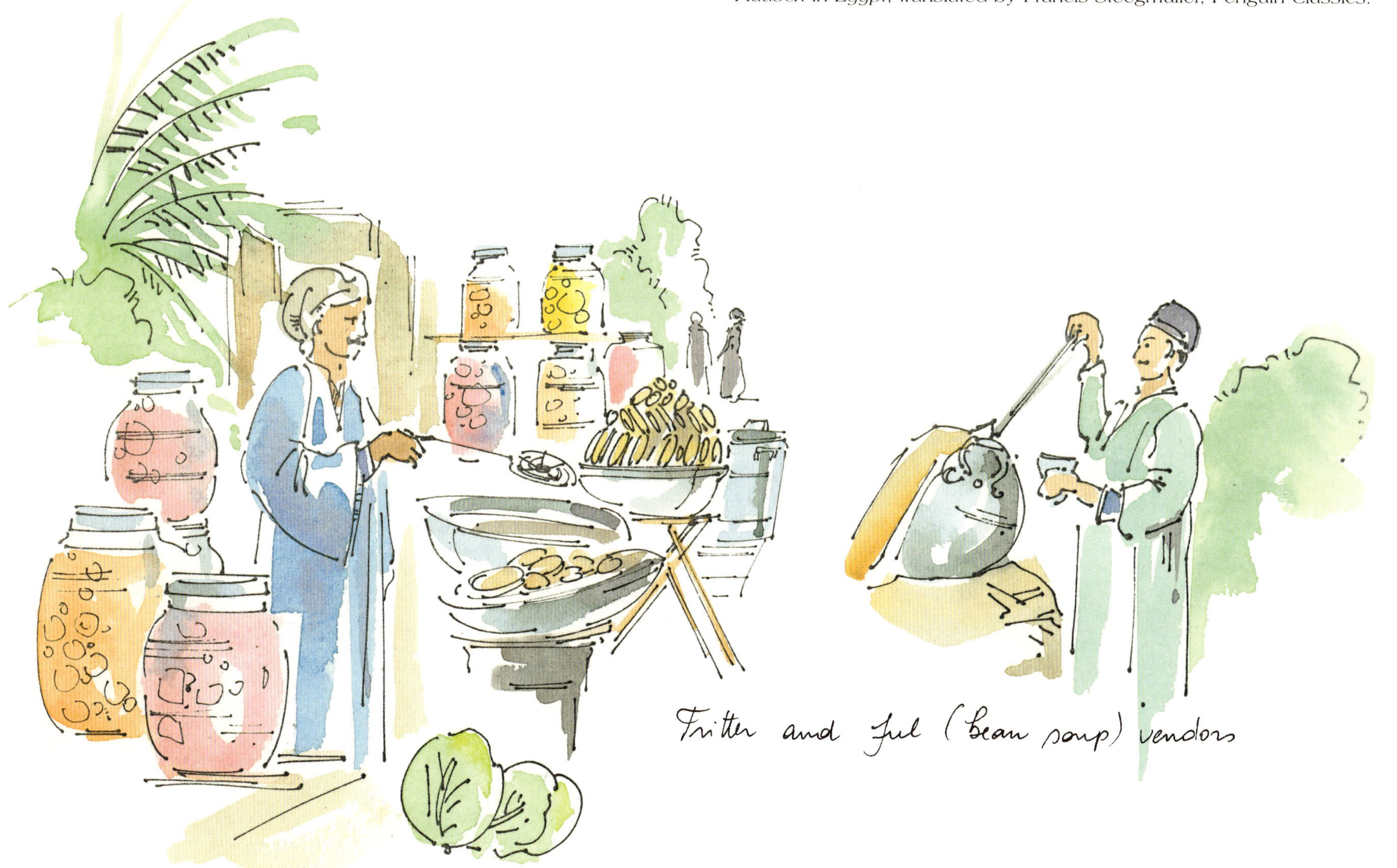

Fritter and Ful (bean soup) vendors

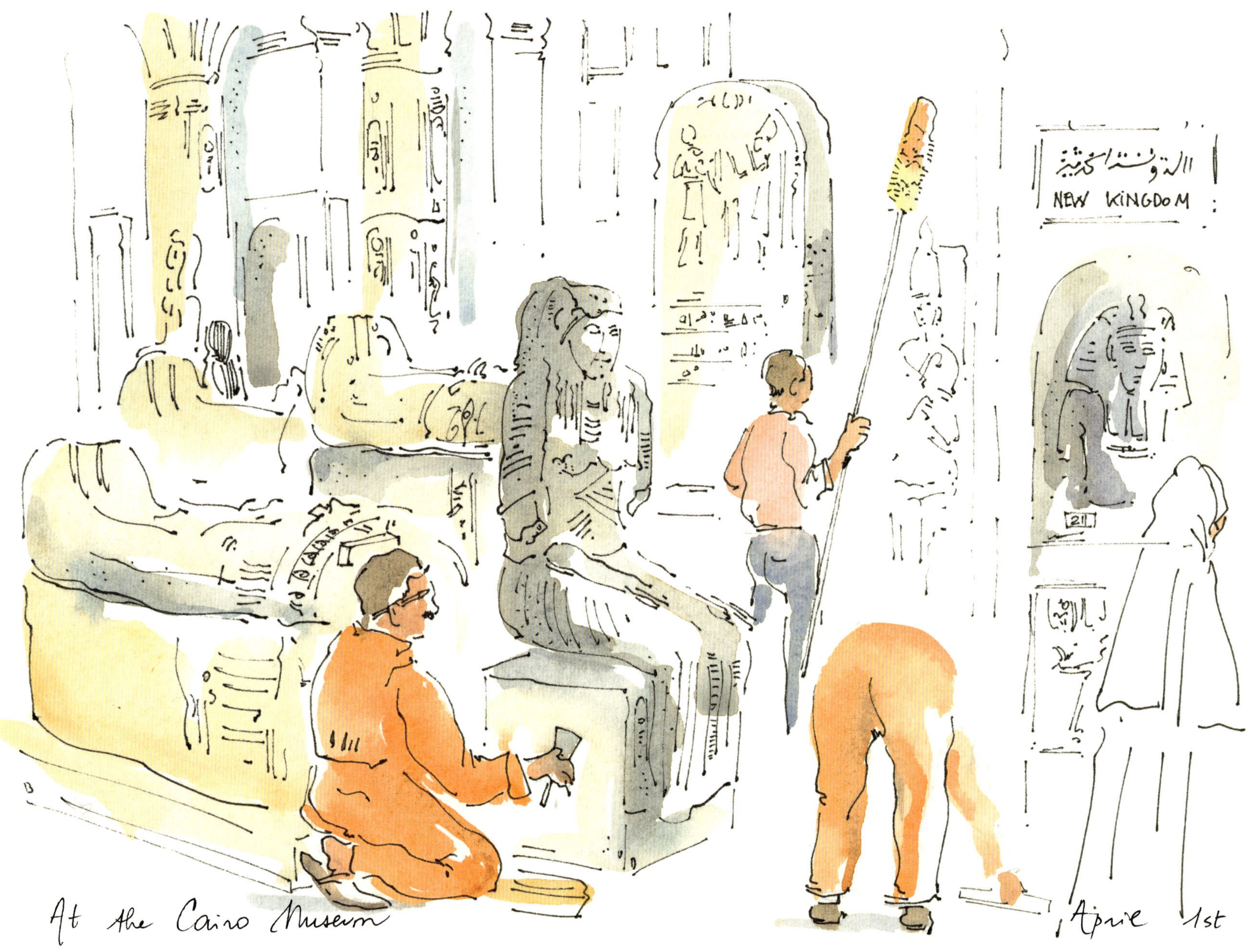

At the Cairo Museum   April 1st

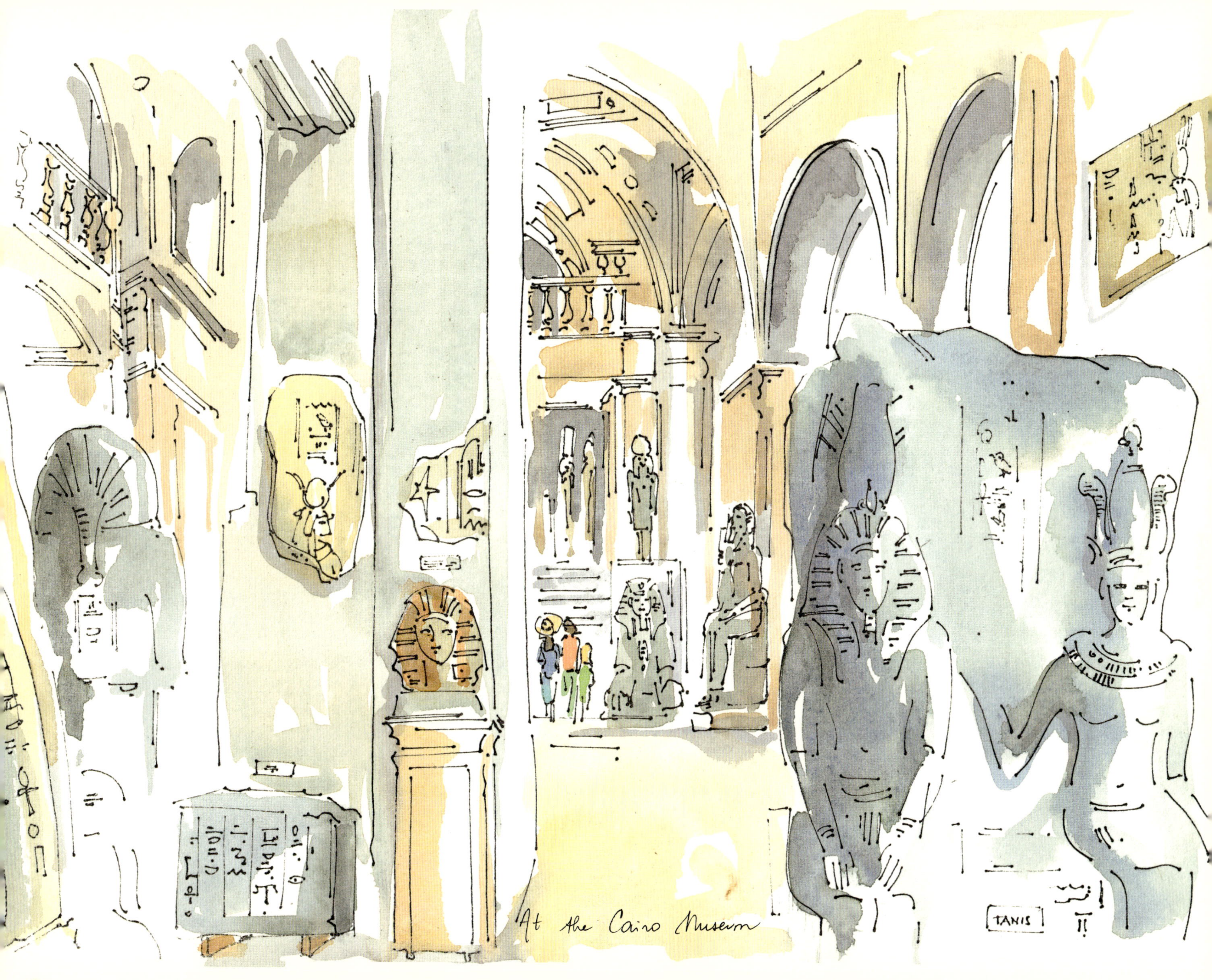

At the Cairo Museum

All that I had before my eyes fell upon
you was a wasted life.
How can my past be taken seriously?
You are my life. " Inta Omri"
Oum Kalsoum (Egypt's most celebrated singer
1908-1975)

The water pipes at Shaly Lodge - Siwa

Nothing is more conducive to poetic reveries than taking small
puffs, while reclining on the cushions of a divan, of this fragrant
smoke, cooled by the water it traverses, that reaches you after
flowing through the red or green morocco tubes you hold in
your arms like a Cairo snake charmer playing with serpents.

Théophile Gautier (1811–1872),
Cinq Lettres d'Égypte (Five Letters from Egypt).

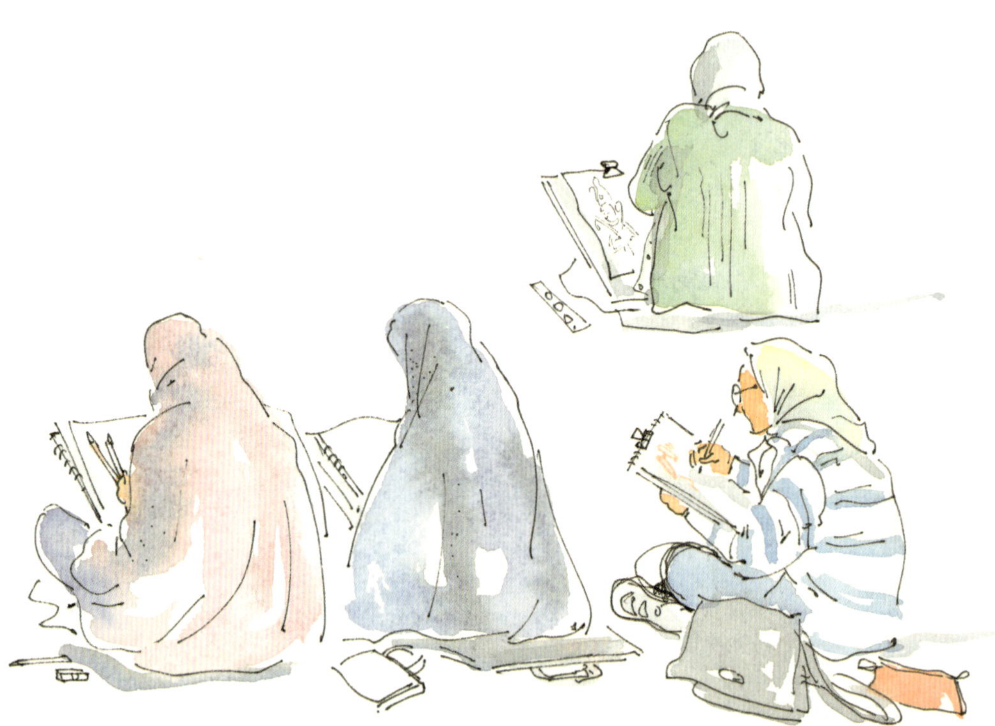

a few fellow artists sketching at the Cairo Museum

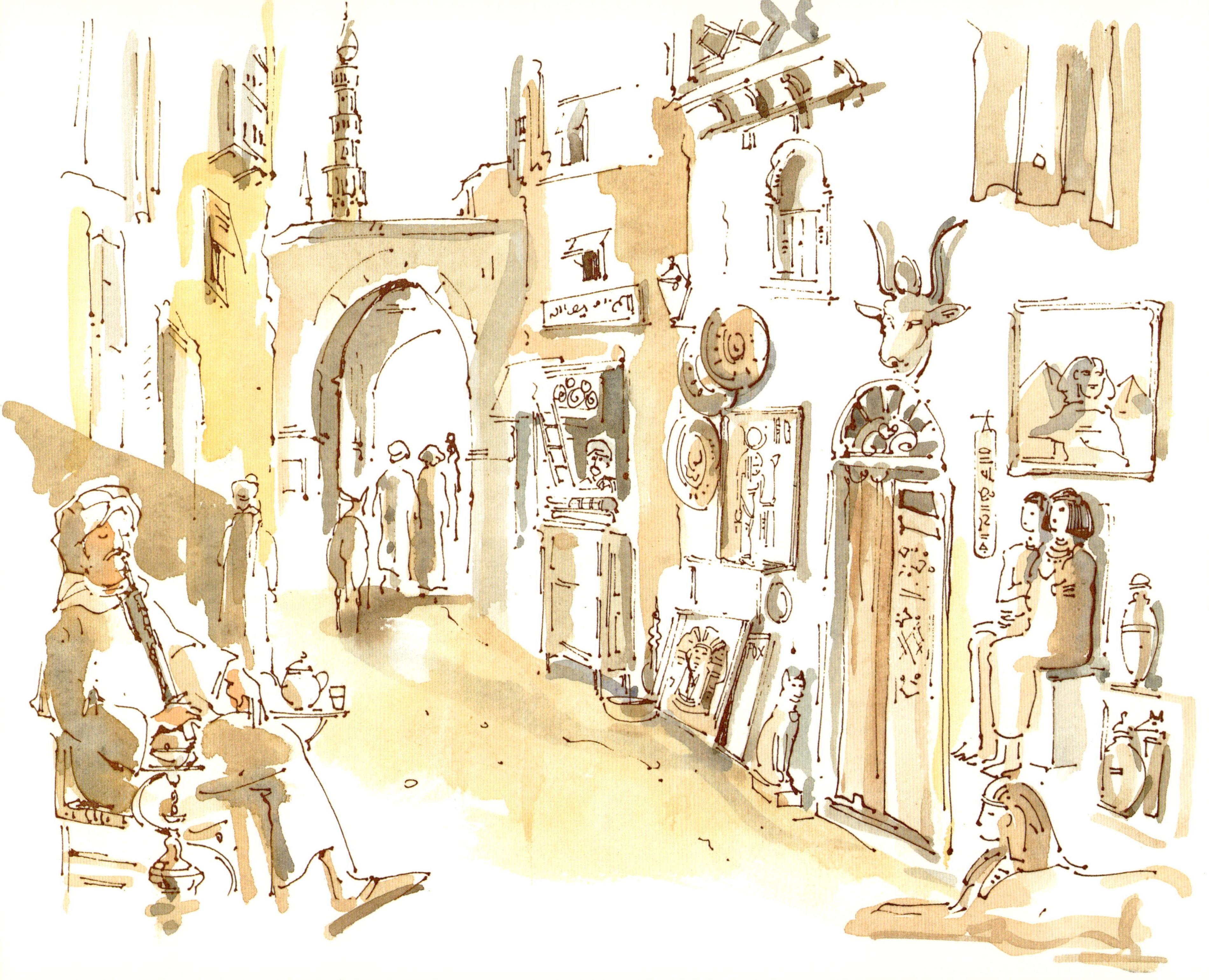

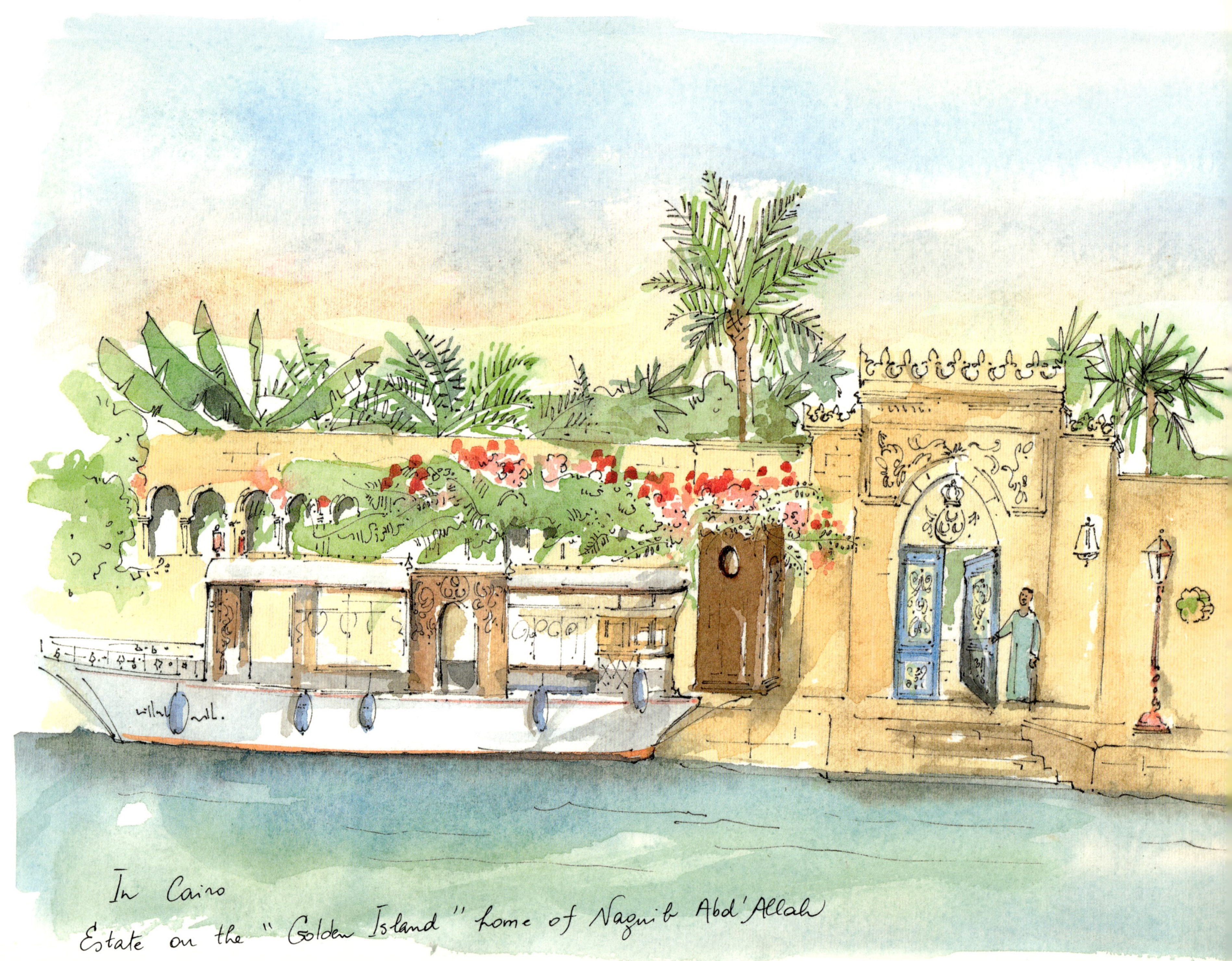

In Cairo
Estate on the " Golden Island " home of Naguib Abd'Allah

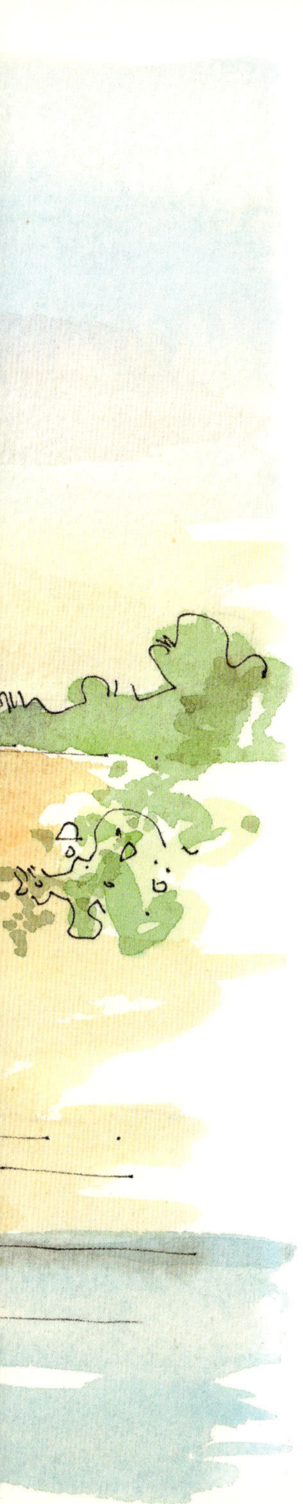

The Sacred Rites of Ammon

When your favorite song plays

Your eyes fill with a burning light

In the evening when the wind stirs

Your heart expands in time with the wind

You swell with Ammon

And sway with the perceived beauty of the worlds

In the evening when the wind stirs

Your heart explodes with a thousand fires brought to life again

Everything must be gathered

By the wind that sings its immense praise

All the prayers of worlds past and future

Rest on your skin in the evening

A caress desired and received

When the wind stirs and your favorite song plays.

Naguib Abd'Allah

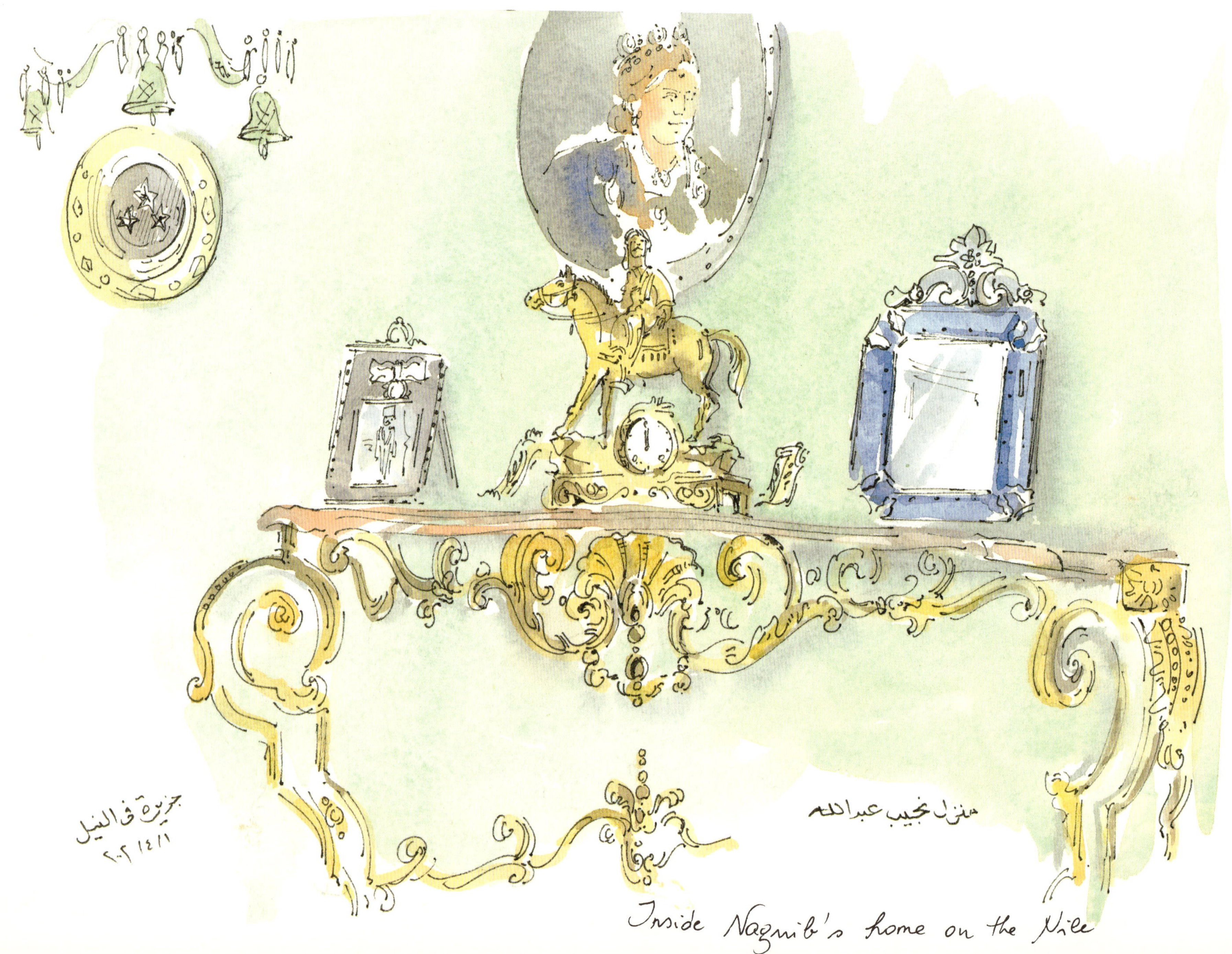

Inside Naguib's home on the Nile

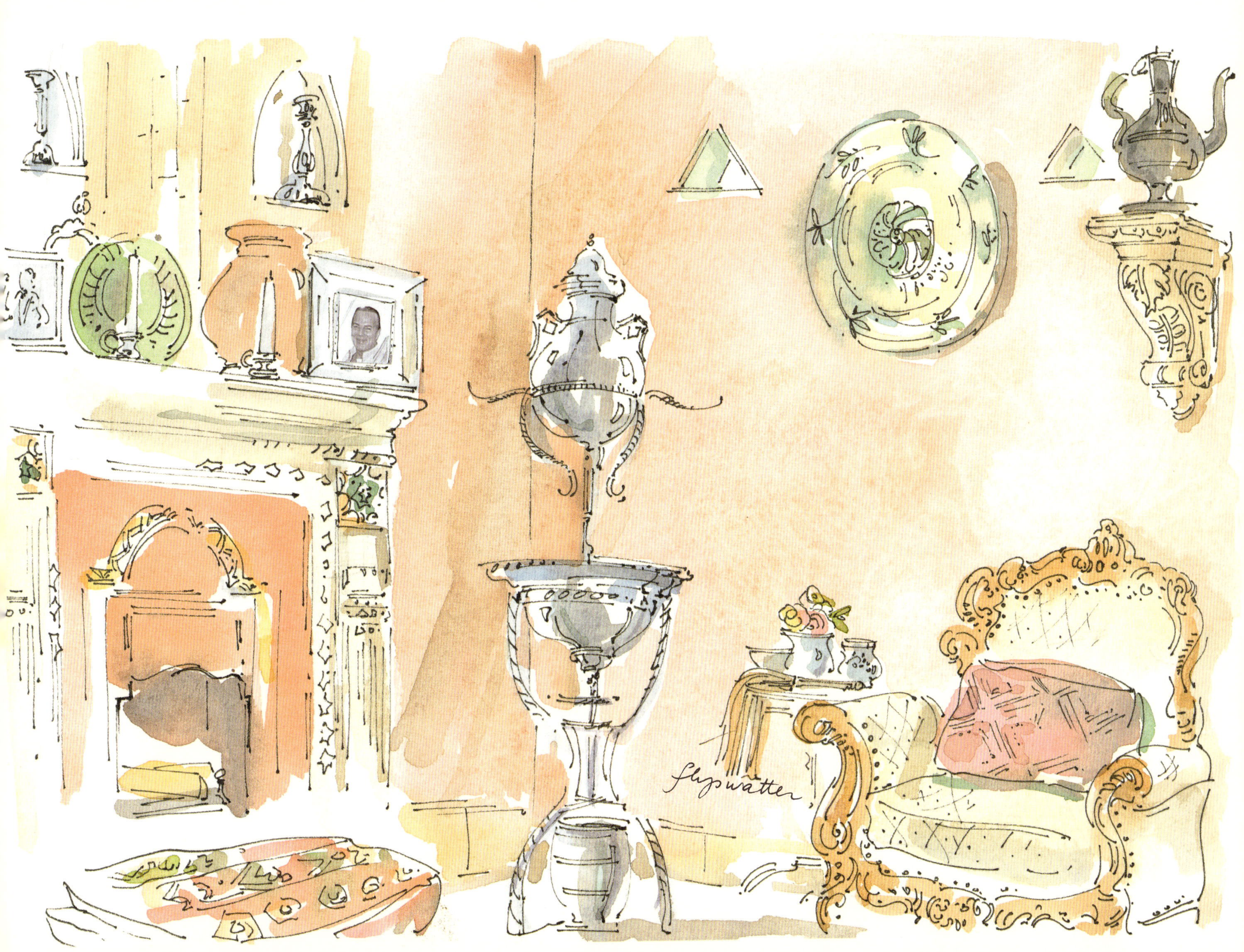

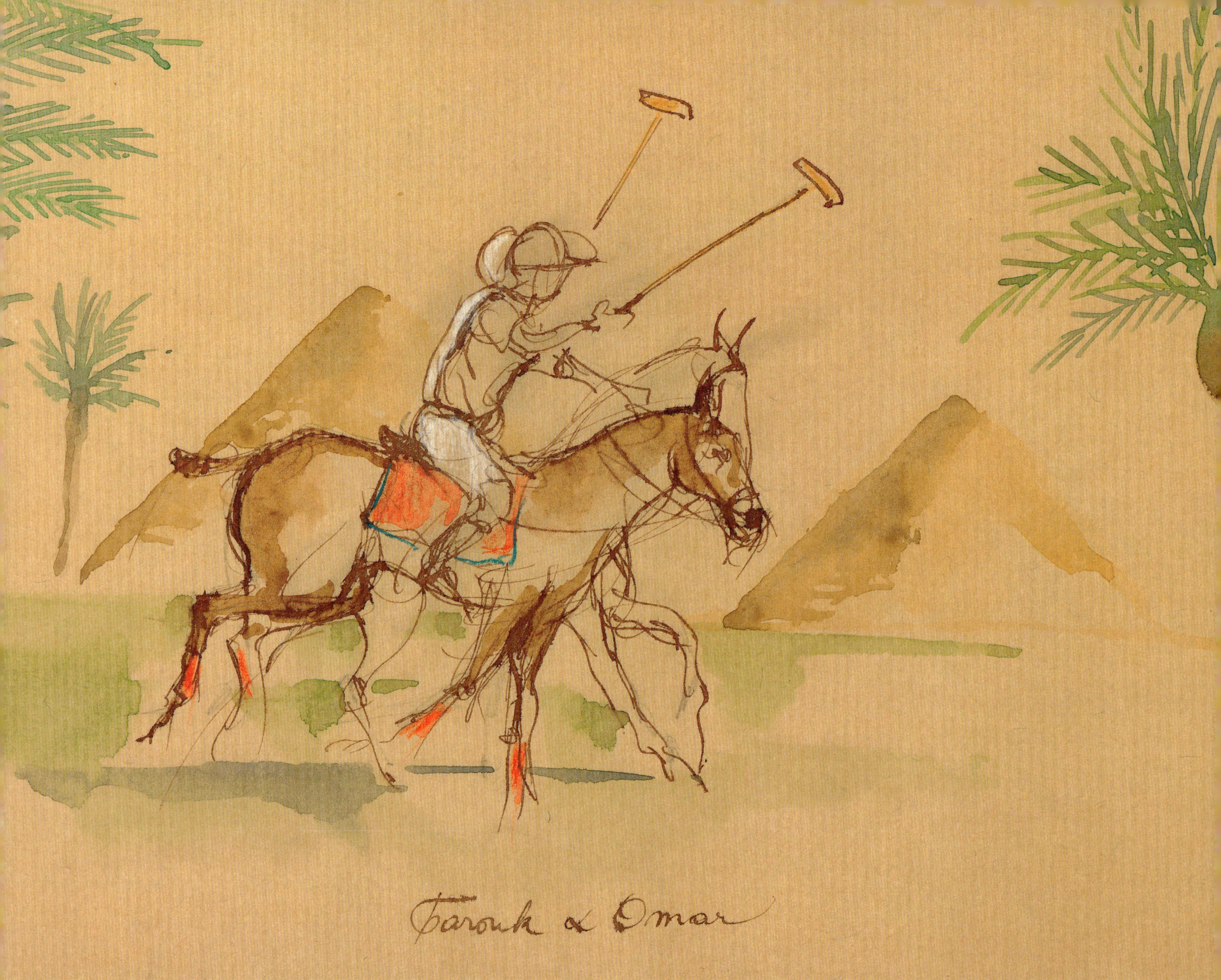

Farouk & Omar

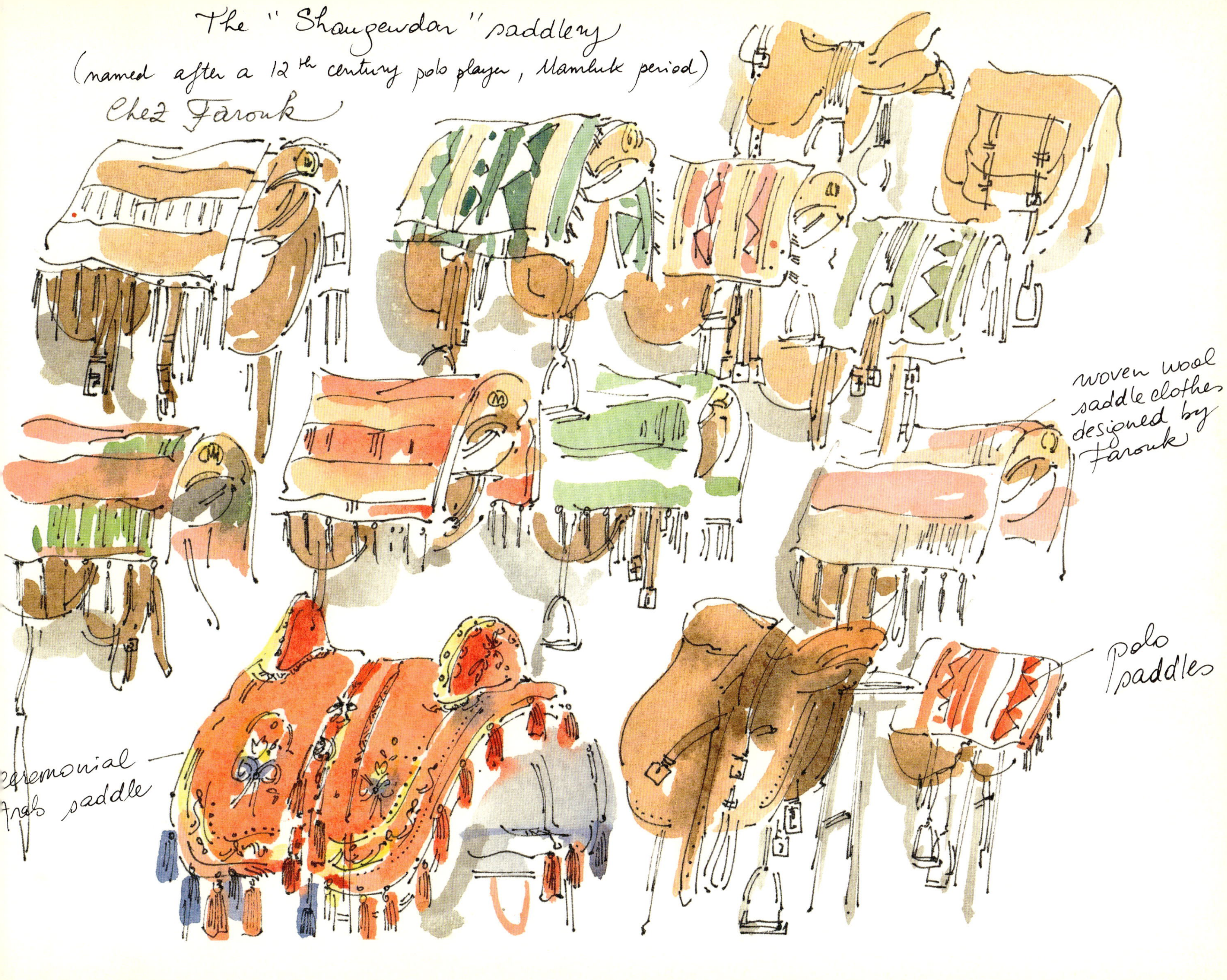

The "Shougendar" saddlery
(named after a 12th century polo player, Mamluk period)
Chez Farouk
woven wool
saddle clothes
designed by
Farouk
polo
saddles
ceremonial
Arab saddle

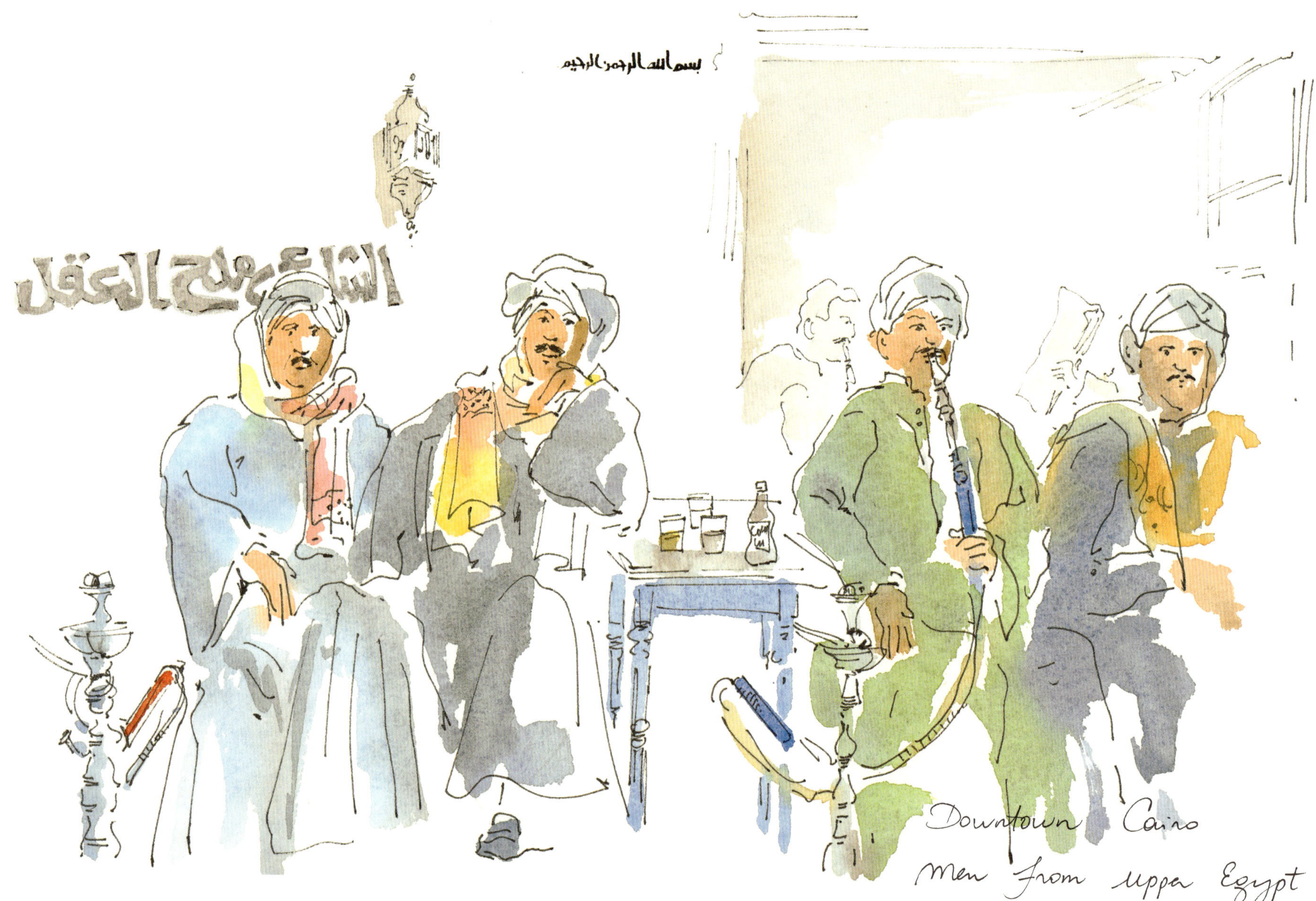
بسم الله الرحمن الرحيم
الشارع صلاح العقل
Downtown Cairo
Men from Upper Egypt

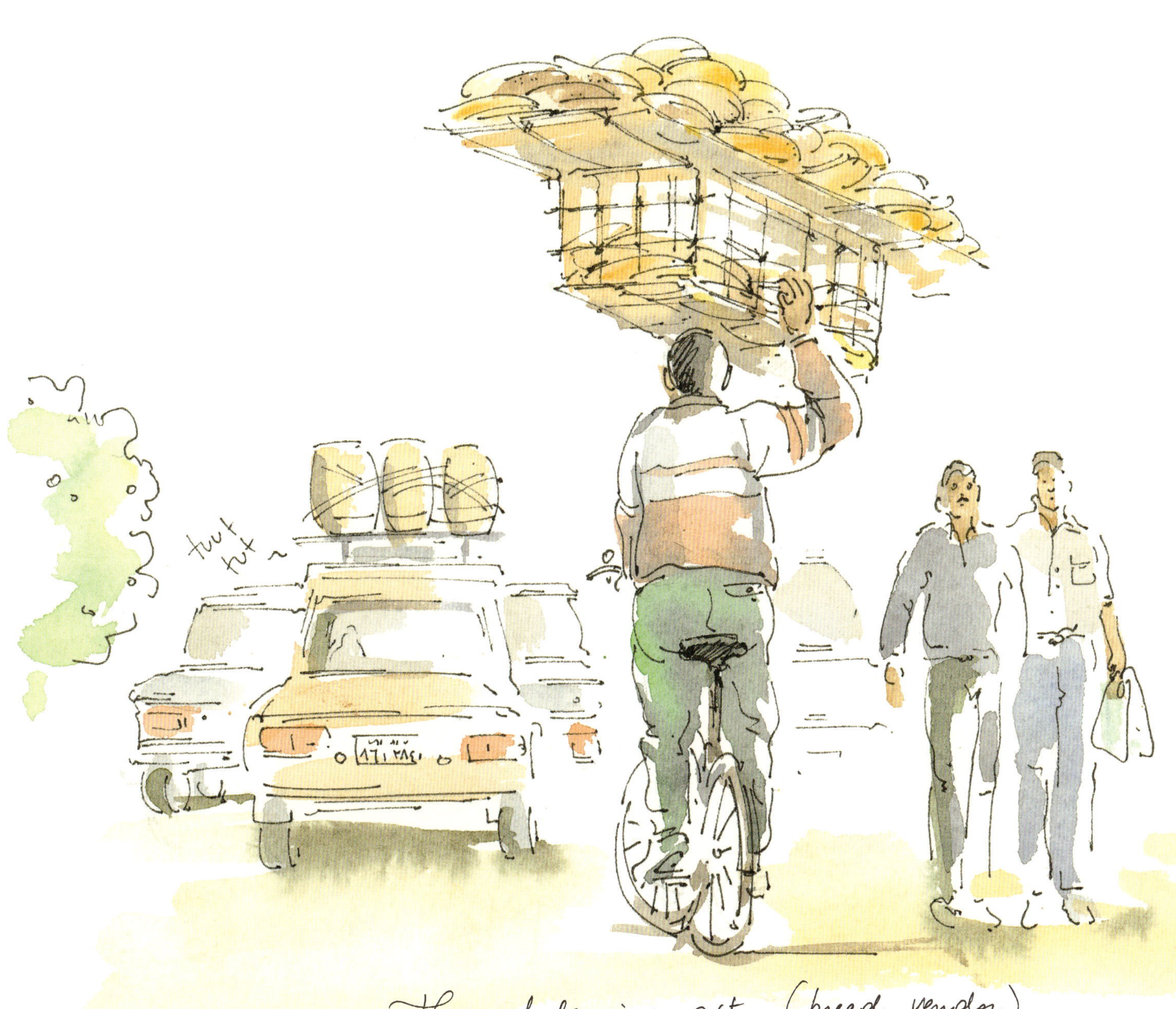

The balancing act (bread vendor)

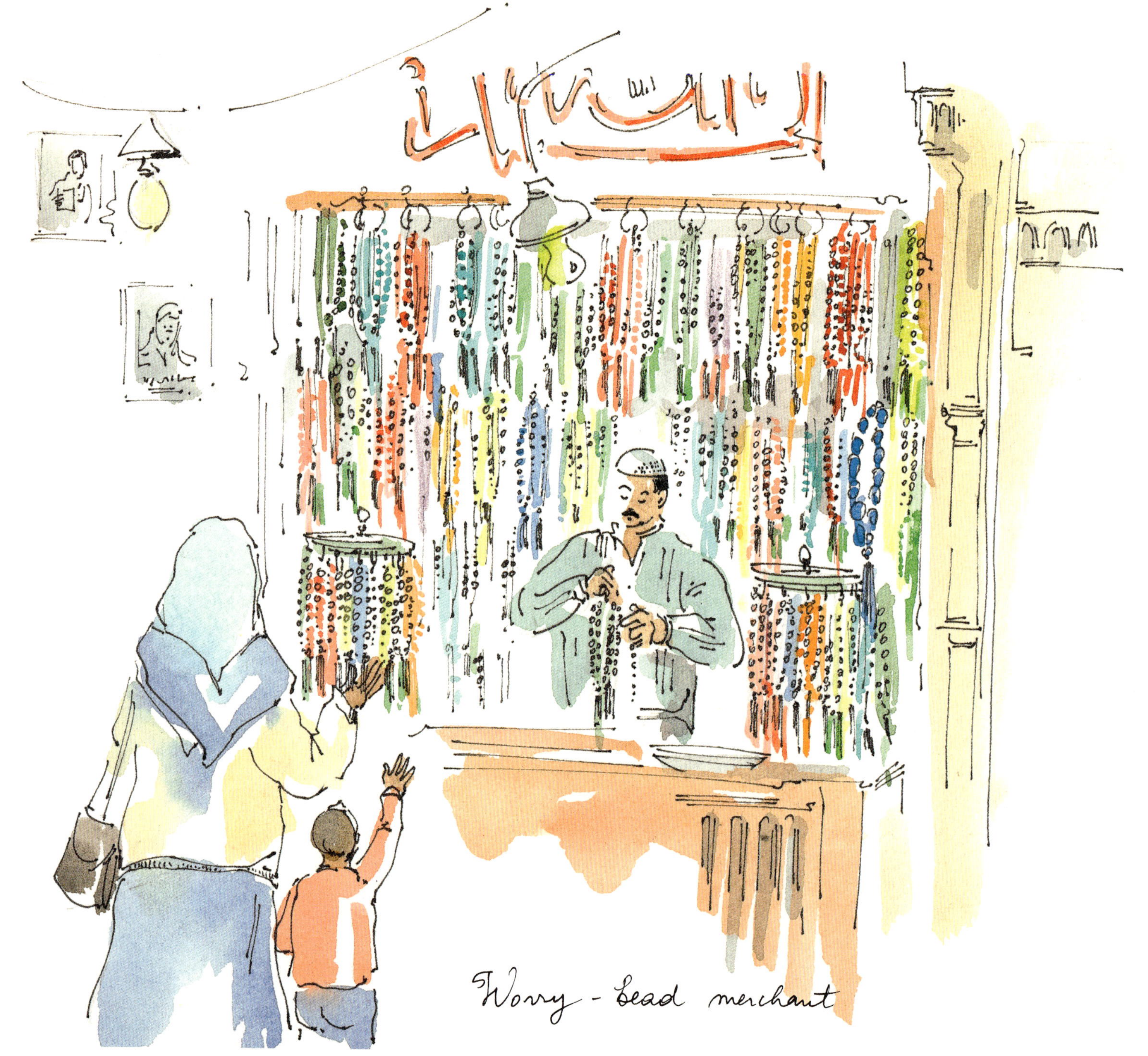

Worry - bead merchant

The entire street is, as you can
well imagine, very busy, very
noisy, filled with stands selling
fried foods, pastries, watermelons.
There are the inevitable street-
singers, wrestlers and monkey-
trainers or snake-charmers.

Gérard de Nerval (French writer, 1808–1855),
"To my friend Théophile Gautier," *Selected Writings*,
translated by Richard Siebarth, Penguin Classics.

Here are hundreds of country folk sitting on the ground behind their
baskets of fruits and vegetables. Some have eggs, butter, and
buffalo-cream for sale, while others sell sugar canes, limes,
cabbages, tobacco, barley, dried lentils, split beans, maize, wheat,
and dura. The women go to and fro with bouquets of live poultry.
The chickens scream; the sellers rave; the buyers bargain at the
top of their voices; the dust flies in clouds; the sun pours down
floods of light and heat; you can scarcely hear yourself speak.

Amelia B. Edwards (British writer, 1831–1892),
A Thousand Miles Up the Nile, Henry T. Coates & Co.

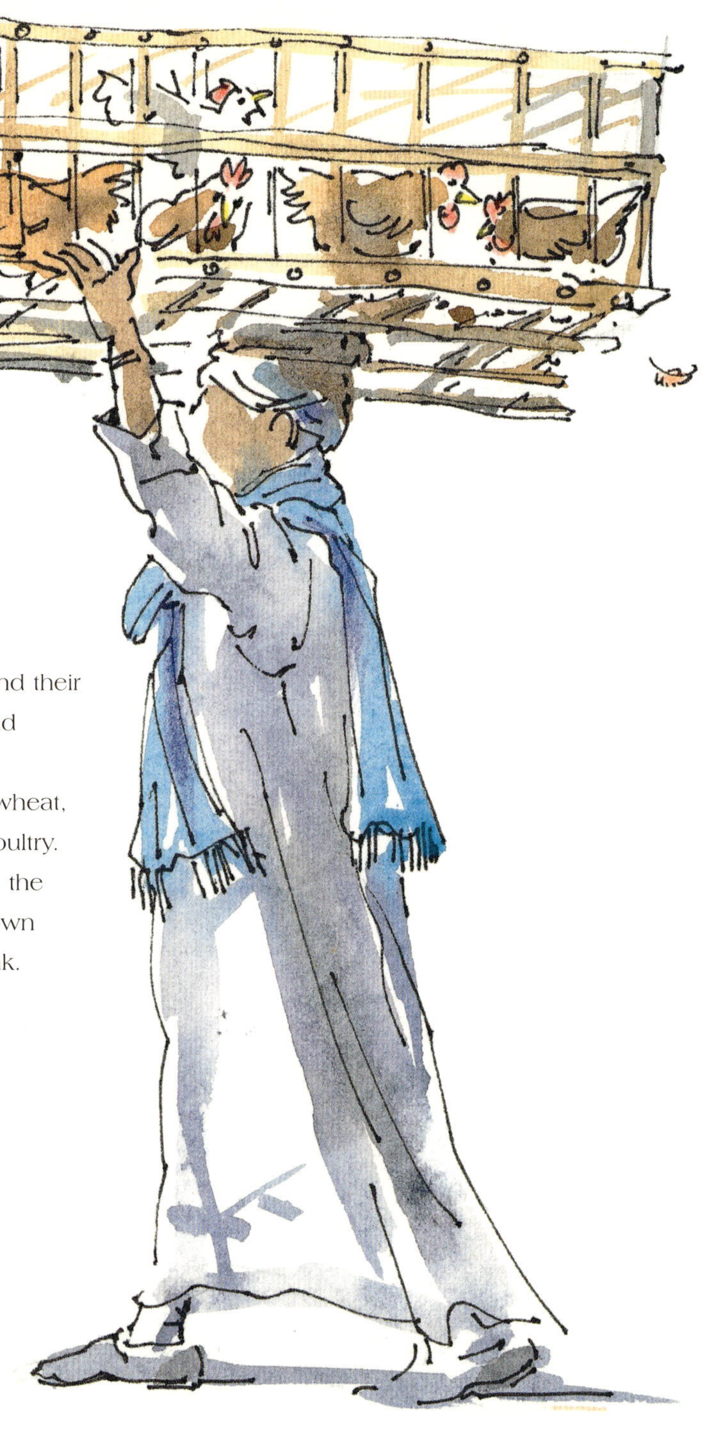

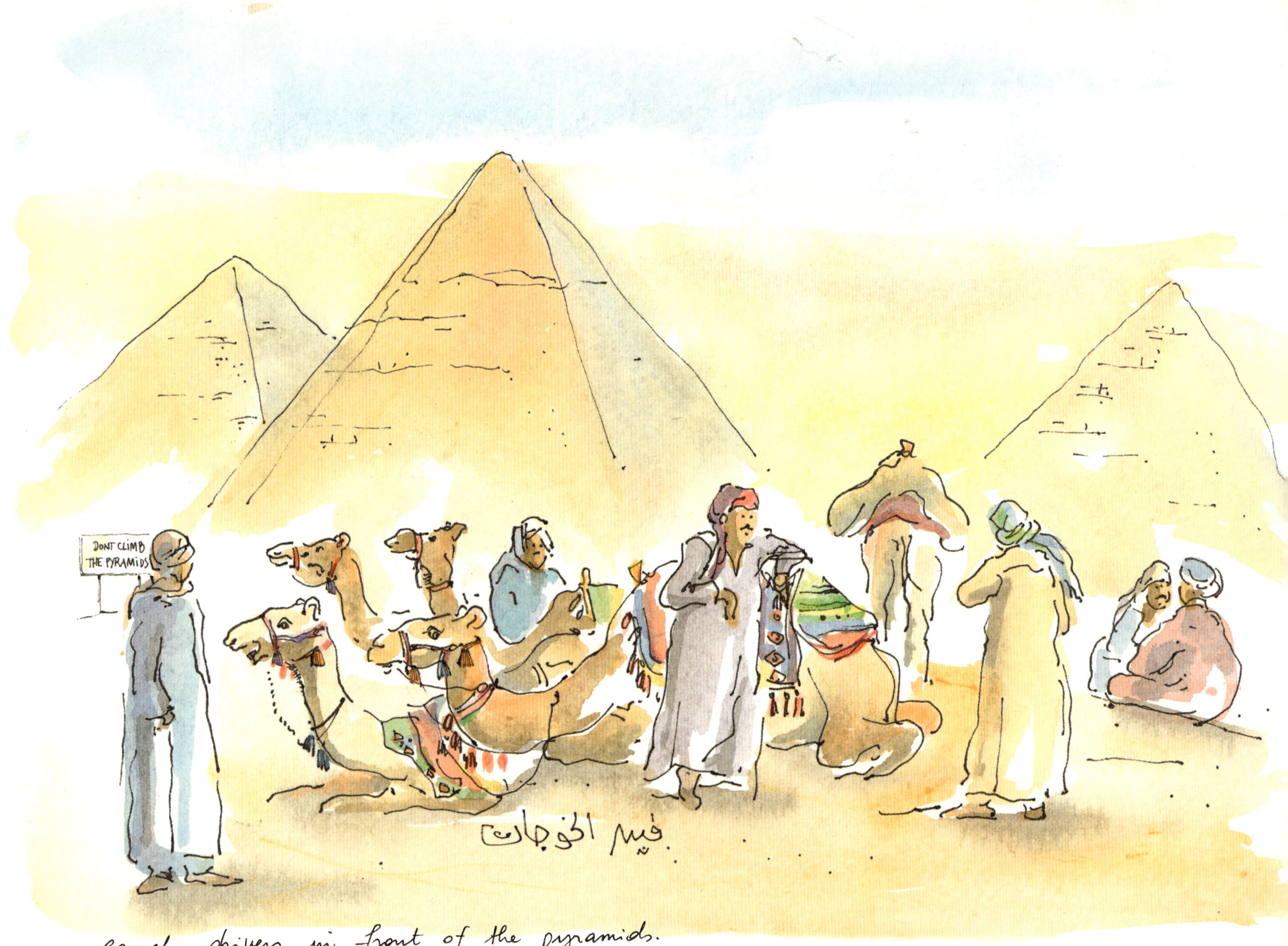

Camel drivers in front of the pyramids.

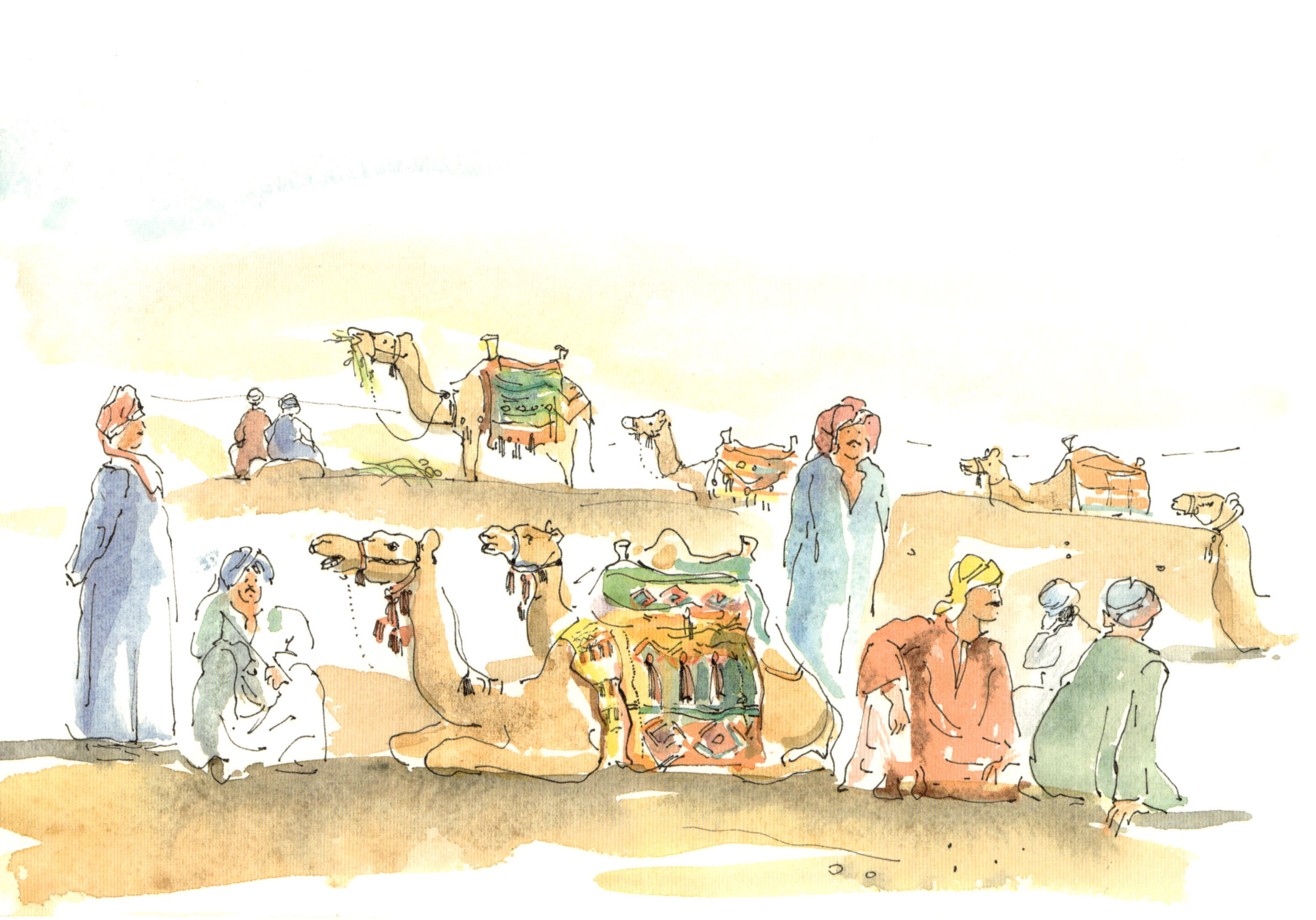

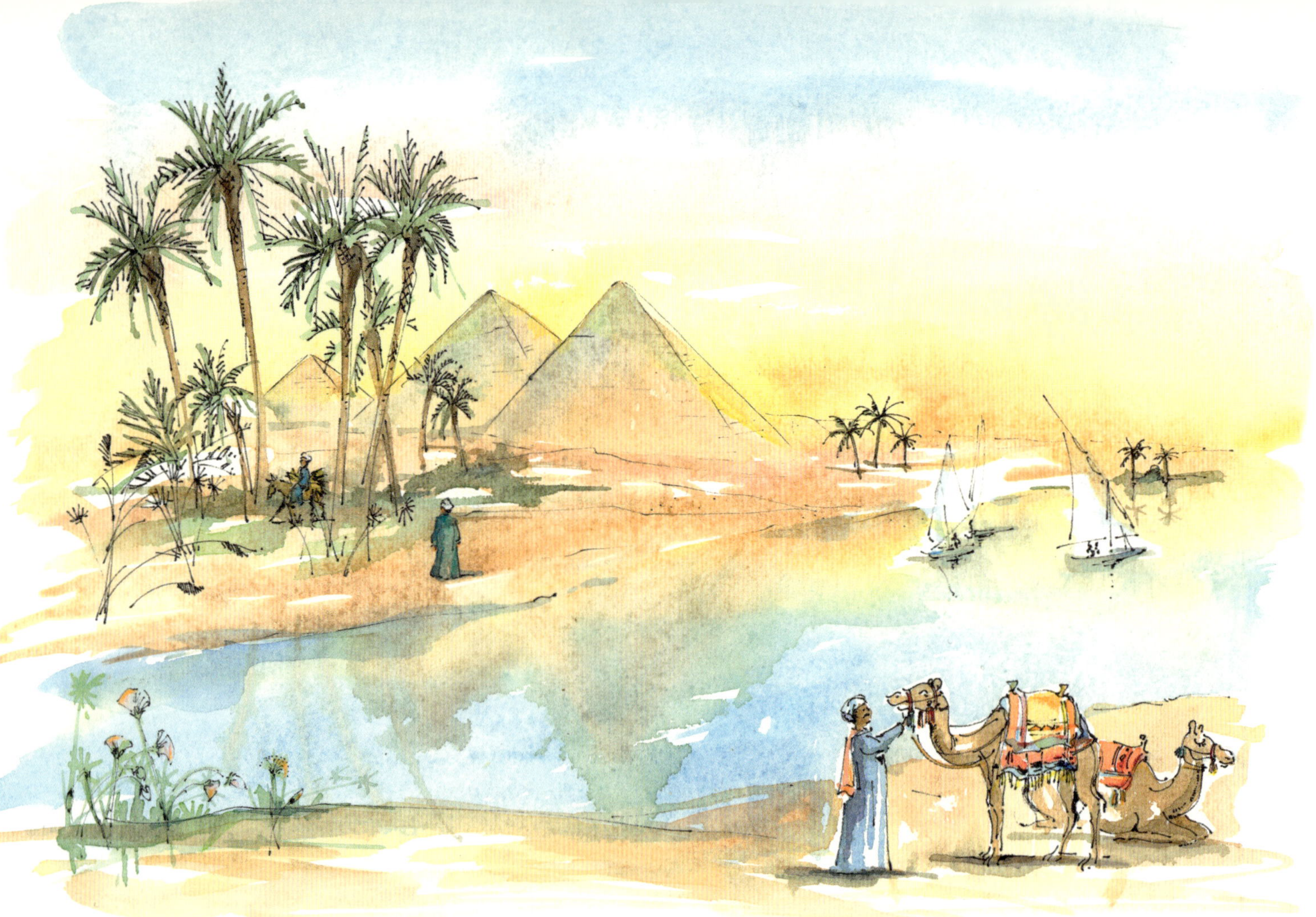

The Blue Vein and the Calm Heart

The Nile pulses up from the south
through Wadis that she has created.
Running and climbing against the northerly gravity
she yearns for the gentle Mediterranean touch
of her unseen lover.

At times her waters turn to mercury and silver
flowing through hard rock. Other times she yawns
her body open and her waters slip past

wheat-brown sand. And even other times,
her waters deepen by a blue, glide through
green reeds and drooping date palms,
their fronds tickling her by.

Until the delta, where she divides herself
and multiplies the times
she will make love to her waiting sea.

Omar F. Younes, 1995

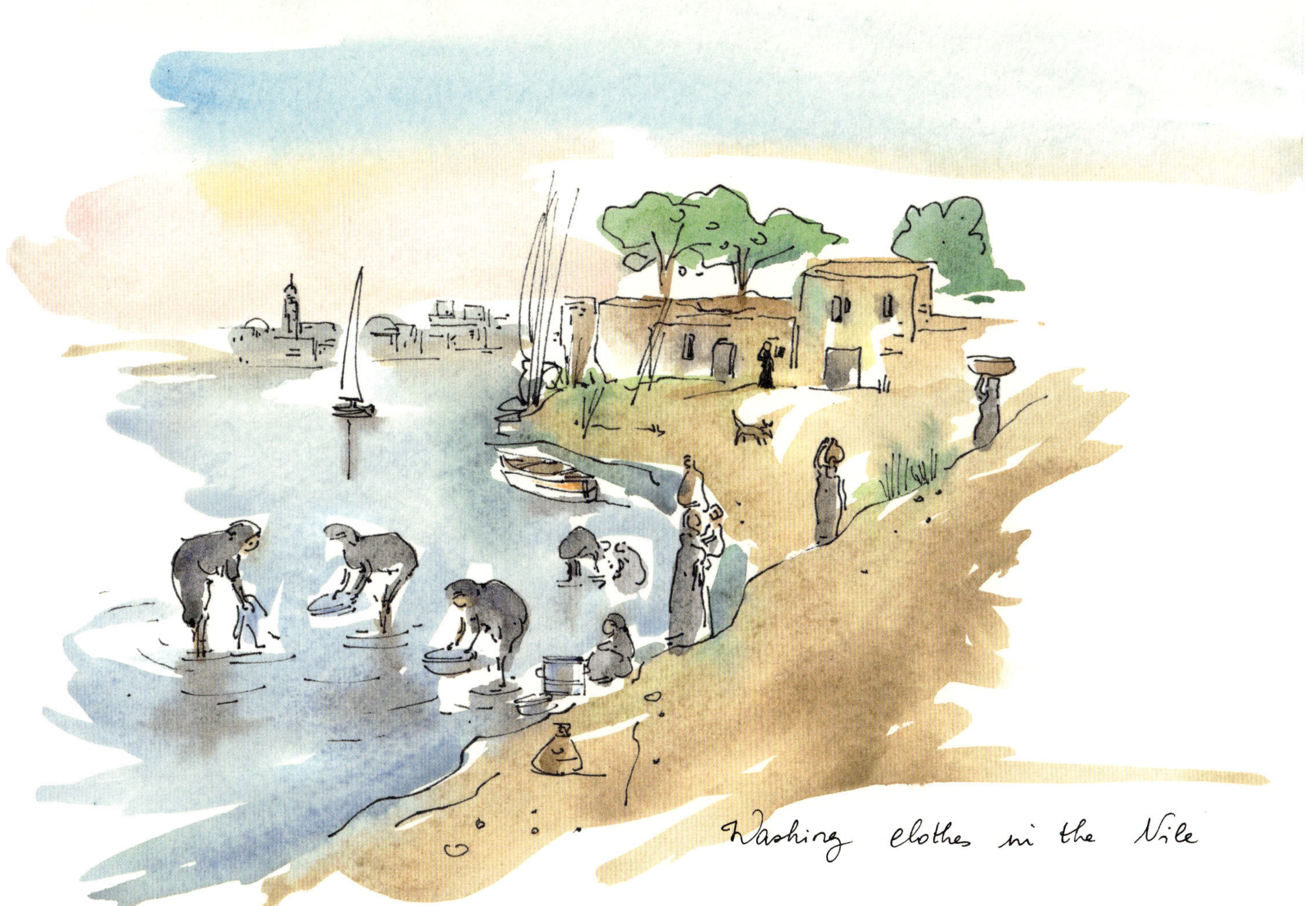

Egypt is the gift of the Nile

Herodotus, *The Histories, Book Two*

The River King created their country, which, without him, would have been nothing more than a desert. And, moreover, he fashioned the people themselves: the water of the Nile seemed to flow from their veins. Subject to a capricious benefactor who had to be cajoled or fought, compelled to work and close ranks, this people became a nation.

Robert Solé, *Dictionnaire amoureux de l'Égypte (The Egypt Lover's Dictionary)*, Éditions Plon, 2001.

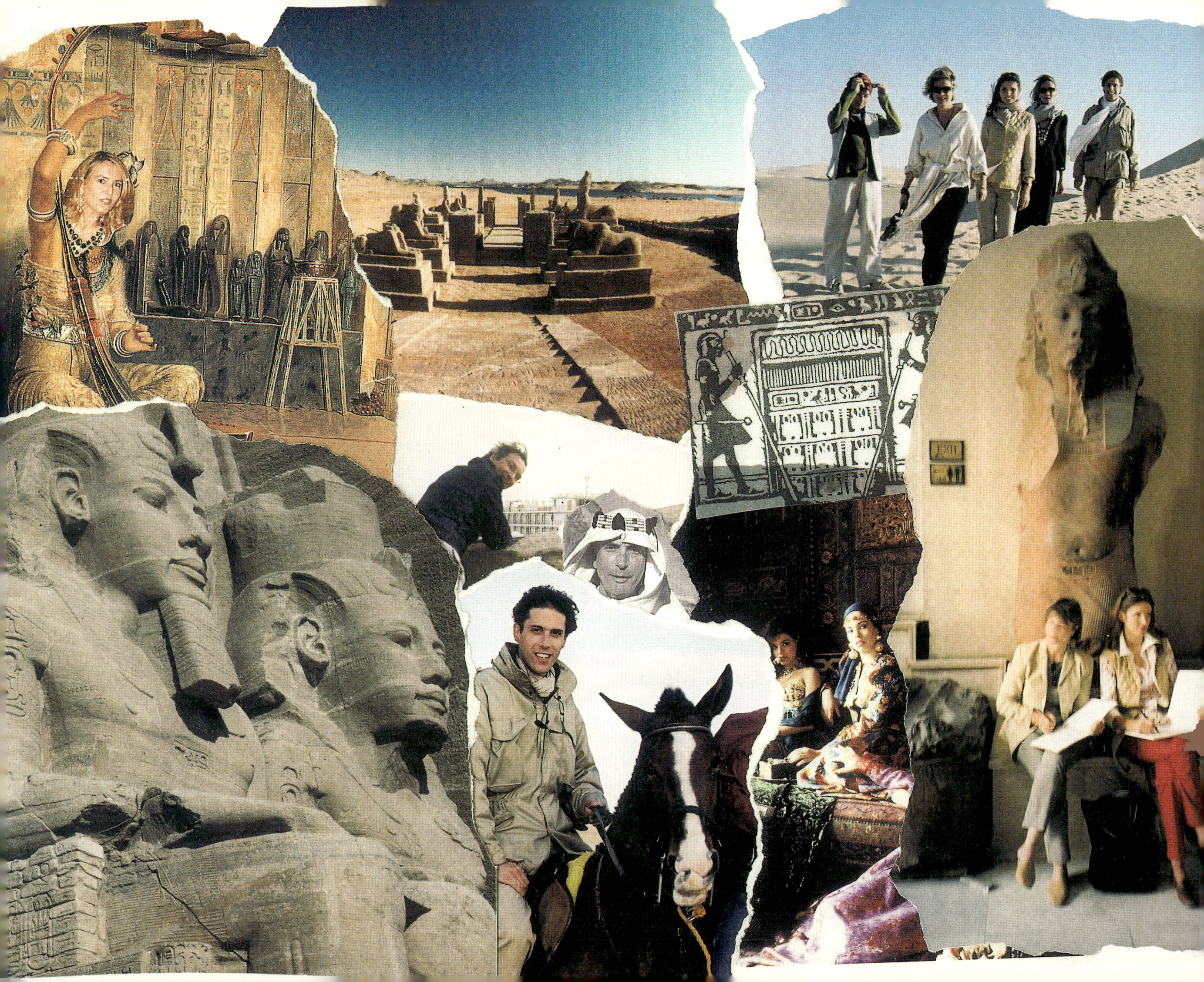

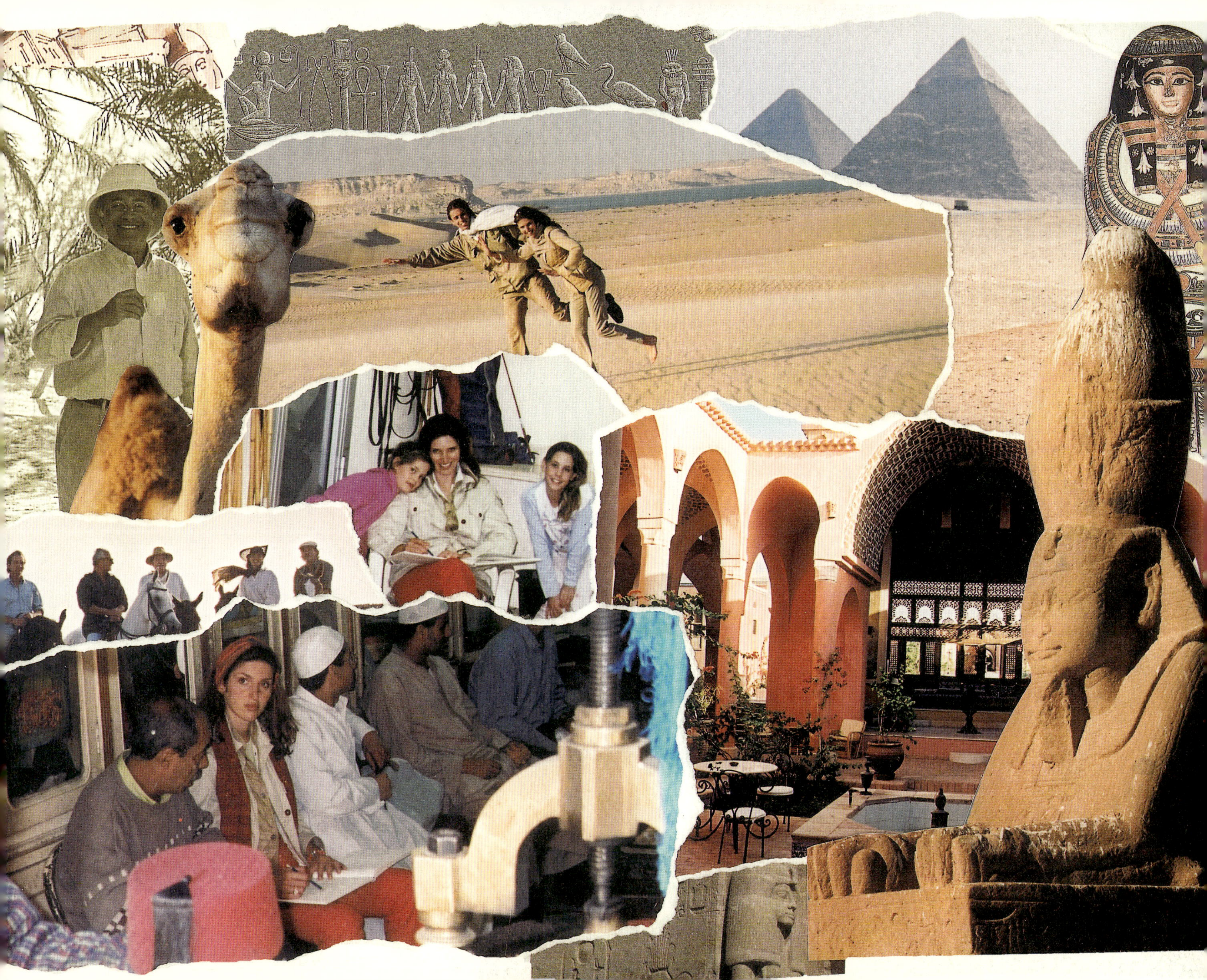

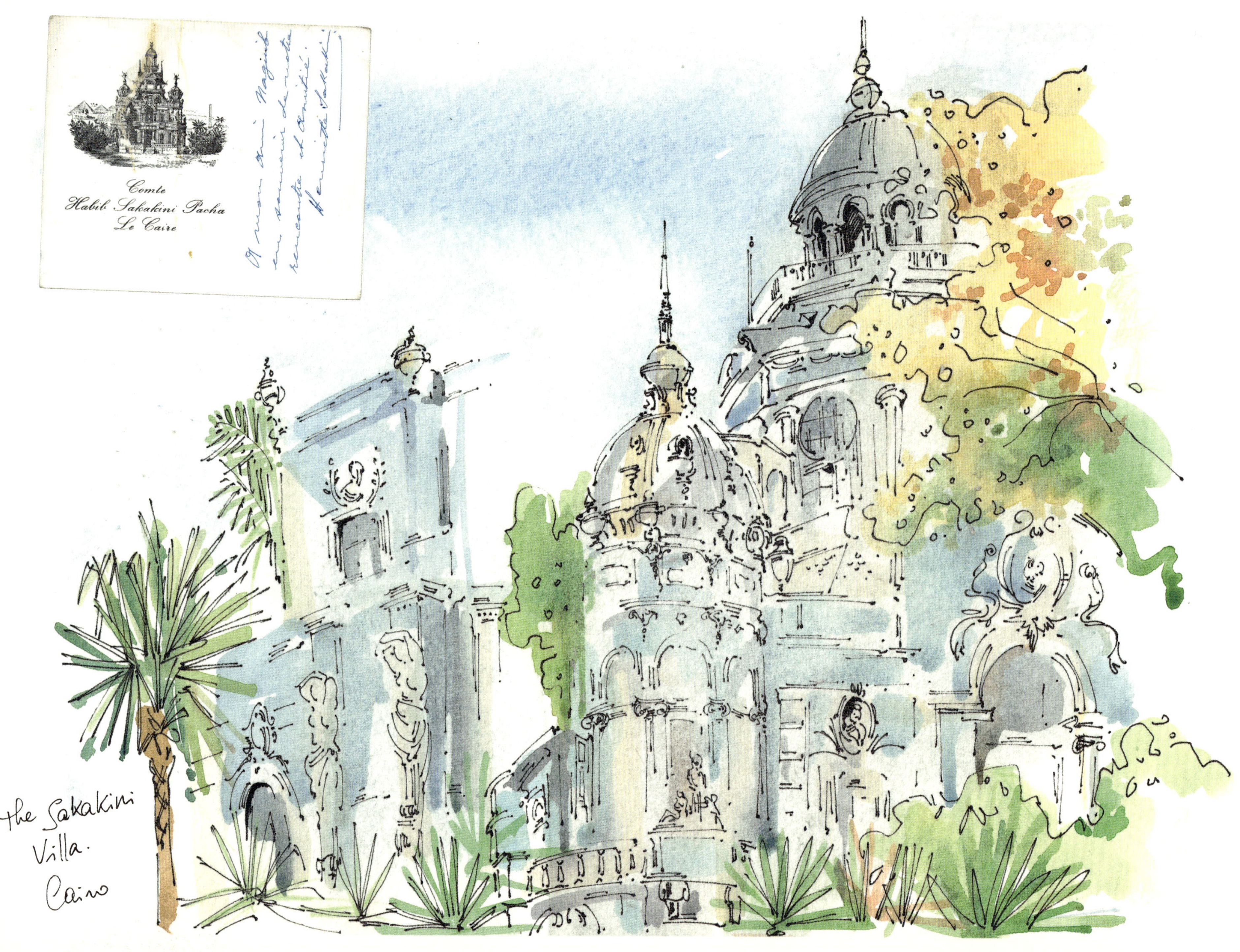
Comte
Habib Sakakini Pacha
Le Caire
the Sakakini
Villa.
Cairo

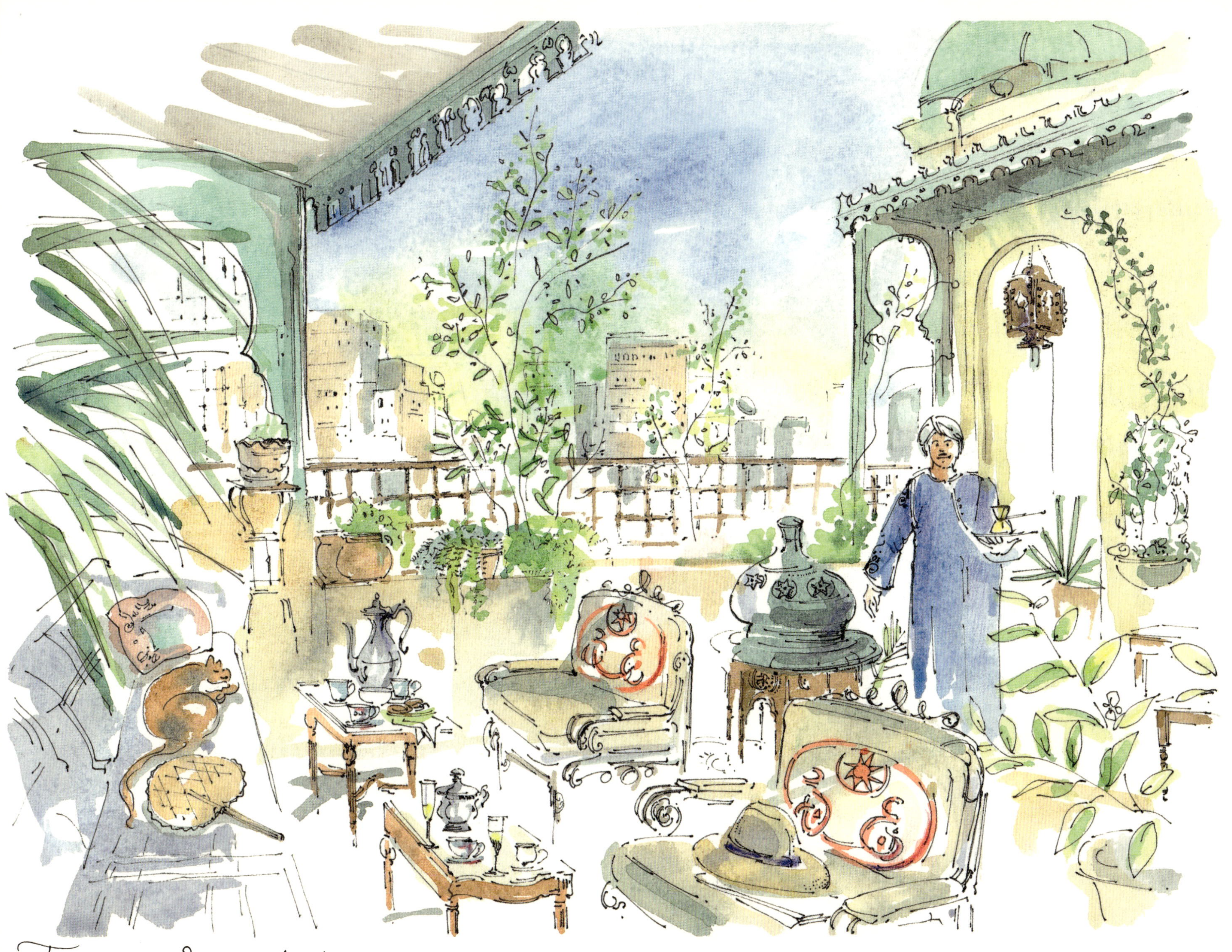

Terrace, Zamalek

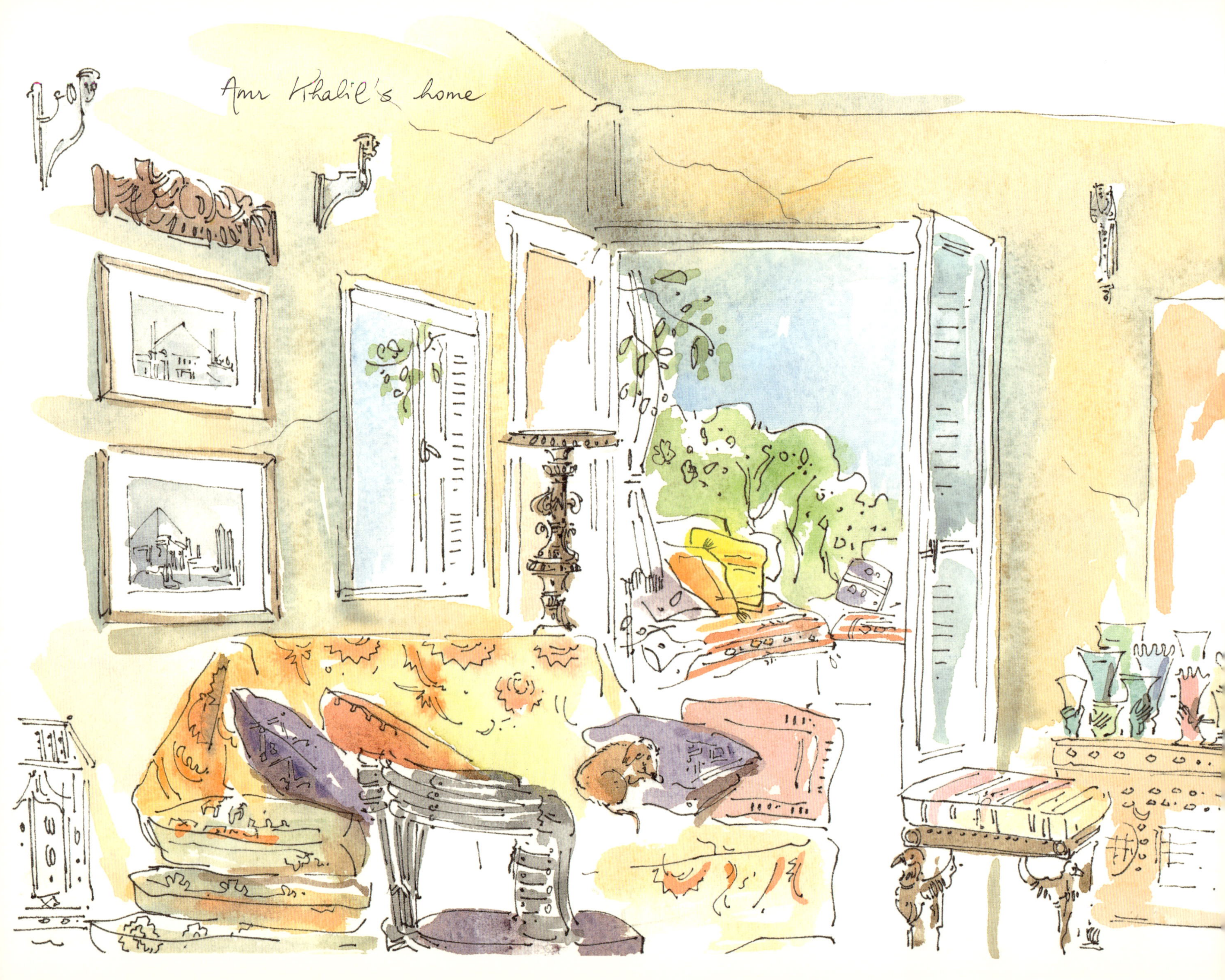
Amr Khalil's home

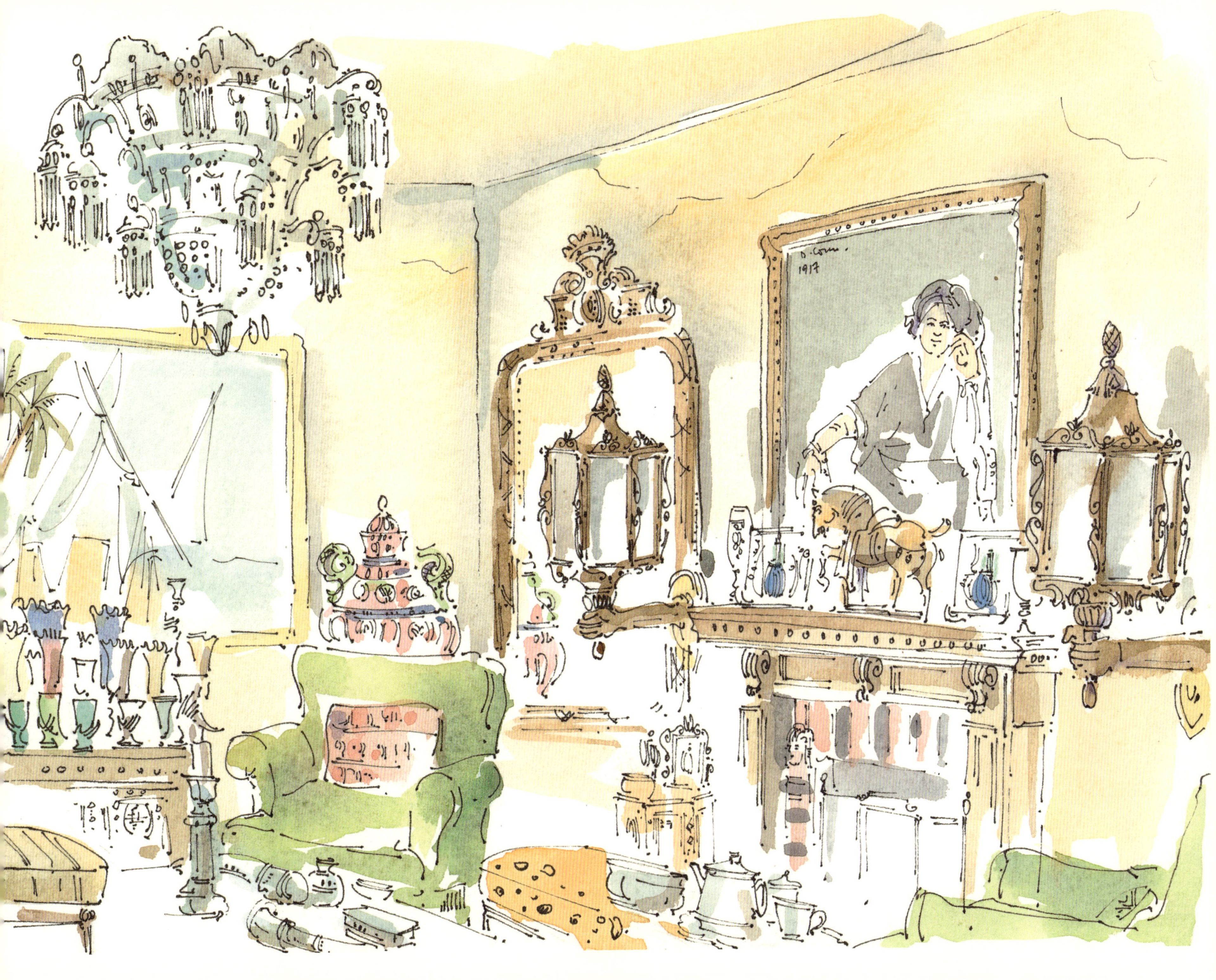

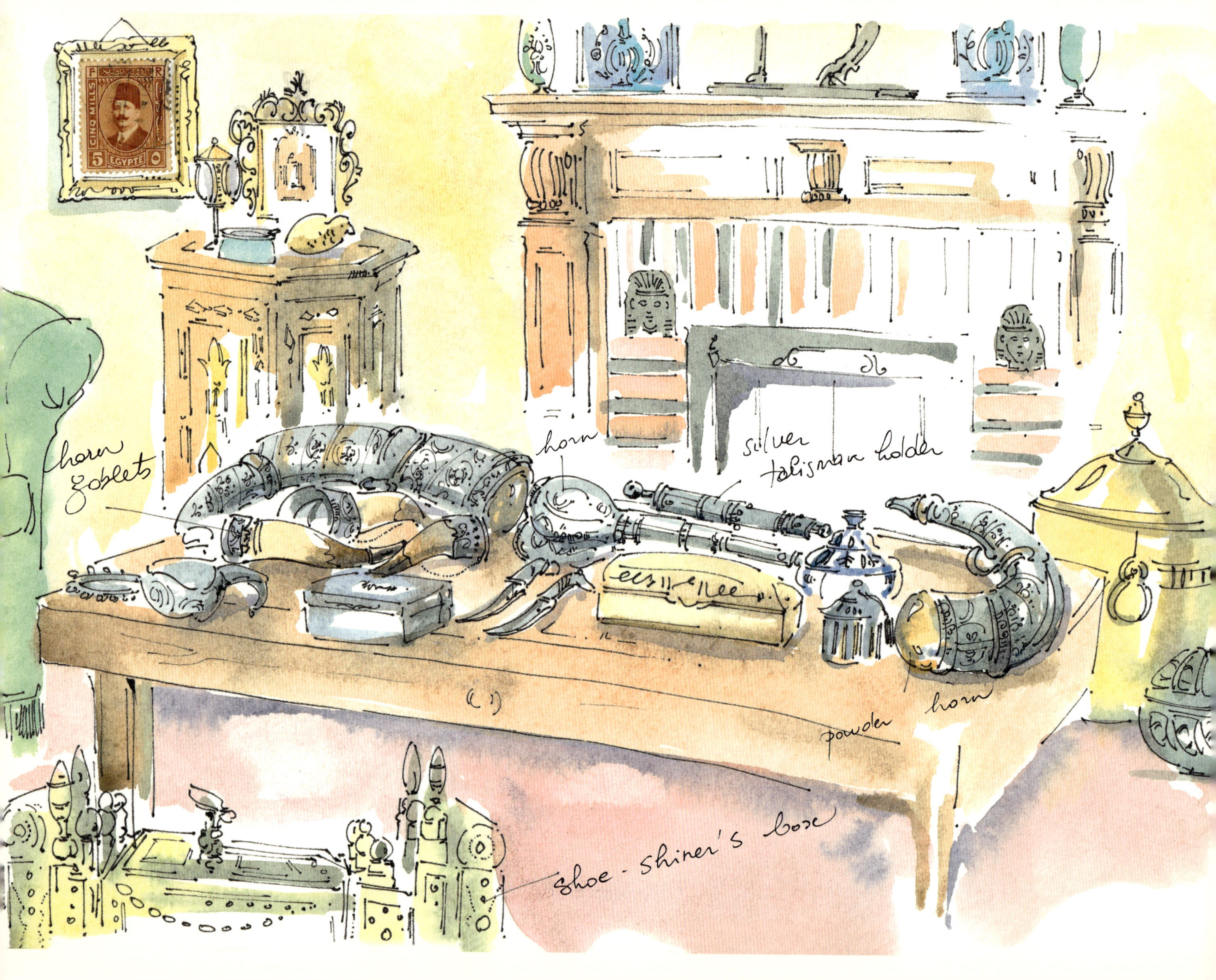

horn goblets
horn
silver talisman holder
horn
powder
shoe-shiner's box

The Harem *by Estelle Arielle Bouchet*

On the other side of the moucharaby, even the window hides itself from the eyes of the street, like the women of the East, who see without being seen. The harem symbolizes this private realm whose veils have always caressed the fantasies of the male psyche. An abundance of lascivious women whose only raison d'être is to serve men and their pleasures – this is one of the harem's erotic connotations, which has deeply embedded itself into the Western collective unconscious and rapidly developed in the eighteenth century when Orientalism came into fashion. Texts such as Montesquieu's *Persian Letters*, the tales of *A Thousand and One Nights*, Shelley and Byron's poetry, and the letters of Lady Mary Wortley Montagu inspired an infatuation with the East in European culture, which reached its zenith in the Orientalist painting of the nineteenth century. European painters depicted the forbidden world of the harem in theatrical, sensuous, and highly colorful works.

From an Eastern point of view, however, the harem does not symbolize licentiousness, but, on the contrary, a structural order based on political, religious, and social values. In fact, the Arabic word "harem" signifies that which is forbidden and, consequently, that which is hidden. The harem represents two concepts: the container—an enclosed space where women from the same family or tribe dwell—and the content—the women themselves. So as not to contravene the concept behind the harem, it is necessary to hide the object of desire and to protect it from all outside temptation. This universe is specifically feminine, its privacy corresponding symbolically to the internalized nature of female sexuality. Unlike Judaism, where traditions are passed on by the mother, Islam is handed down by the father. This paternal transmission partly explains the scrupulous enclosure to which women are subjected, which aims to guarantee complete control over offspring.

Only eunuchs were allowed to enter this strictly feminine realm. Deprived of the ability to procreate, they presented no danger for the community. Sultans, sheikhs, and untitled men of substantial means could have their own harem. The Manial Palace on the banks of the Nile contains a harem where one can easily imagine the sensual women who once devoted themselves to the arts of belly dancing, music, fragrance, and incense, and reading fortunes in Turkish coffee grounds. Magical arts were also widely practiced in the harem.

The Turkish Sultaness Nejla Orhan confides that, at the Ottoman court, "to get rid of an unwanted guest, we used to place coarse grains of salt behind his chair that we carefully swept away after he left: the unhappy guest would never come back." The practice of magic was a natural accompaniment of ancestral beliefs in which superstitions and the profane occupy a central place. We are far from the Judeo-Christian or Islamic monotheism that formally condemns these practices trespassing against divine providence. Even today, some protect themselves with turquoise, the relic of a pharaonic tradition where stones and colors carry talismanic powers warding off the "evil eye." Children always wear turquoise, in the same way that children in ancient Rome carried a branch of coral. On the banks of the Nile, the spirit of Scheherazade lives on.

"When nothing existed, love existed and when nothing will remain, love will remain. It is the first and the last. It is the bridge of truth, it is beyond everything one may say. It is a companion in the tomb. It is the vine that attaches itself to the tree and draws its luxuriant life from the heart it devours."

Night 989, *A Thousand and One Nights*

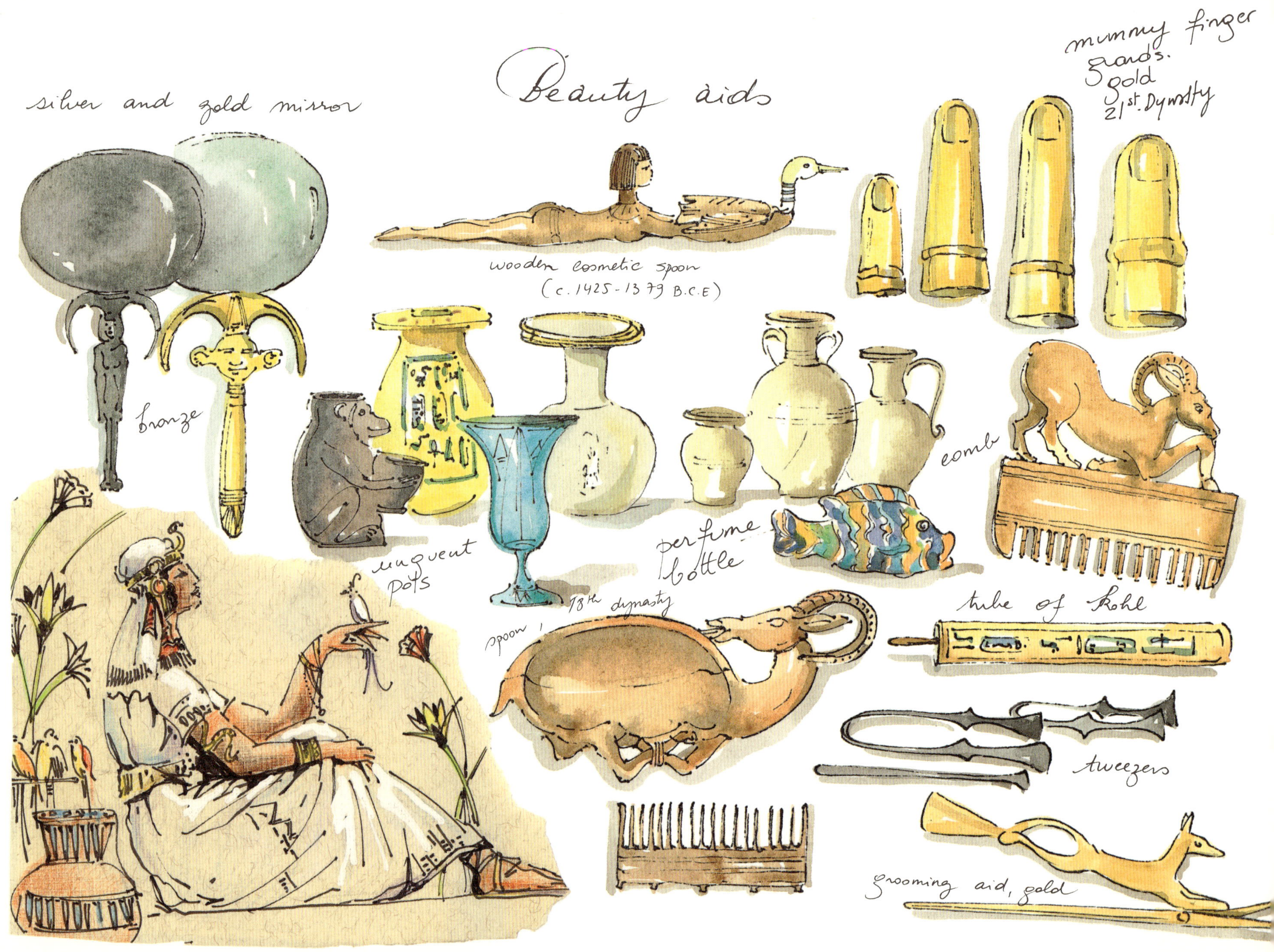

silver and gold mirror
Beauty aids
mummy finger
guards.
gold
21st Dynasty
bronze
wooden cosmetic spoon
(c. 1425 - 1379 B.C.E)
unguent
pots
perfume
bottle
comb
spoon
18th dynasty
tube of kohl
tweezers
grooming aid, gold

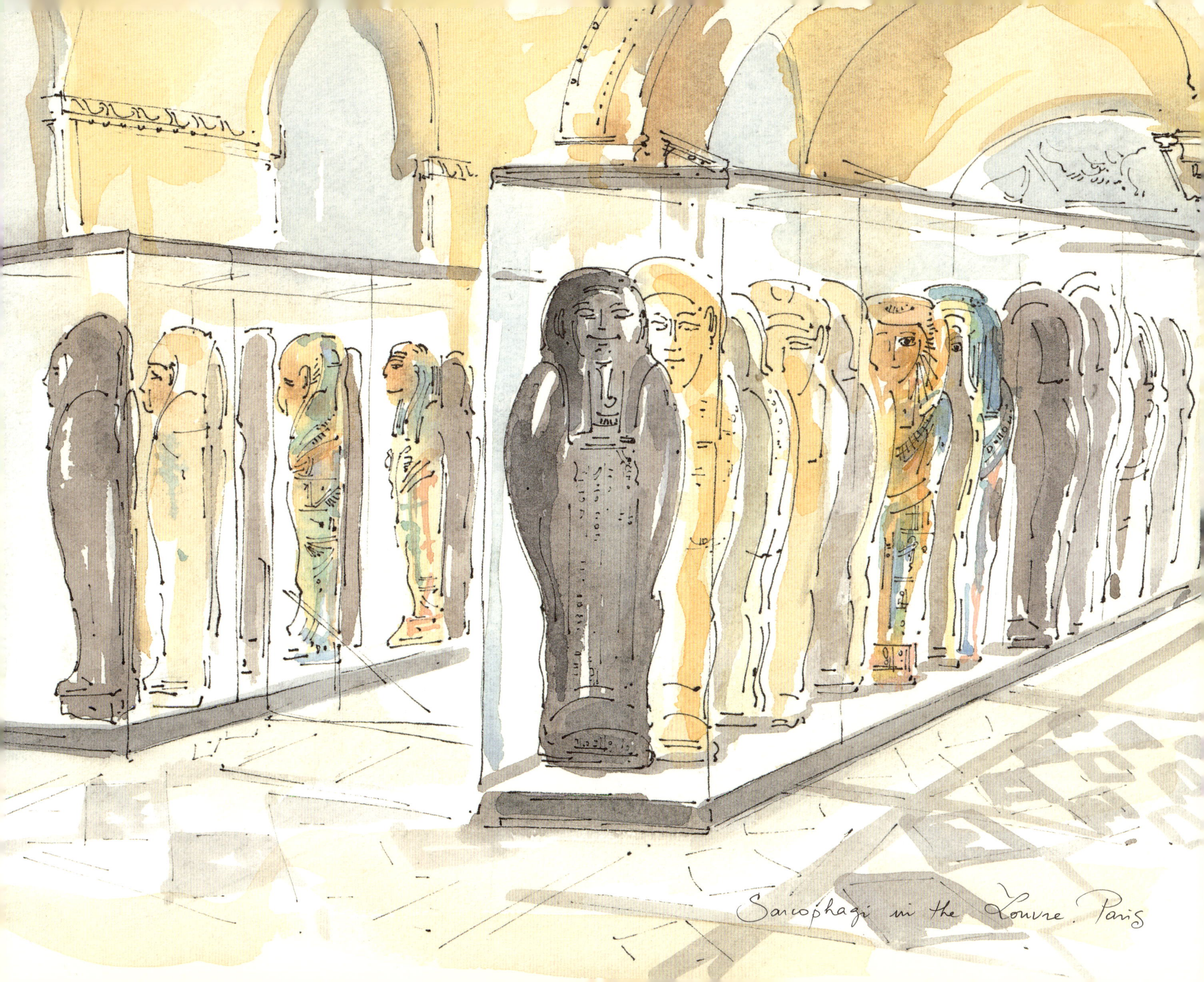

Sarcophagi in the Louvre, Paris

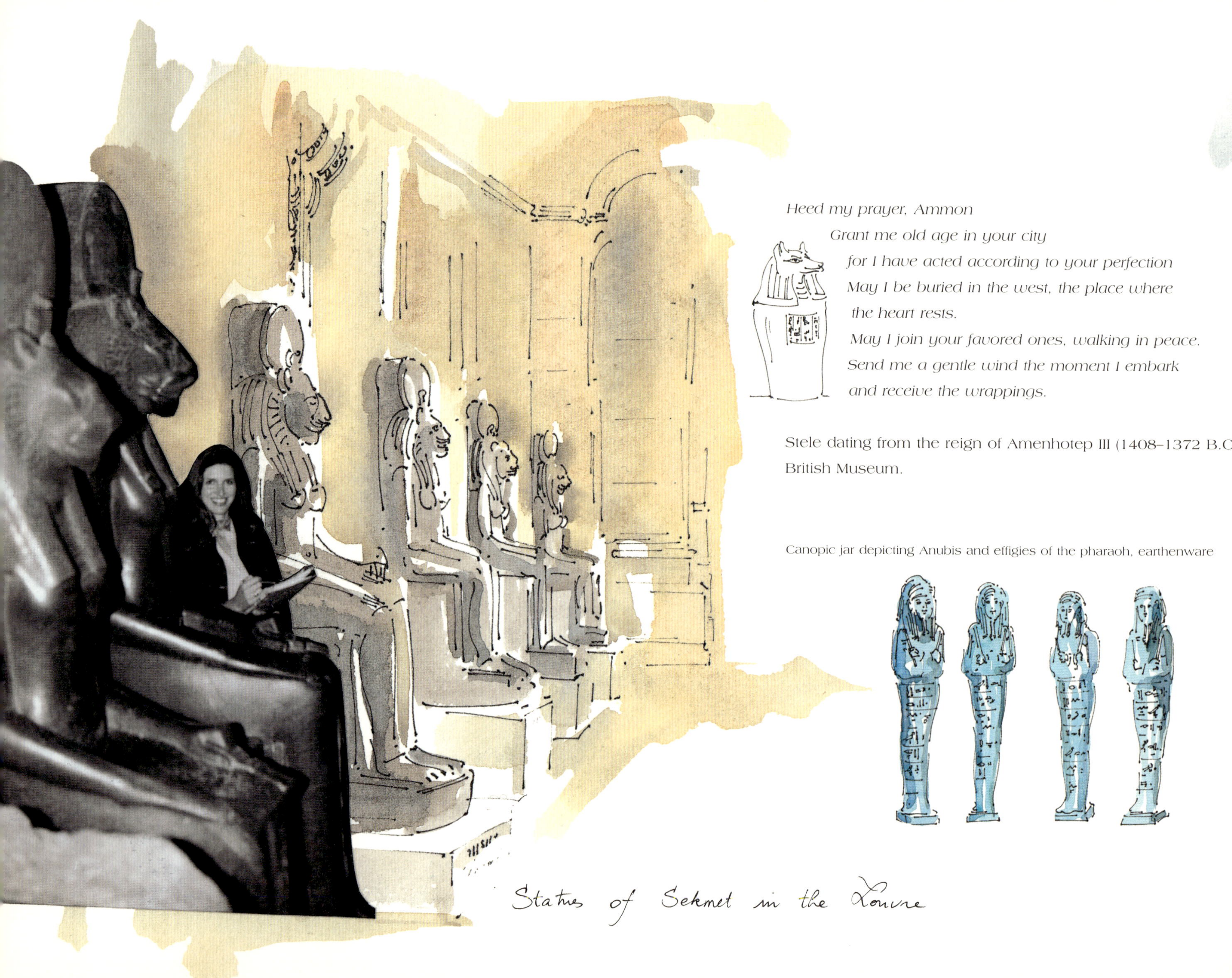

Heed my prayer, Ammon
Grant me old age in your city
for I have acted according to your perfection
May I be buried in the west, the place where
the heart rests.
May I join your favored ones, walking in peace.
Send me a gentle wind the moment I embark
and receive the wrappings.

Stele dating from the reign of Amenhotep III (1408–1372 B.C.E
British Museum.

Canopic jar depicting Anubis and effigies of the pharaoh, earthenware

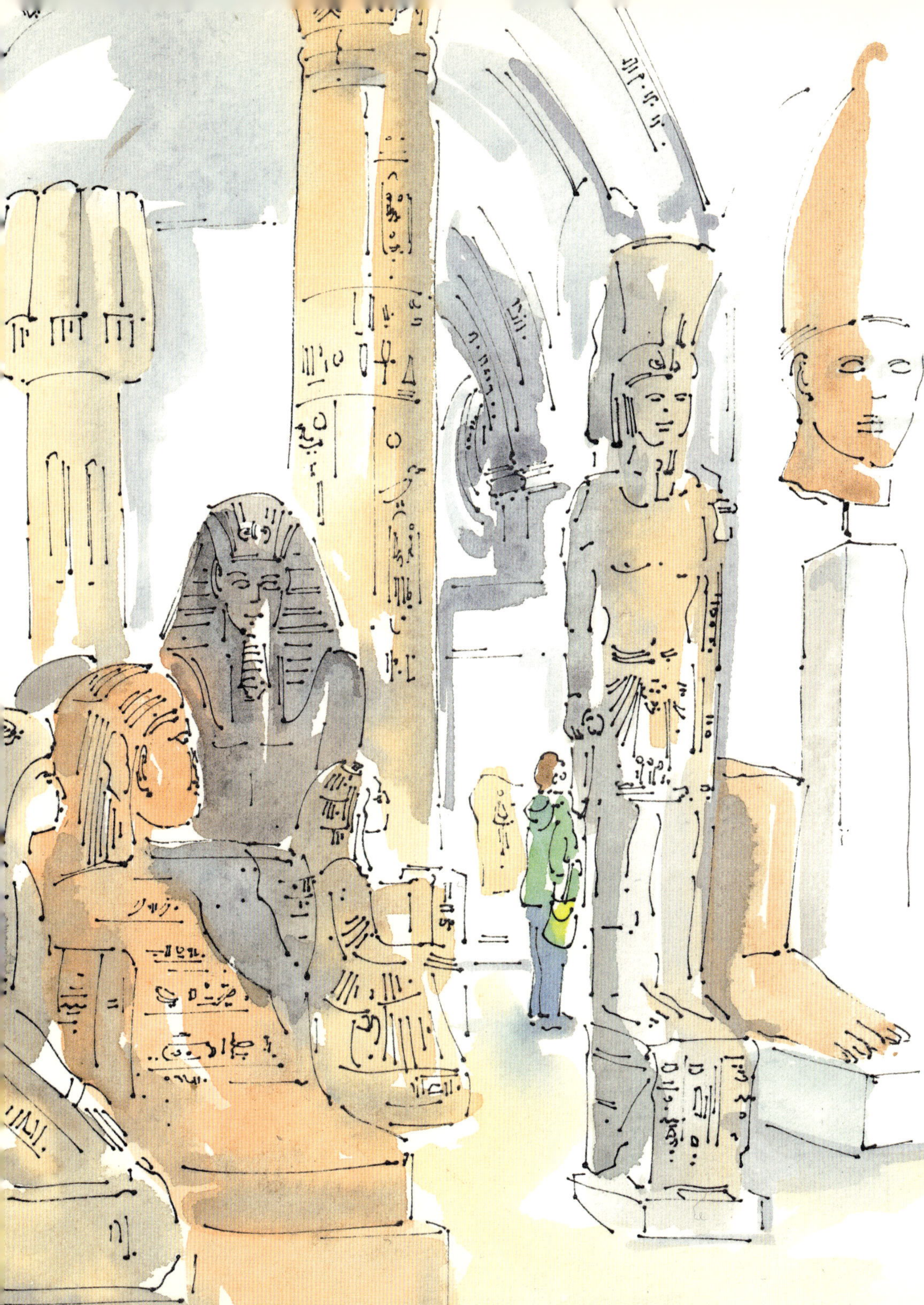

Aisha, the old henna artist

I devote my days to my appearance. Aisha, the henna artist, helps me look beautiful. Aisha truly loves me. She is as small and dark as I am tall and blonde. Aged but energetic, she keeps under the veil of her advanced years the noble beauty handed down from generation to generation by her millennial people.

I watch her as, with obvious pain, she climbs the steps of the terrace overlooking the patio. She is heavy and proud, wearing gipsy-style on her head a turquoise-and-green floral scarf that contains her abundant hair, which she has dyed red herself, tamed into a thick braid. The gentle folds of her long midnight-blue *galabia* conceal the secret of this African woman whose body and face are tattooed, to whom pleasure is forbidden. Yet every part of her body, every breath of her soul vibrates, absorbs, and infinitely radiates a colorful, grandiose fantasy.

Aisha prepares women for marriage, taking care of the sacred temple of their bodies. She initiates them into the ancient rites of love.

Aisha is a magician, but not one of those witches who spread unhappiness and discord.

Aisha is the priestess of love, of unity in its purest sense. Aisha is harmonic and lavishes her music on all

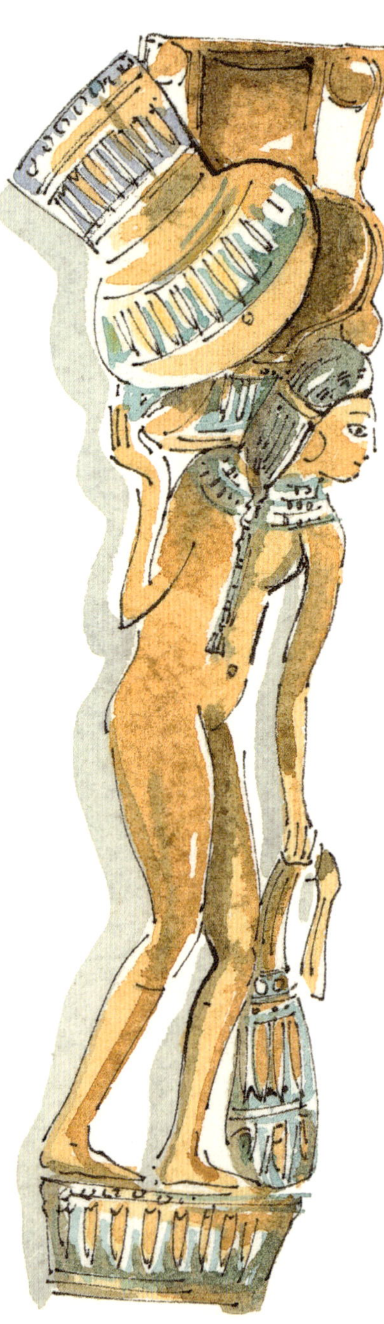

who care to hear: a lesson of balance and joy. The color of her scarf reminds me of the green of Islam, of the green and gold that I will wear tonight to honor Karim. Green, symbol of the *Kitab* (book, that is, the Koran). The "Holy War," the Crusaders fighting the green; perhaps this is why in France, where I was born, it is said that green brings bad luck. But how could God have put an unlucky color into nature?

Green is the friend of water, the friend of life.
The green Nile, the turquoise green of Sinai.

I thirst for absolute green. In distant Arabia, in this land where the Koran was inspired by the Prophet, in the midst of desert, sand, and drought, green was in short supply.

Akdhar, the talismanic color of Islam. Symbolic green. The green of your eyes when they find your native land again, the green of mine when they marry yours. Blessed land, the blessed people whose pacifism Herodotus praised.

The green of nature, the green of life, the green of peace. The grandeur and strength of the sap that rises through the tree to nourish it. Green is one in its multiplicity.

Nejma, Om'Nazem, *Al Baraka*

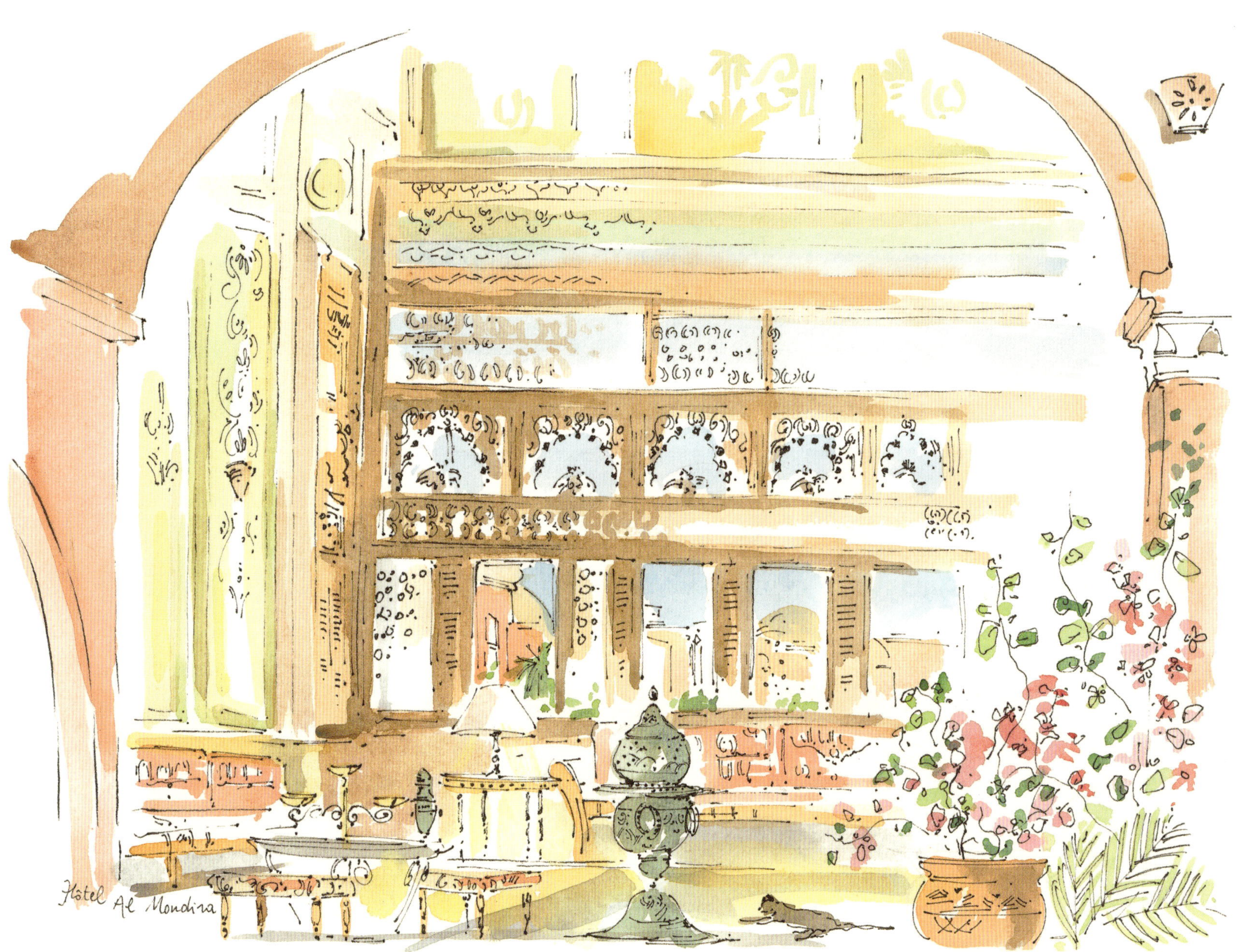

Hôtel Al Moudira

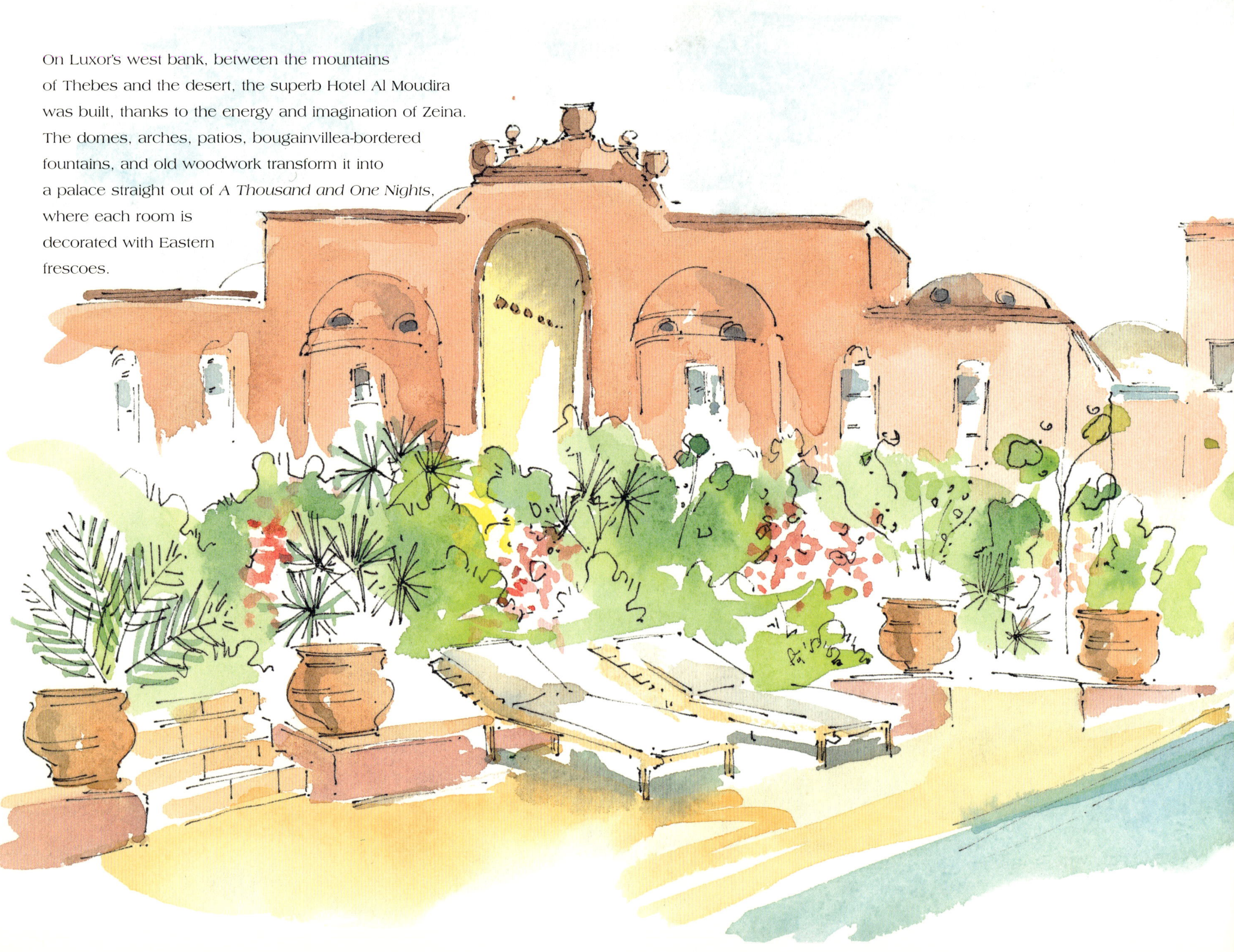

On Luxor's west bank, between the mountains
of Thebes and the desert, the superb Hotel Al Moudira
was built, thanks to the energy and imagination of Zeina.
The domes, arches, patios, bougainvillea-bordered
fountains, and old woodwork transform it into
a palace straight out of *A Thousand and One Nights*,
where each room is
decorated with Eastern
frescoes.

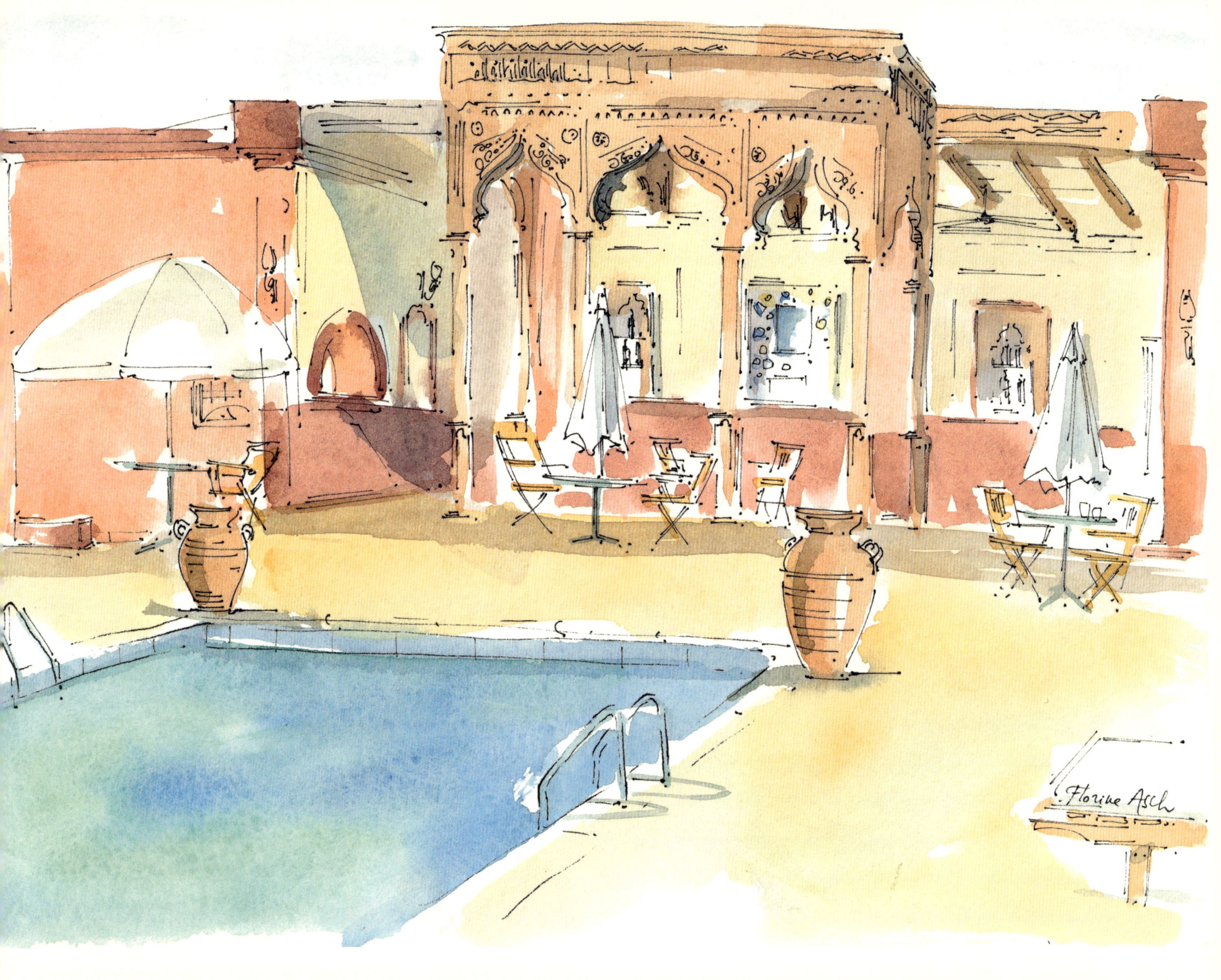

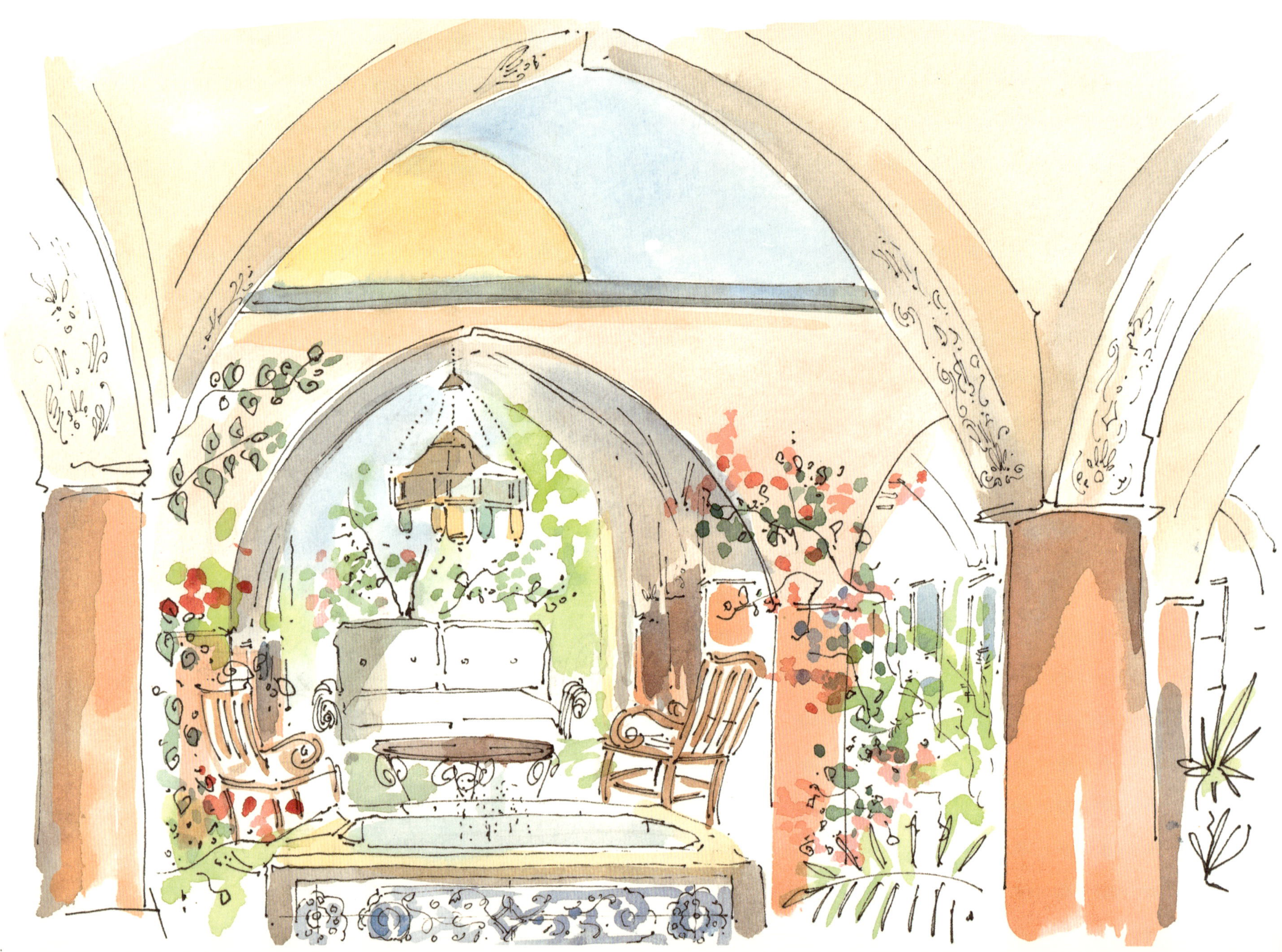

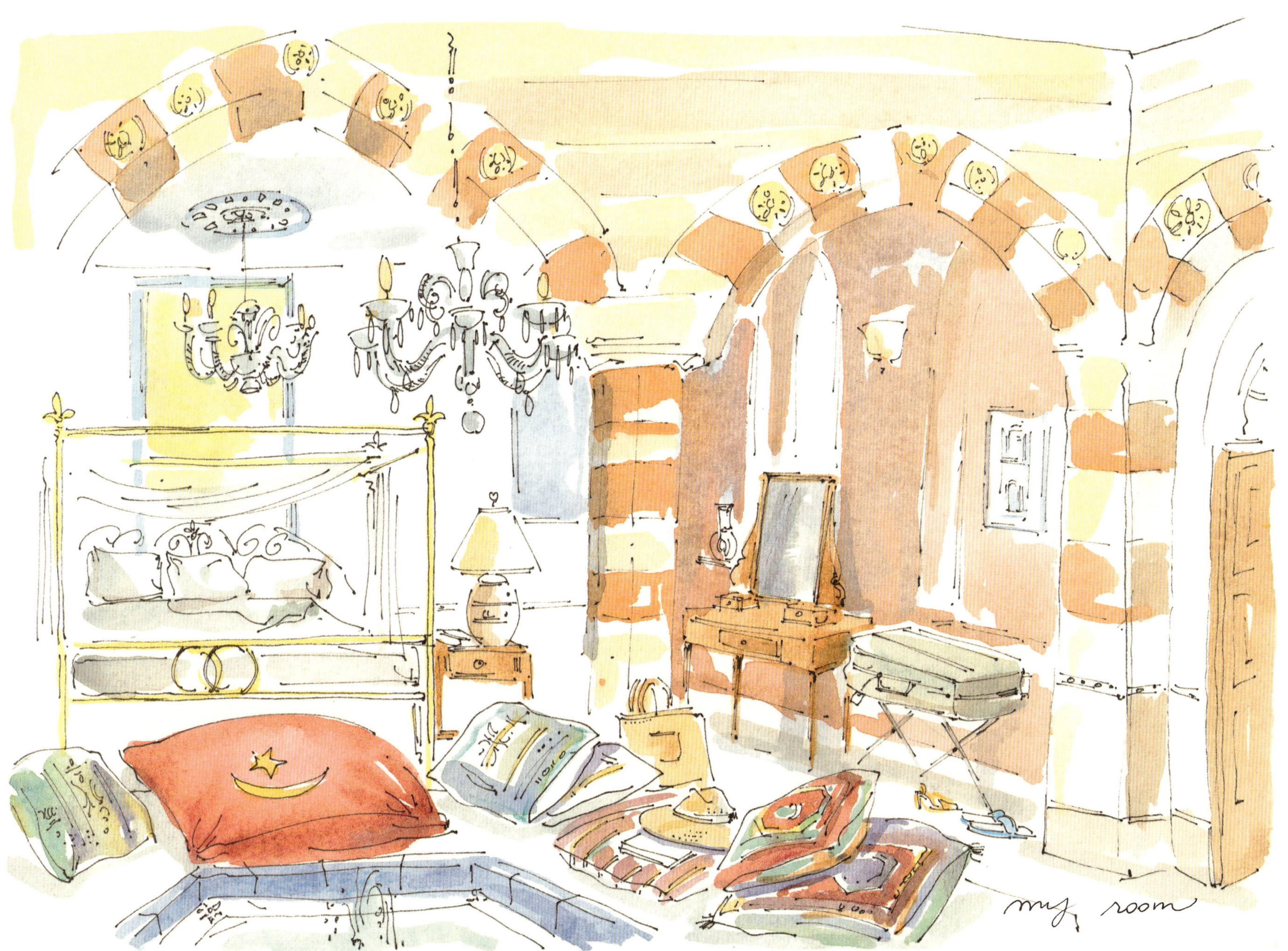
room

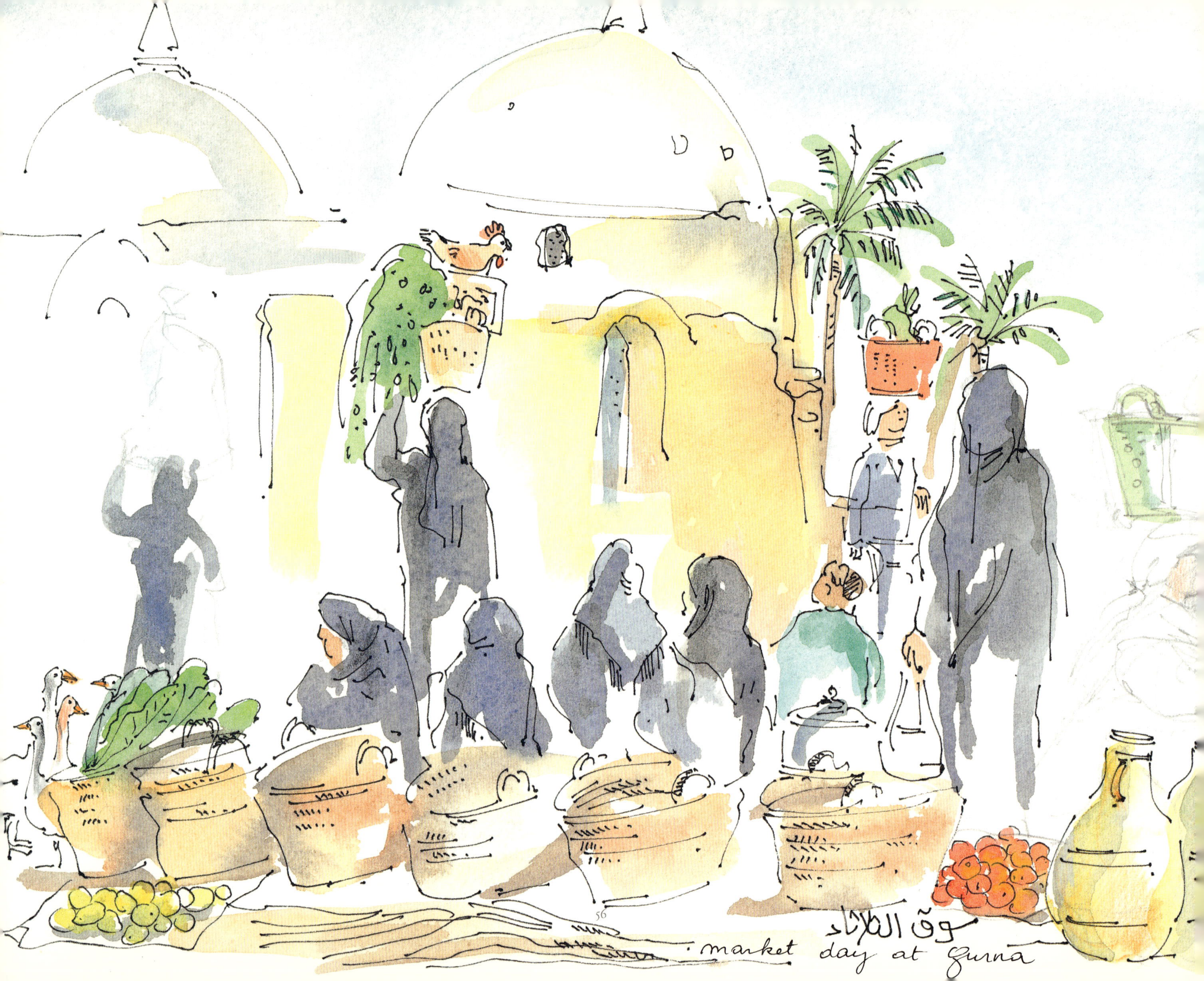

market day at Qurna

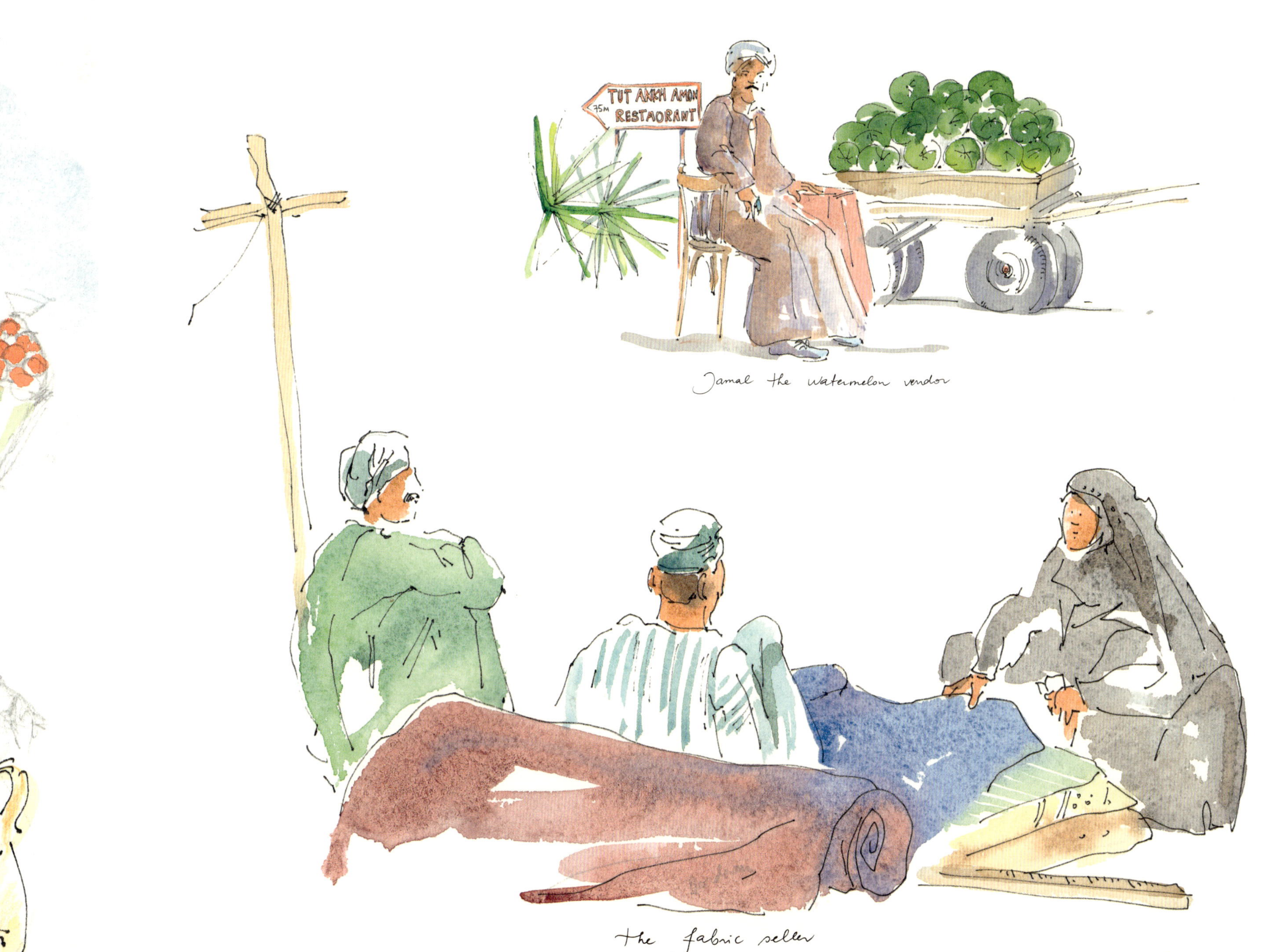

Jamal the Watermelon vendor

the fabric seller

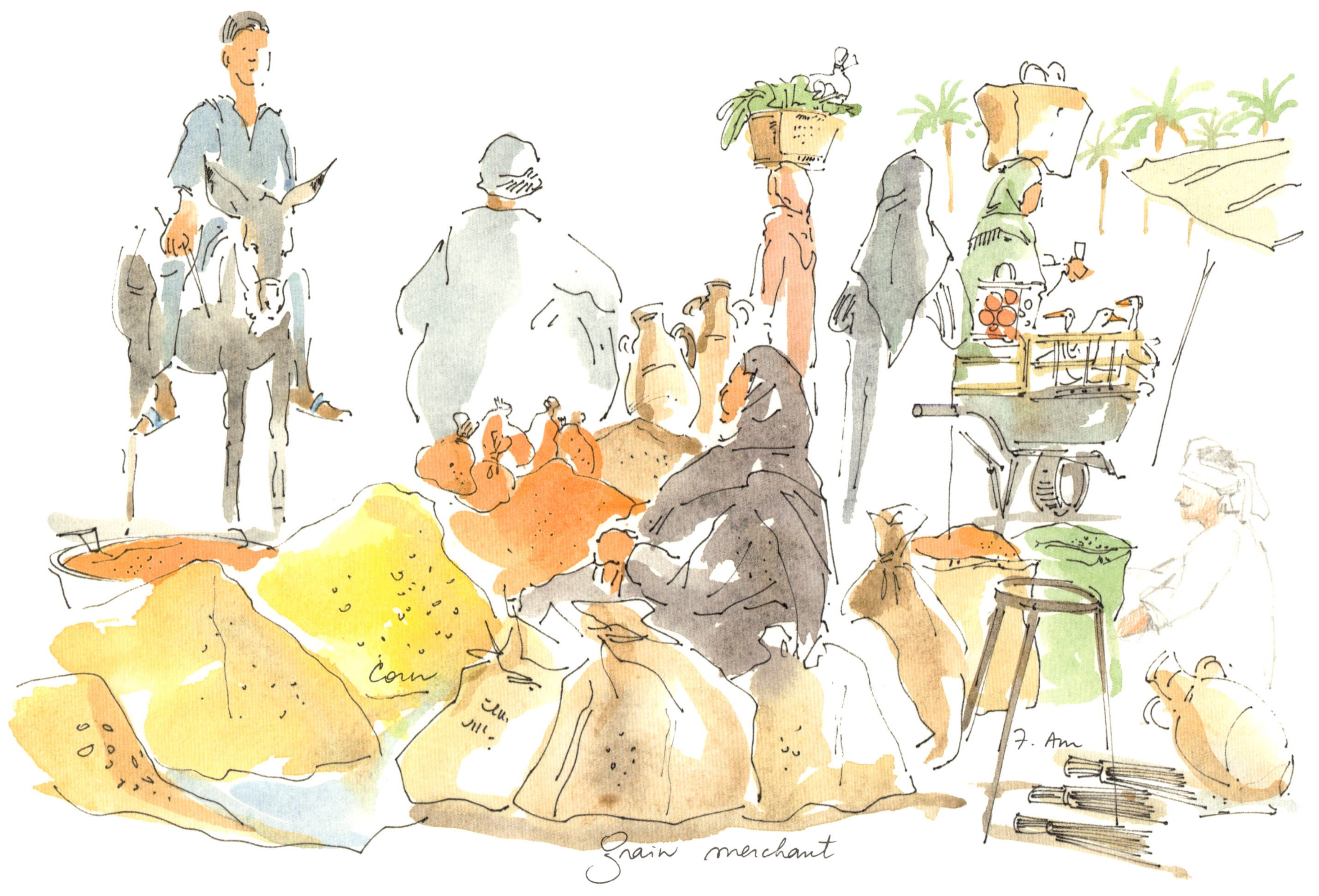

Corn
Grain merchant
7. Am

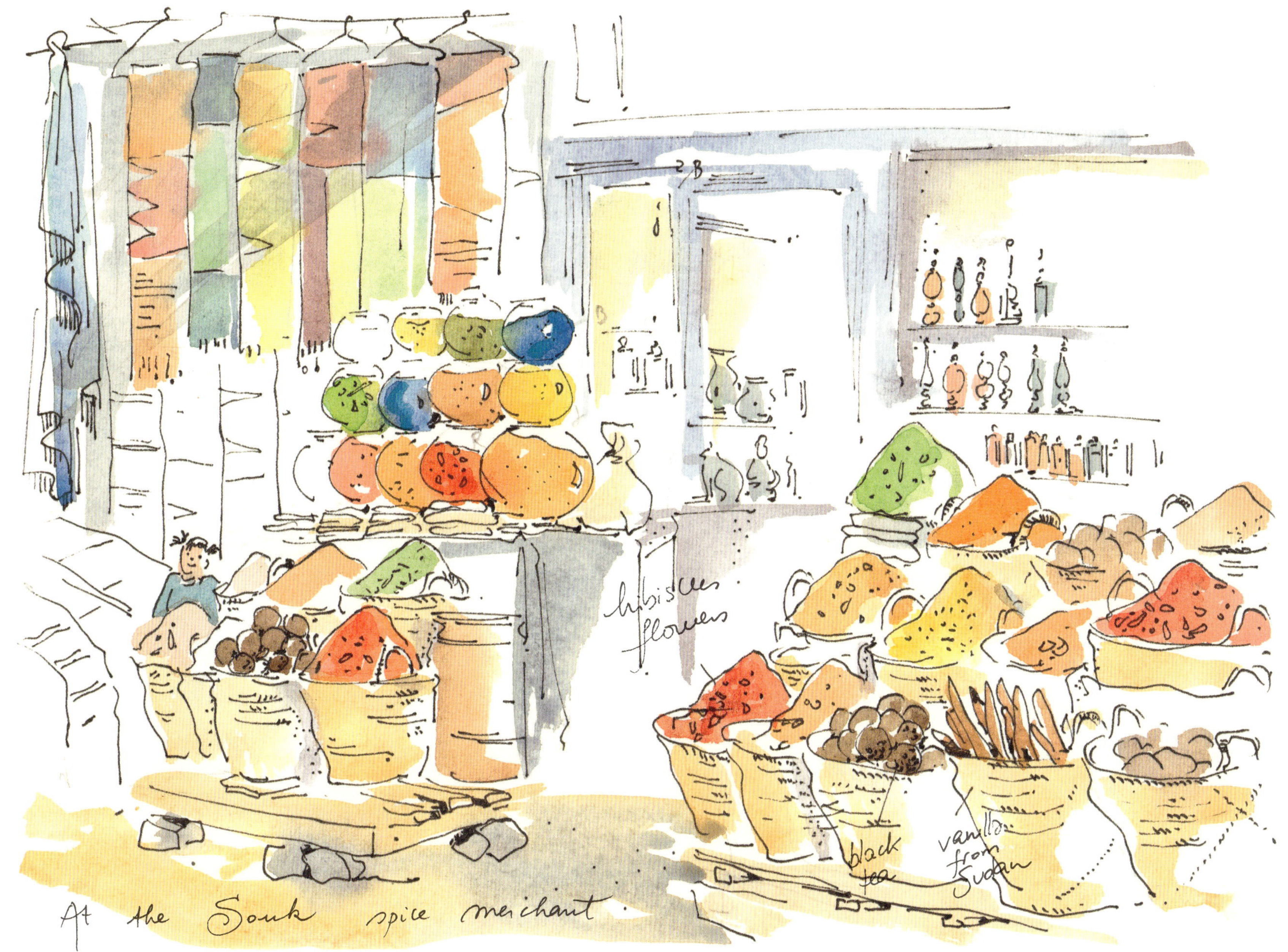

hibiscus flowers
black tea
vanilla from Sudan
At the Souk   spice merchant

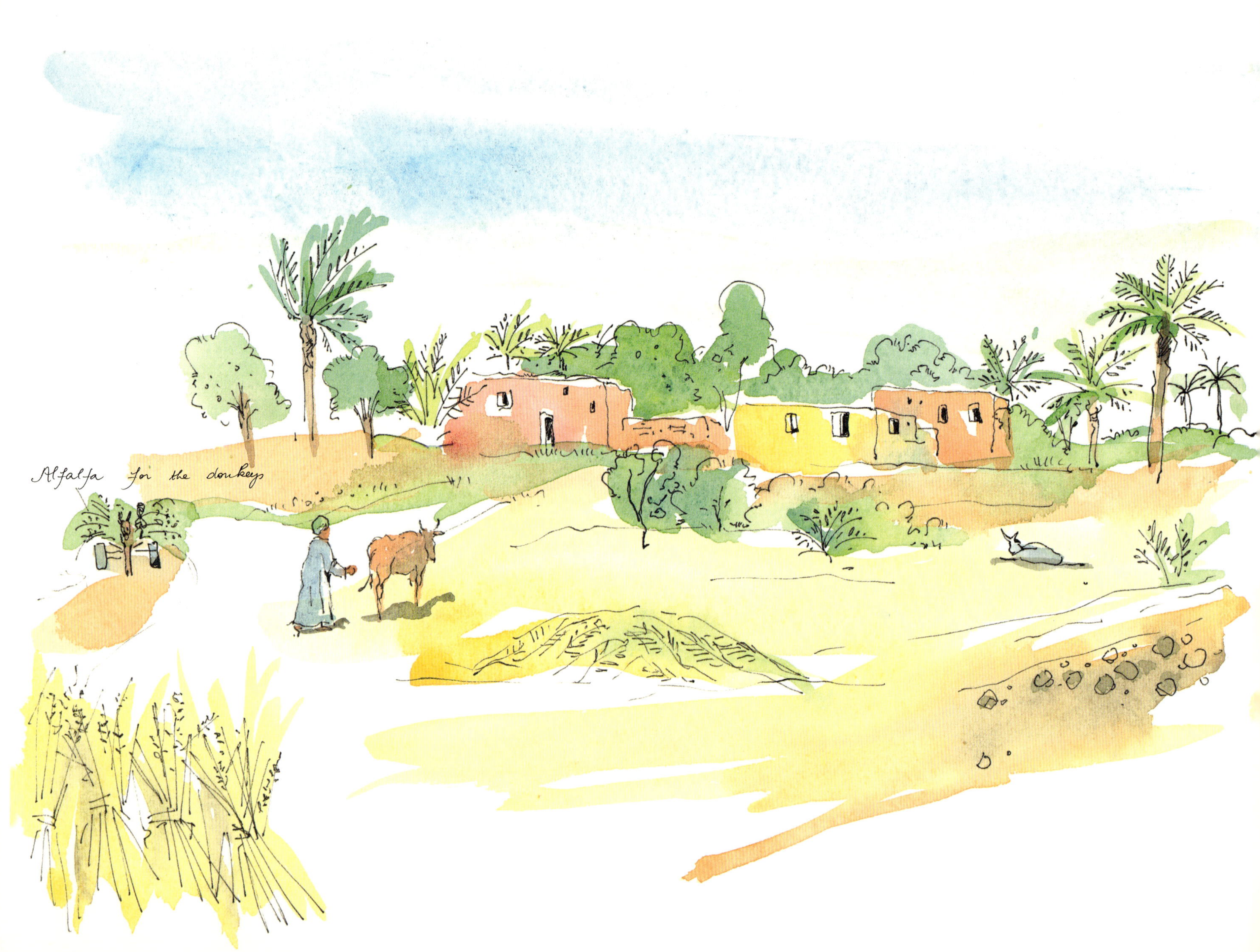

Alfalfa for the donkeys

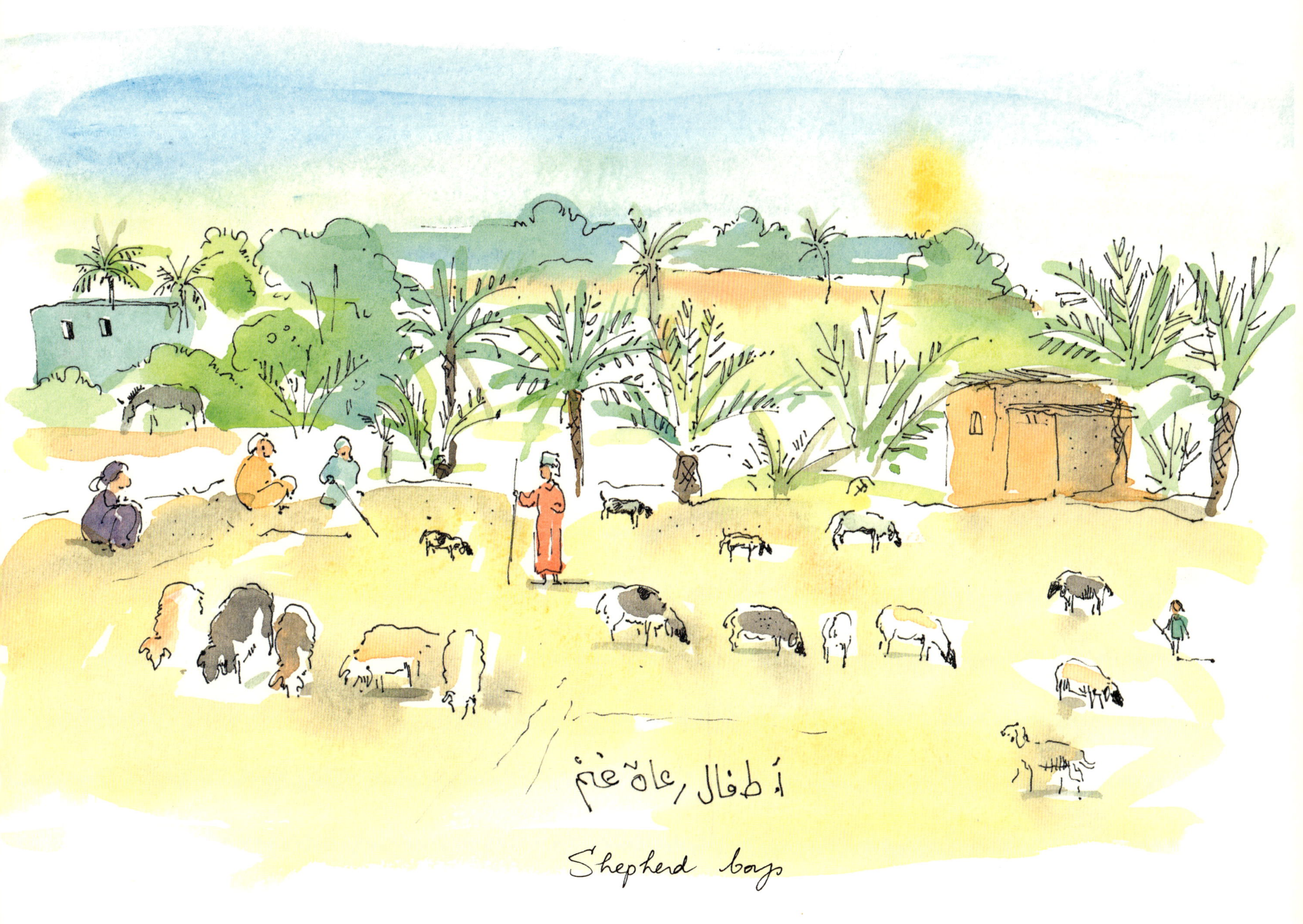

أطفال رعاة غنم

Shepherd boys

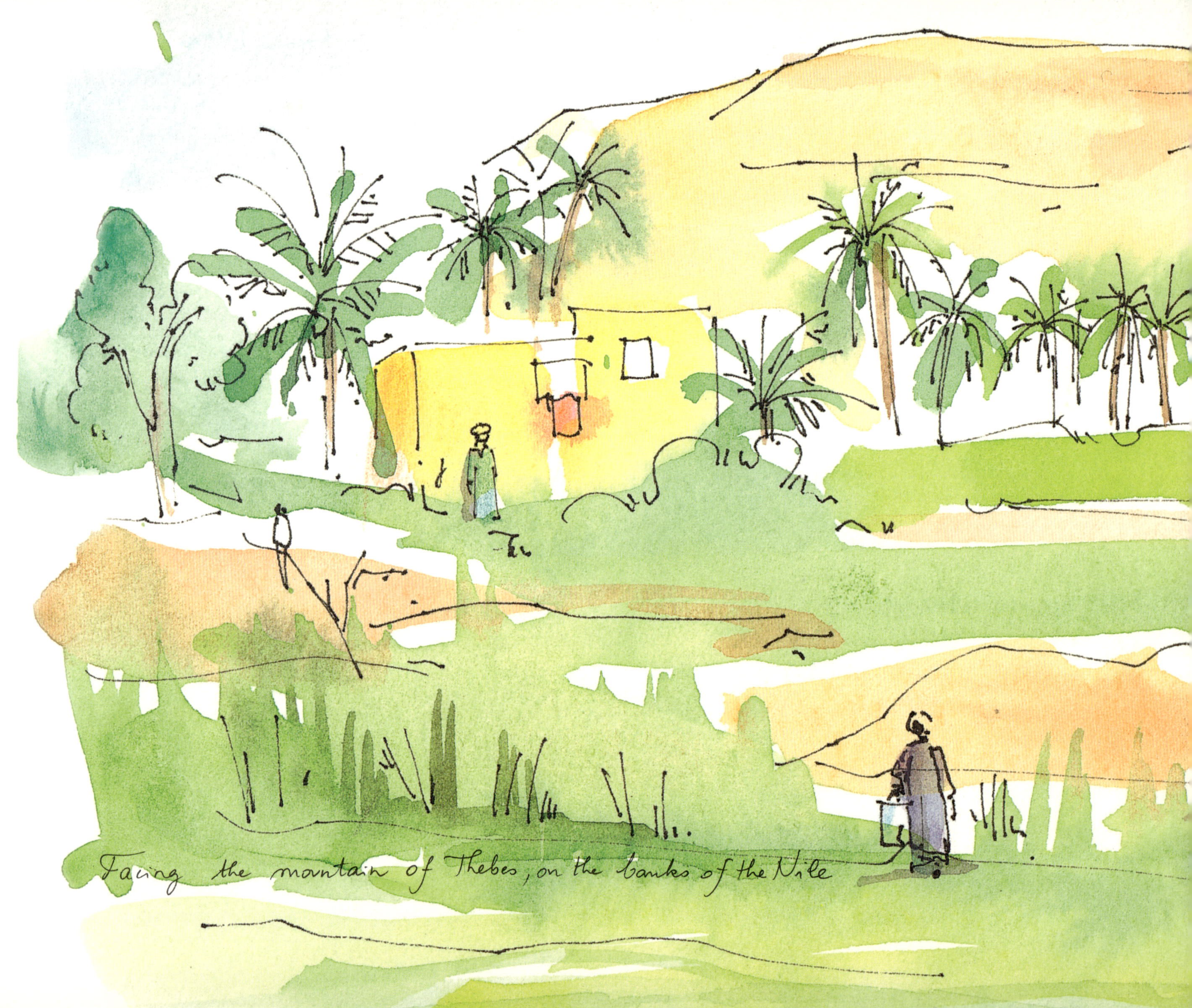

Facing the mountain of Thebes, on the banks of the Nile

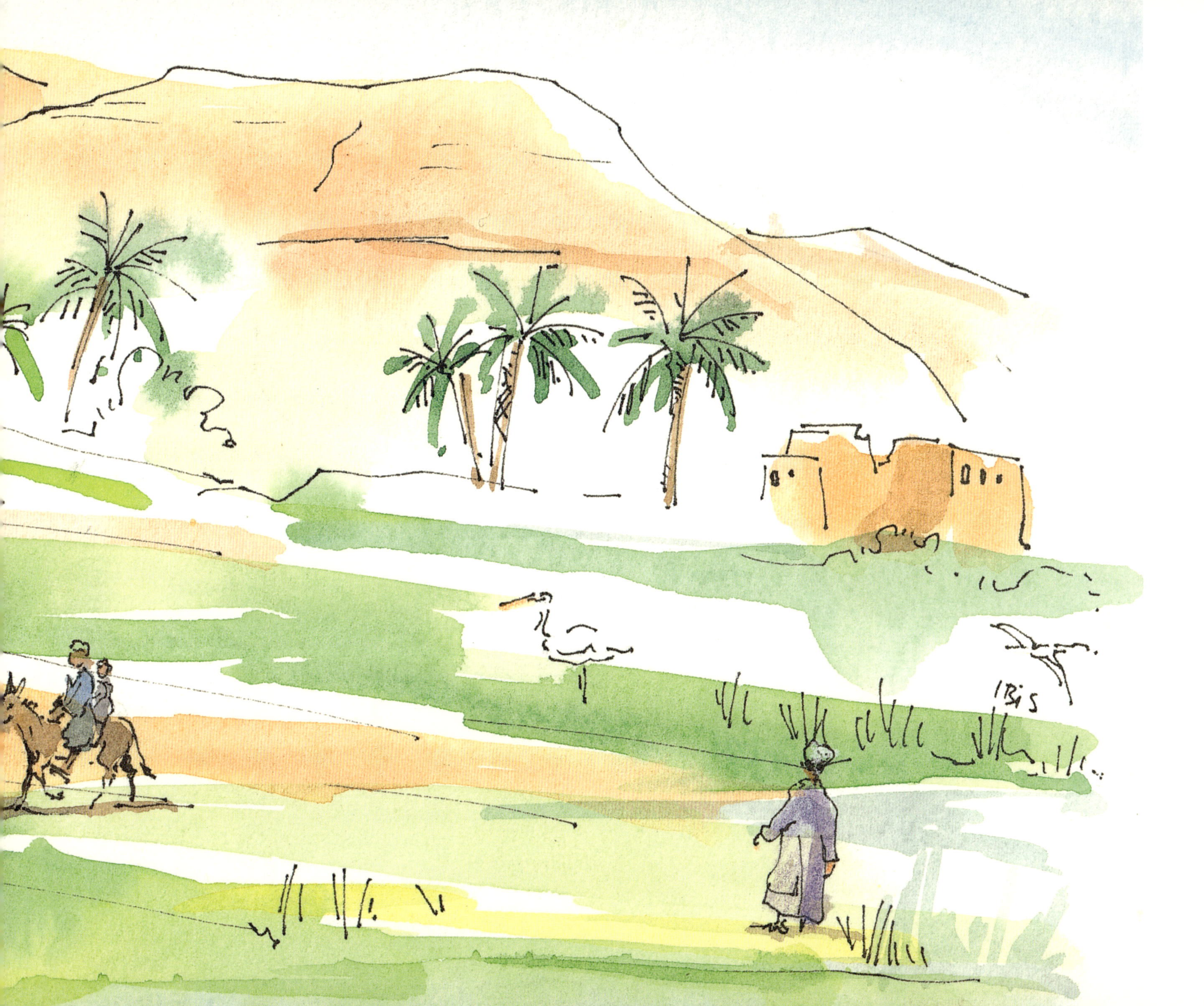
IBIS

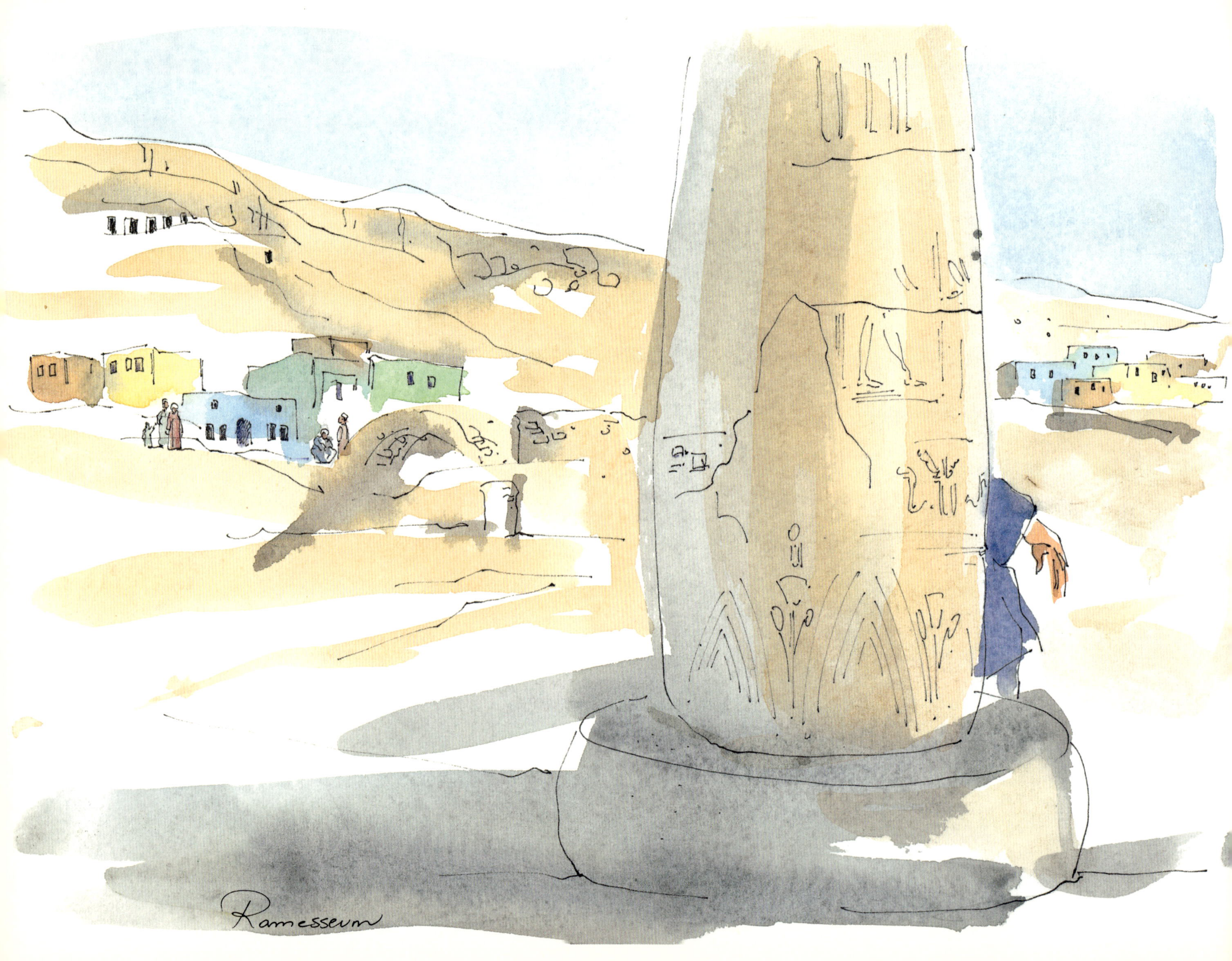

Ramesseum

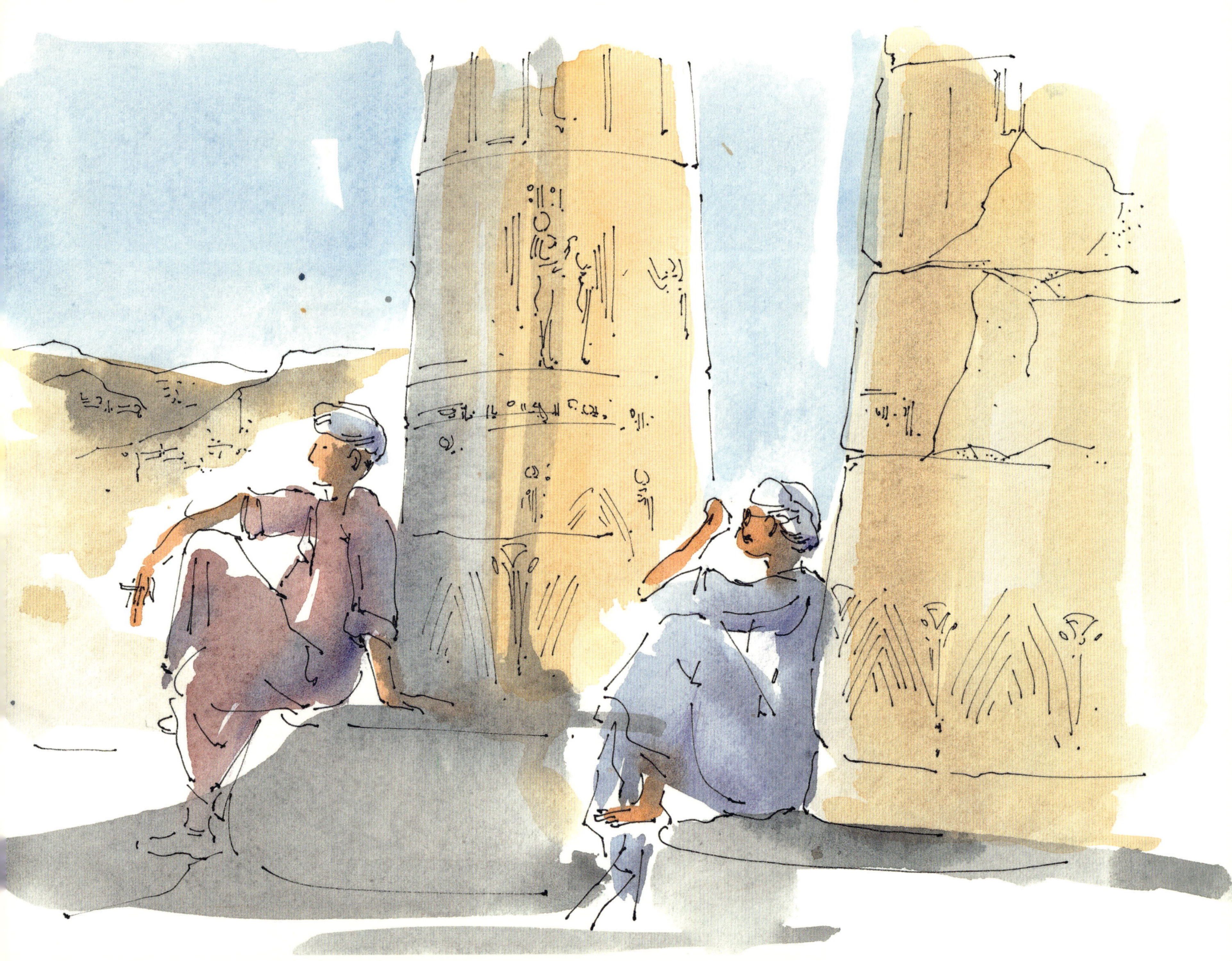

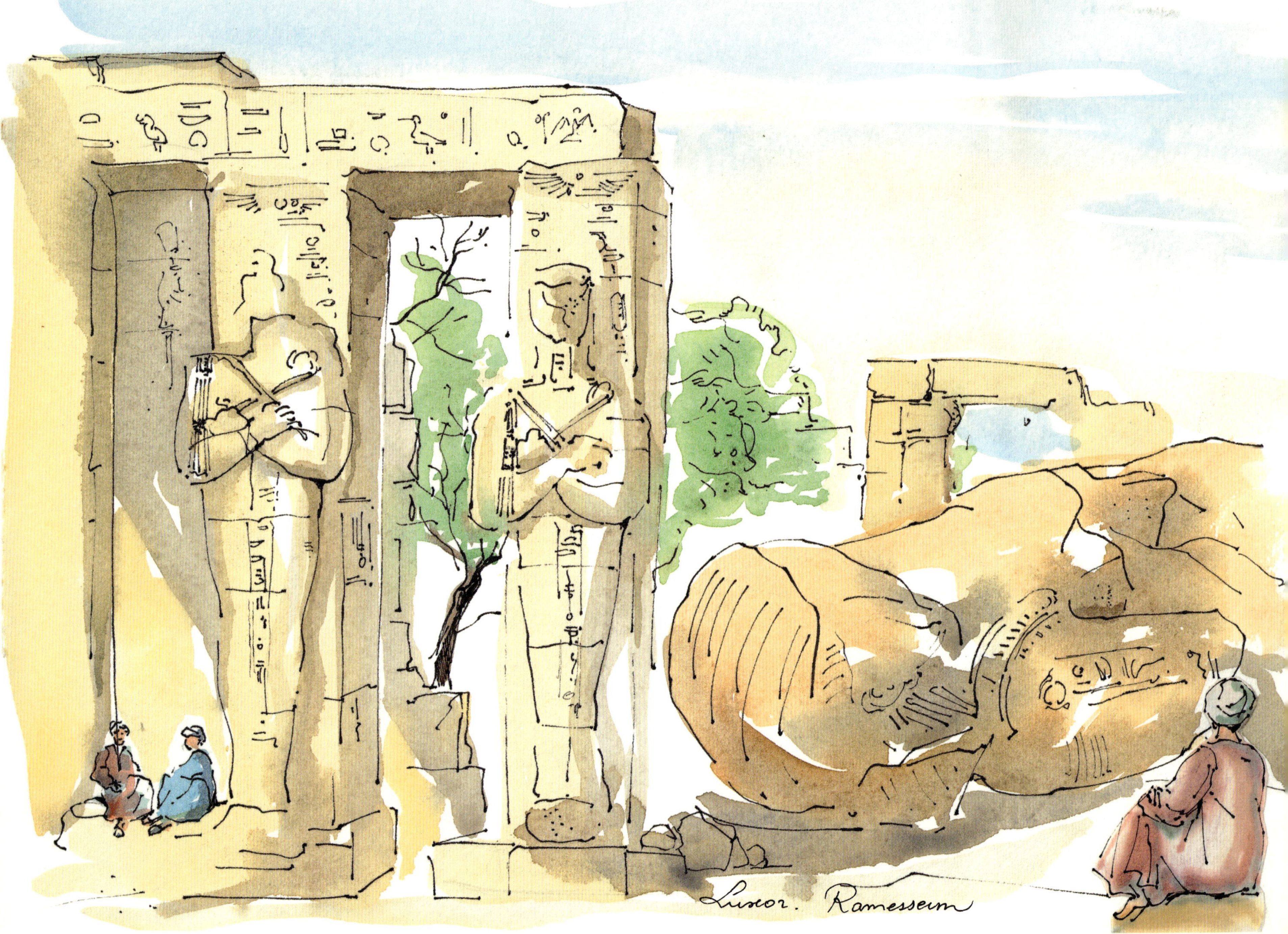

Luxor. Ramesseum

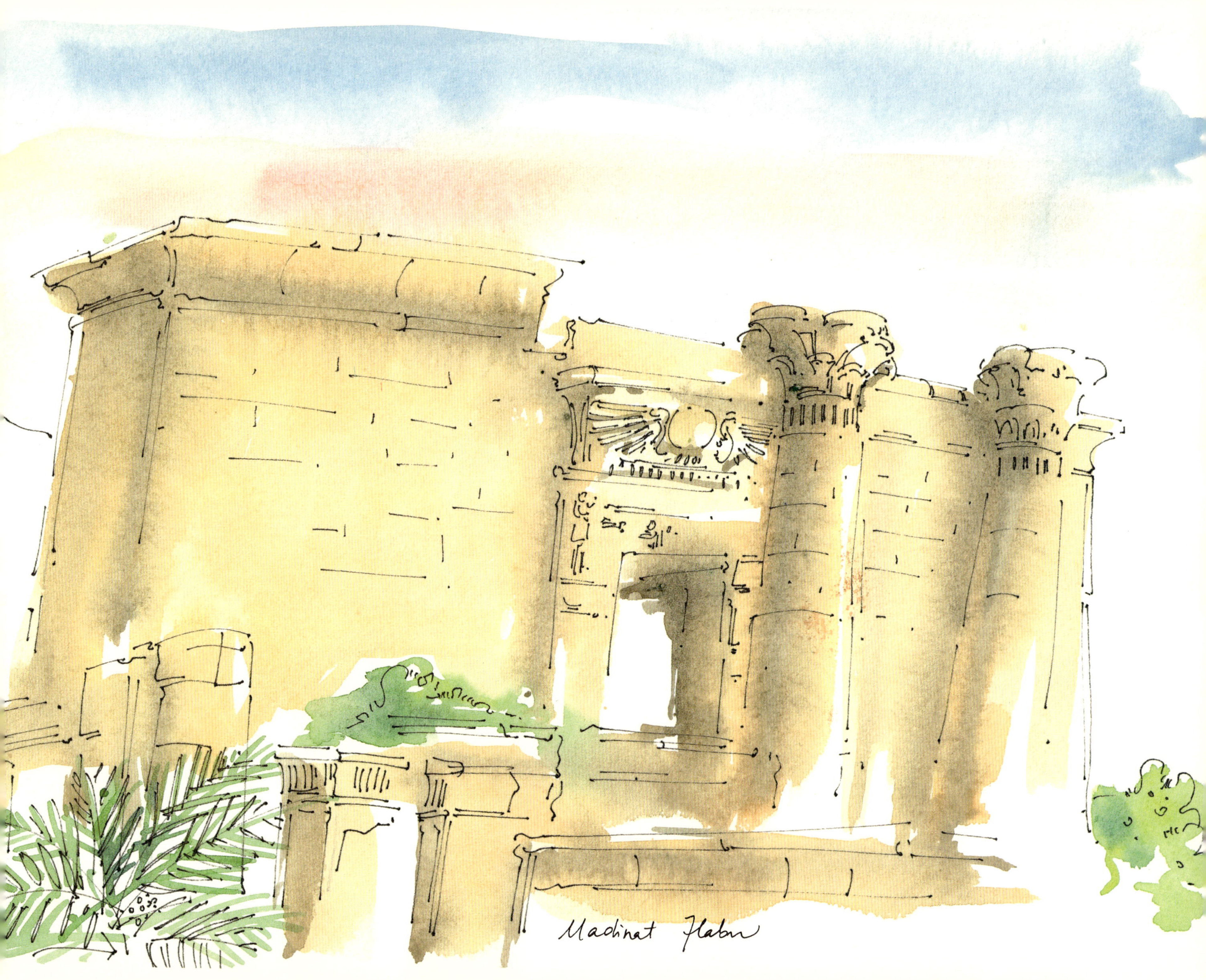

Madinat Habu

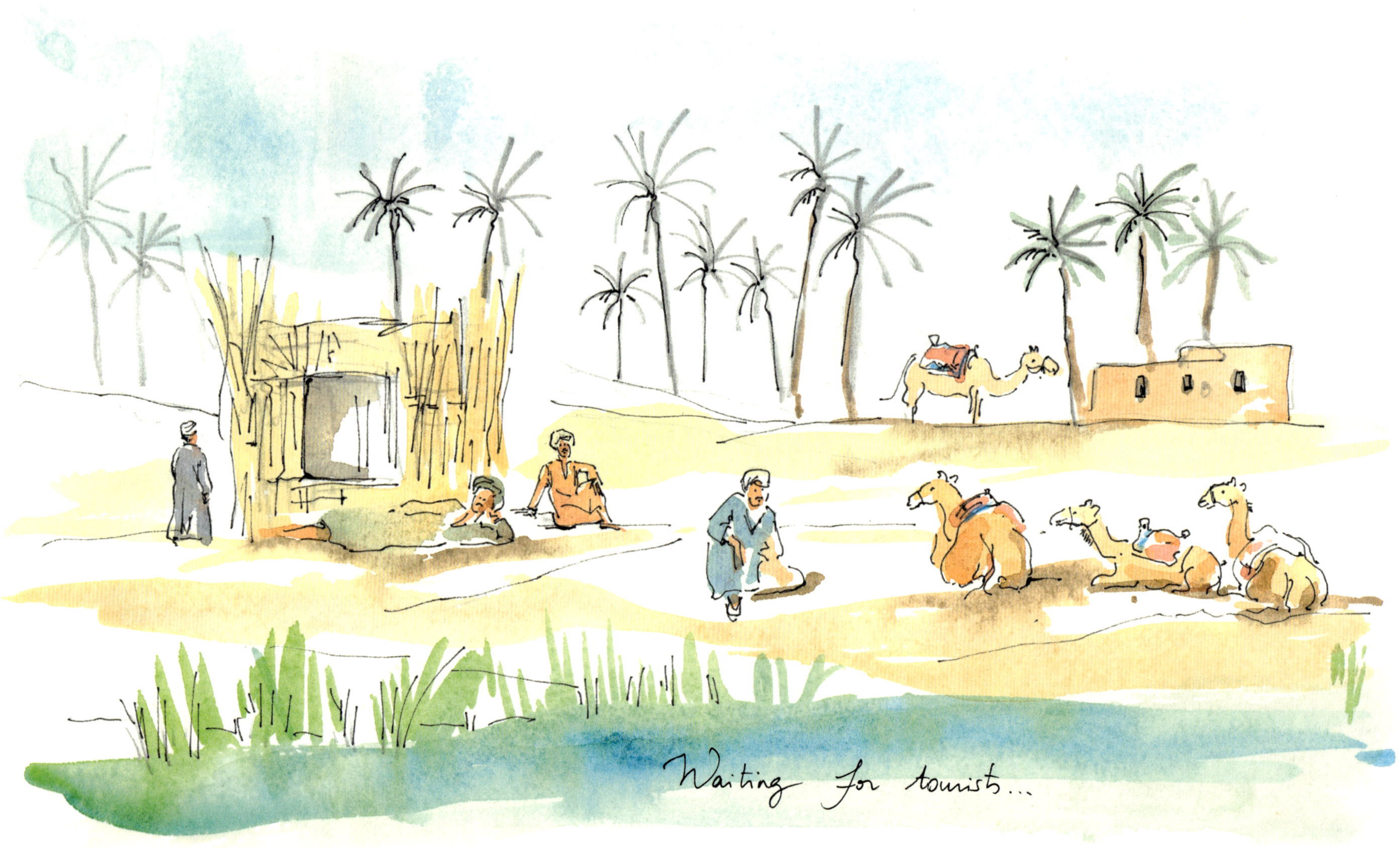

Waiting for tourists...

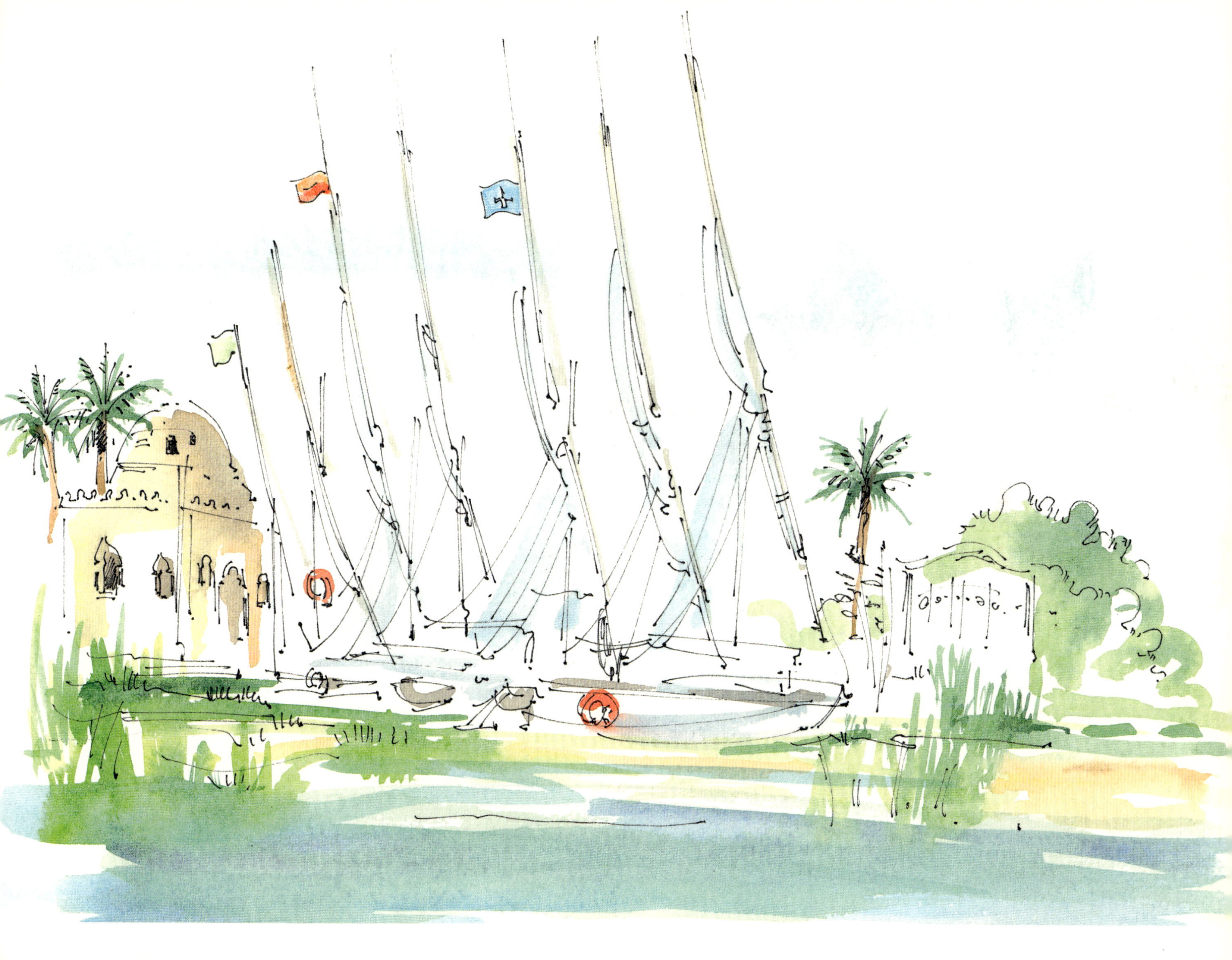

Hail to thee, O Nile! Who manifests thyself over this land,

and comes to give life to Egypt!

Mysterious is thy issuing forth from the darkness,

on this day whereon it is celebrated!

Watering the orchards created by Re, to cause all the cattle

to live, you give the earth to drink, inexhaustible one!

Lord of the fish, during the inundation, no bird alights

on the crops. You create the grain, you bring forth the barley,

assuring perpetuity to the temples. If you cease your toil

and your work, then all that exists is in anguish. If the gods

suffer in heaven, then the faces of men waste away.

But all is changed for mankind when He comes;

He is endowed with the qualities of Nun. If He shines,

the earth is joyous, every stomach is full of rejoicing,

every spine is happy, every jaw-bone crushes (its food).

He brings the offerings, as chief of provisioning;

He is the creator of all good things, as master of energy,

full of sweetness in his choice. If offerings are made it is

thanks to Him. He brings forth the herbage for the flocks,

and sees that each god receives his sacrifices.

All that depends on Him is a precious incense.

He spreads himself over Egypt, filling the granaries,

renewing the marts, watching over the goods of the unhappy.

No dwelling is there which may contain you!

None penetrates within your heart!

He shines when He issues forth from the darkness,

to cause his flocks to prosper. It is his force that gives

existence to all things; nothing remains hidden for him.

Let men clothe themselves to fill his gardens.

When you shine in the royal city, the rich man is sated

with good things, the poor man even disdains the lotus;

all that is produced is of the choicest; all the plants exist

for your children. If you have refused to grant nourishment,

the dwelling is silent, devoid of all that is good,

the country falls exhausted.

O inundation of the Nile, offerings are made unto you,

men are immolated to you, great festivals are instituted

for you. Birds are sacrificed to you, gazelles are taken

for you in the mountain, pure flames are prepared for you.

Come and prosper! Come and prosper! O Nile,

come and prosper! O you who make men to live through

his flocks and his flocks through his orchards!

Come and prosper, come, O Nile, come and prosper!

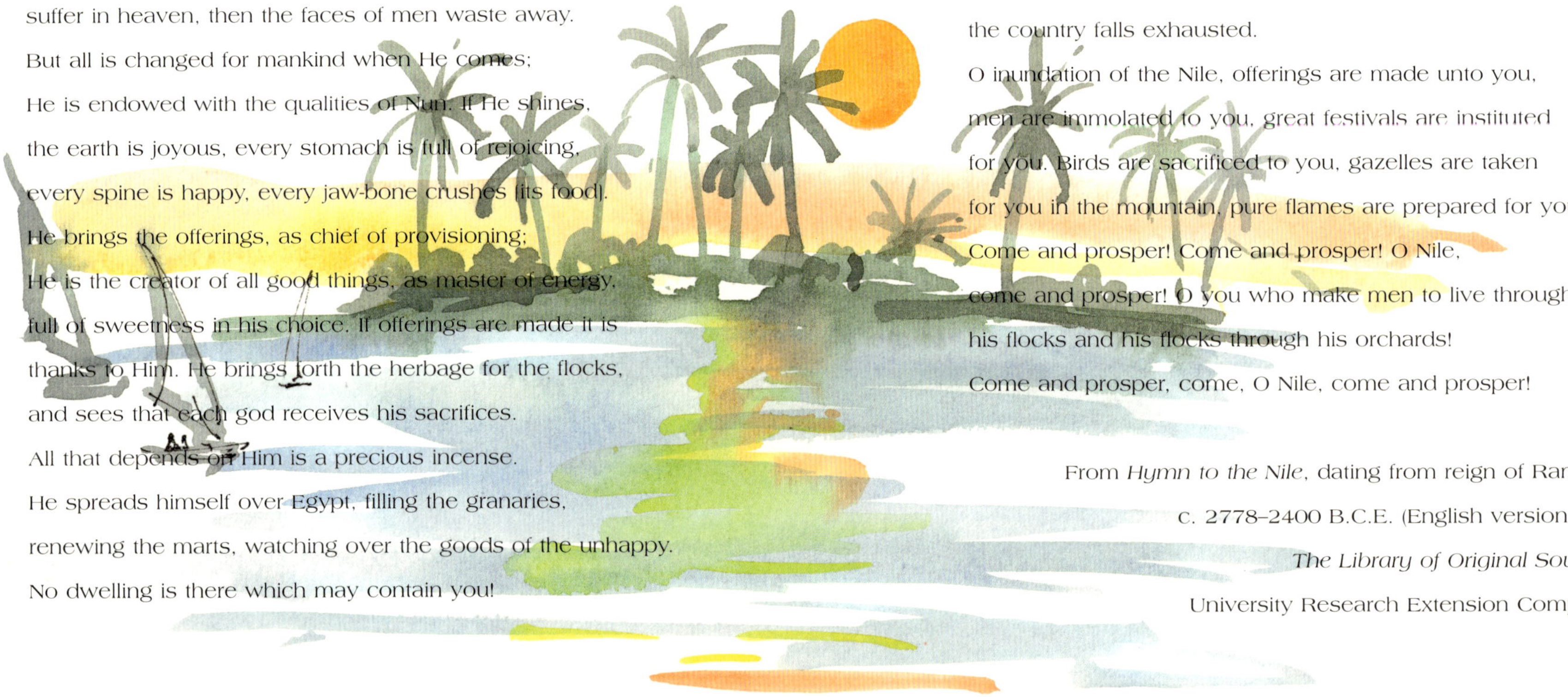

From *Hymn to the Nile*, dating from reign of Ramses,

c. 2778–2400 B.C.E. (English version from

The Library of Original Sources,

University Research Extension Company)

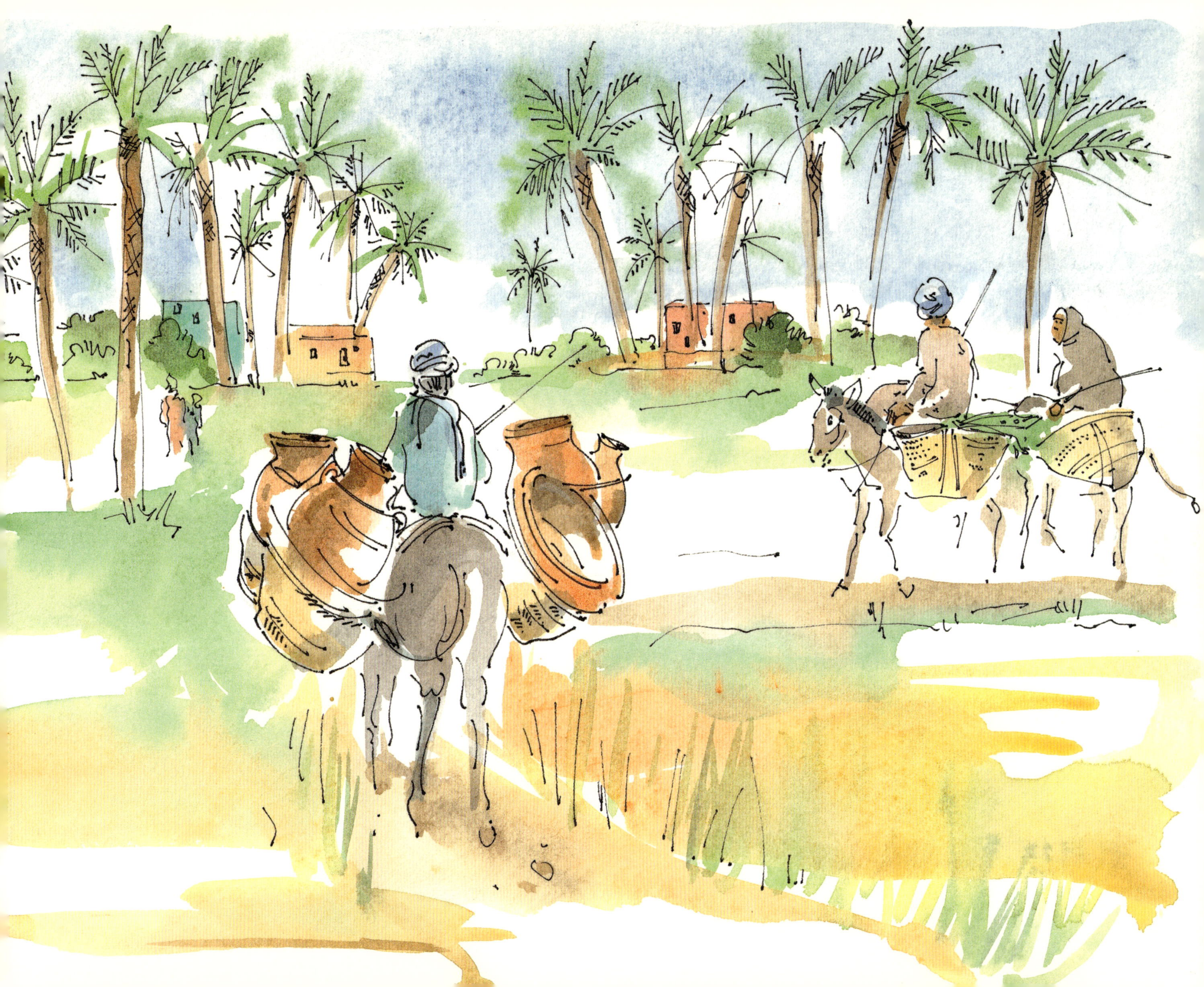

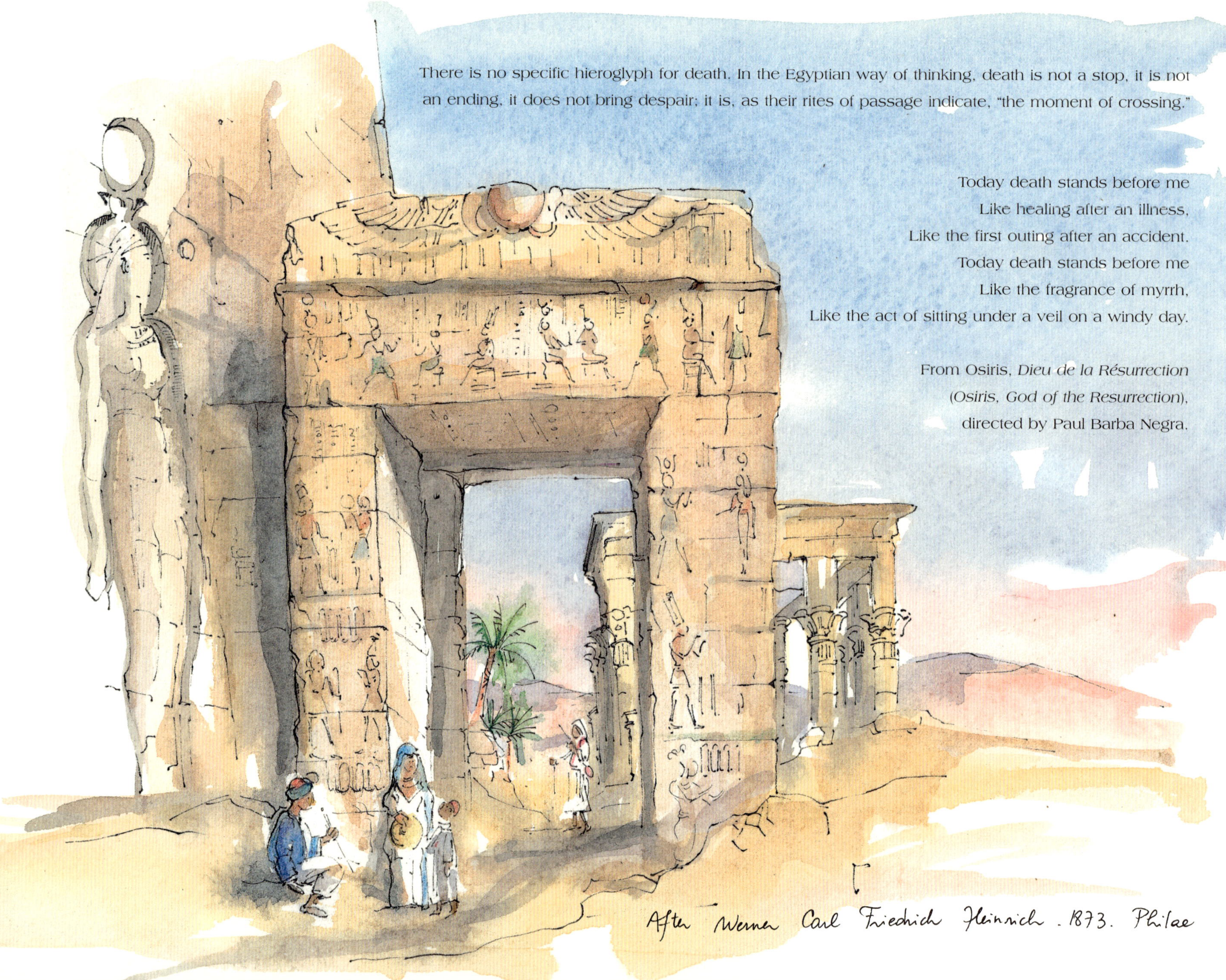

There is no specific hieroglyph for death. In the Egyptian way of thinking, death is not a stop, it is not an ending, it does not bring despair; it is, as their rites of passage indicate, "the moment of crossing."

Today death stands before me
Like healing after an illness,
Like the first outing after an accident.
Today death stands before me
Like the fragrance of myrrh,
Like the act of sitting under a veil on a windy day.

From Osiris, *Dieu de la Résurrection*
(*Osiris, God of the Resurrection*),
directed by Paul Barba Negra.

After Werner Carl Friedrich Heinrich . 1873 . Philae

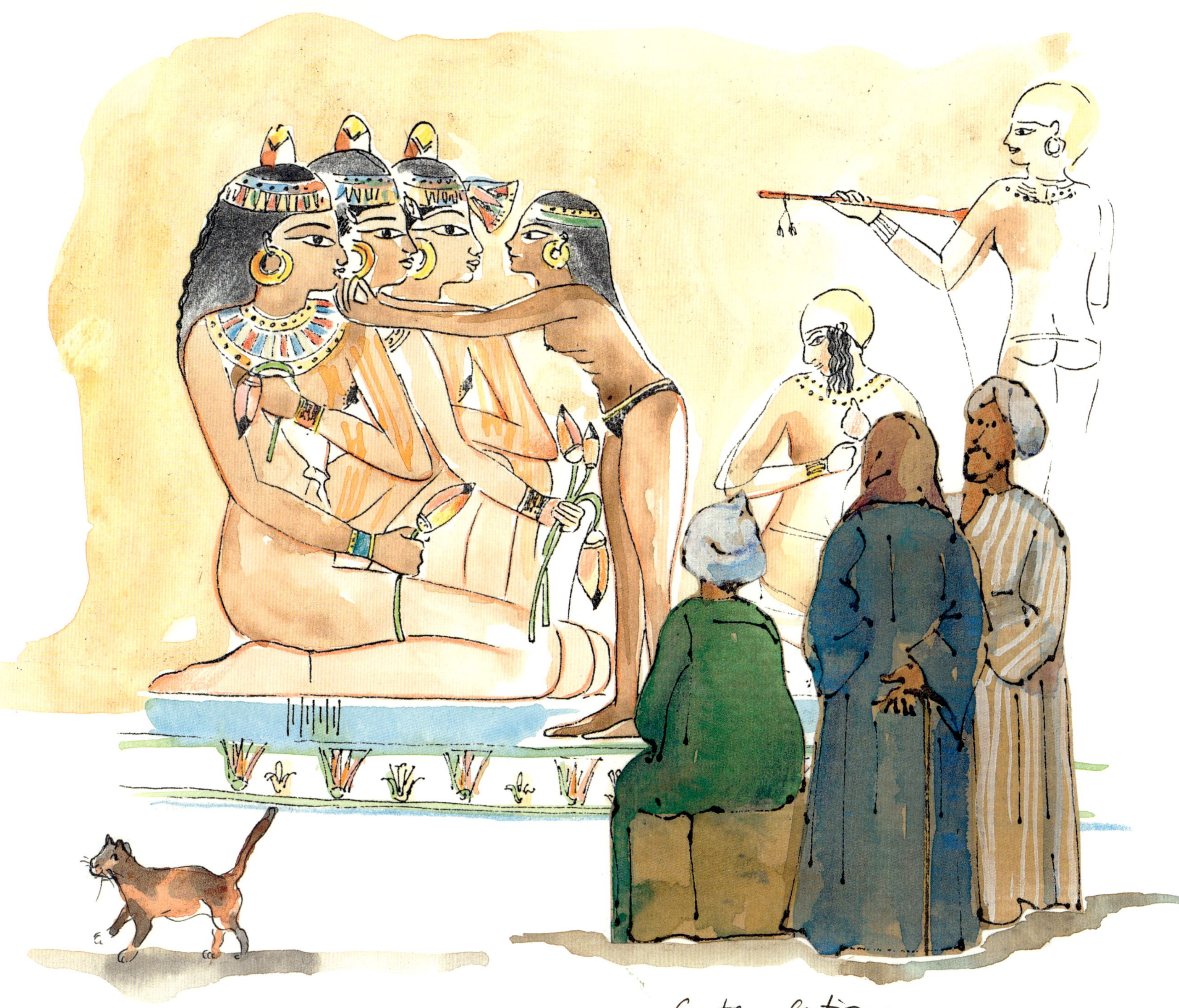

Contemplation

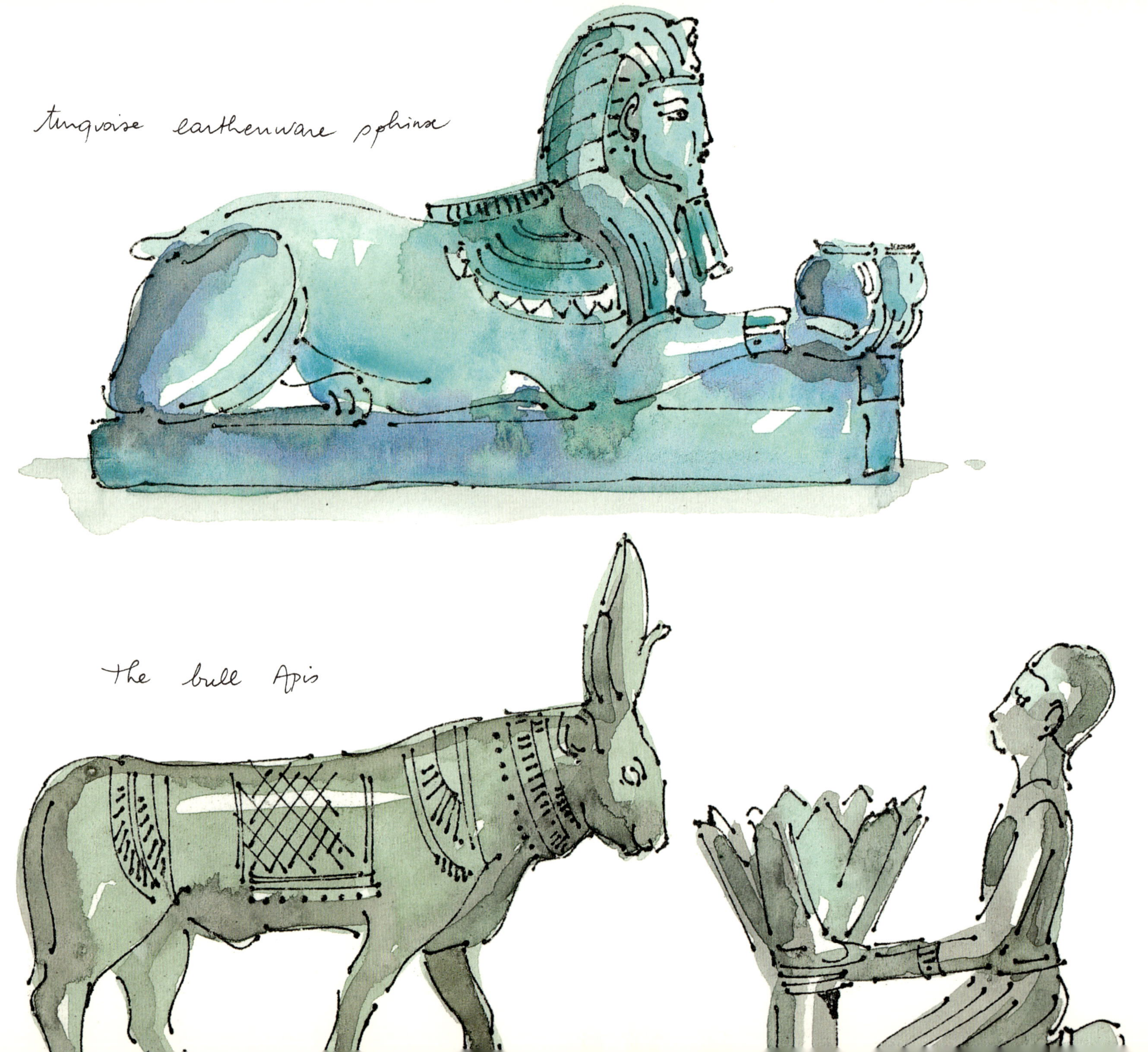

turquoise earthenware sphinx

the bull Apis

Tiy

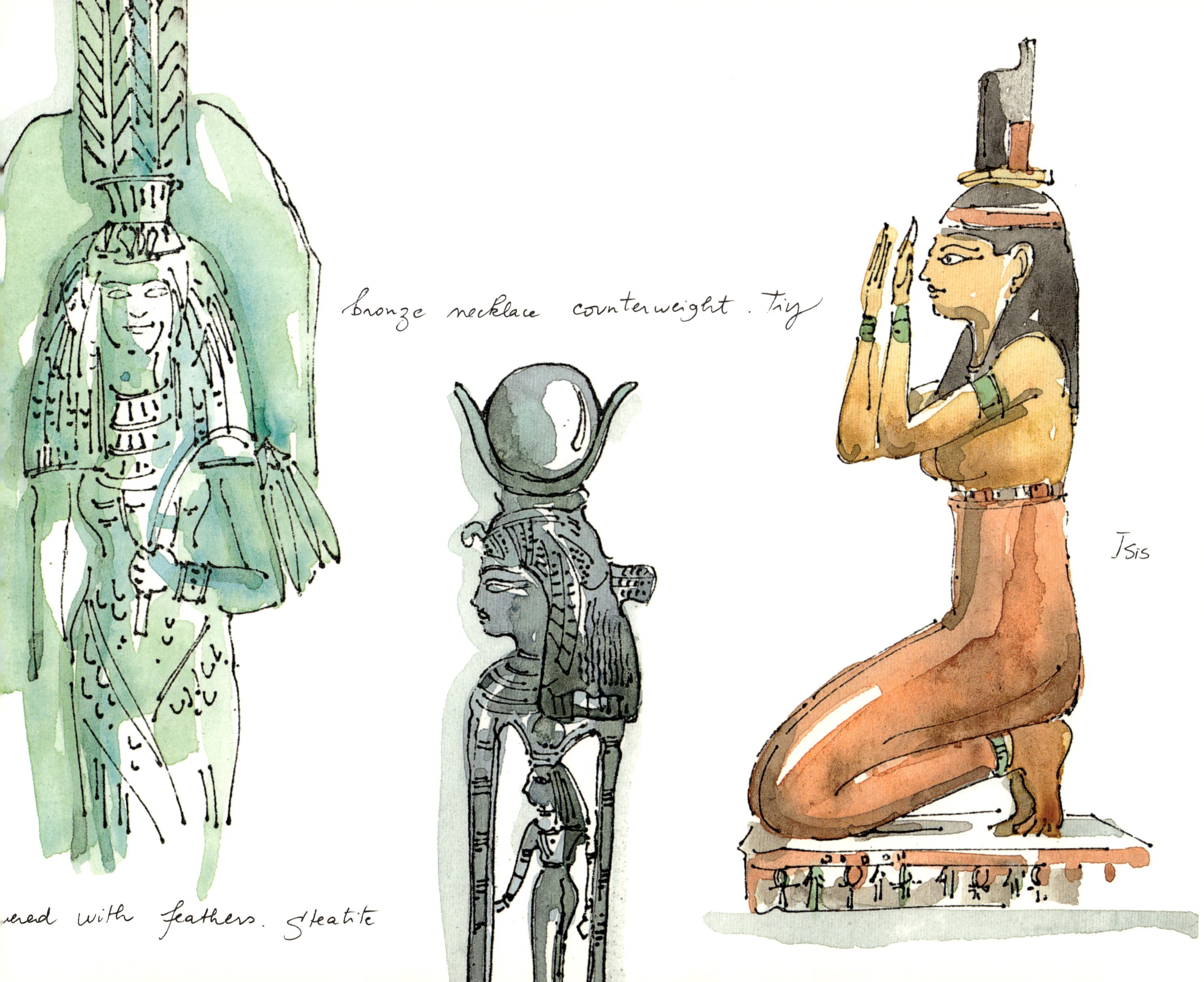
bronze necklace counterweight. Tiy
Isis
...ered with feathers. Steatite

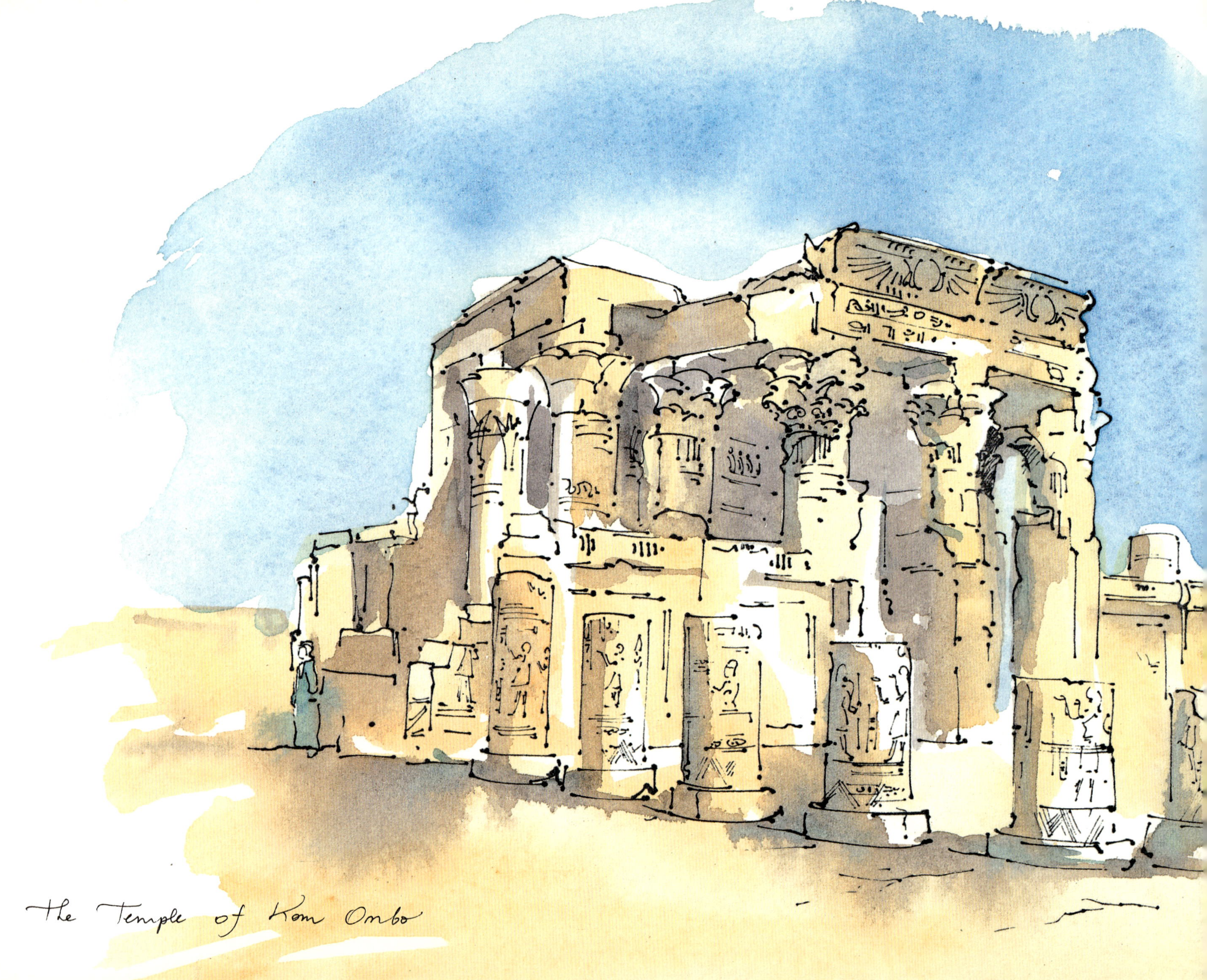

The Temple of Kom Ombo

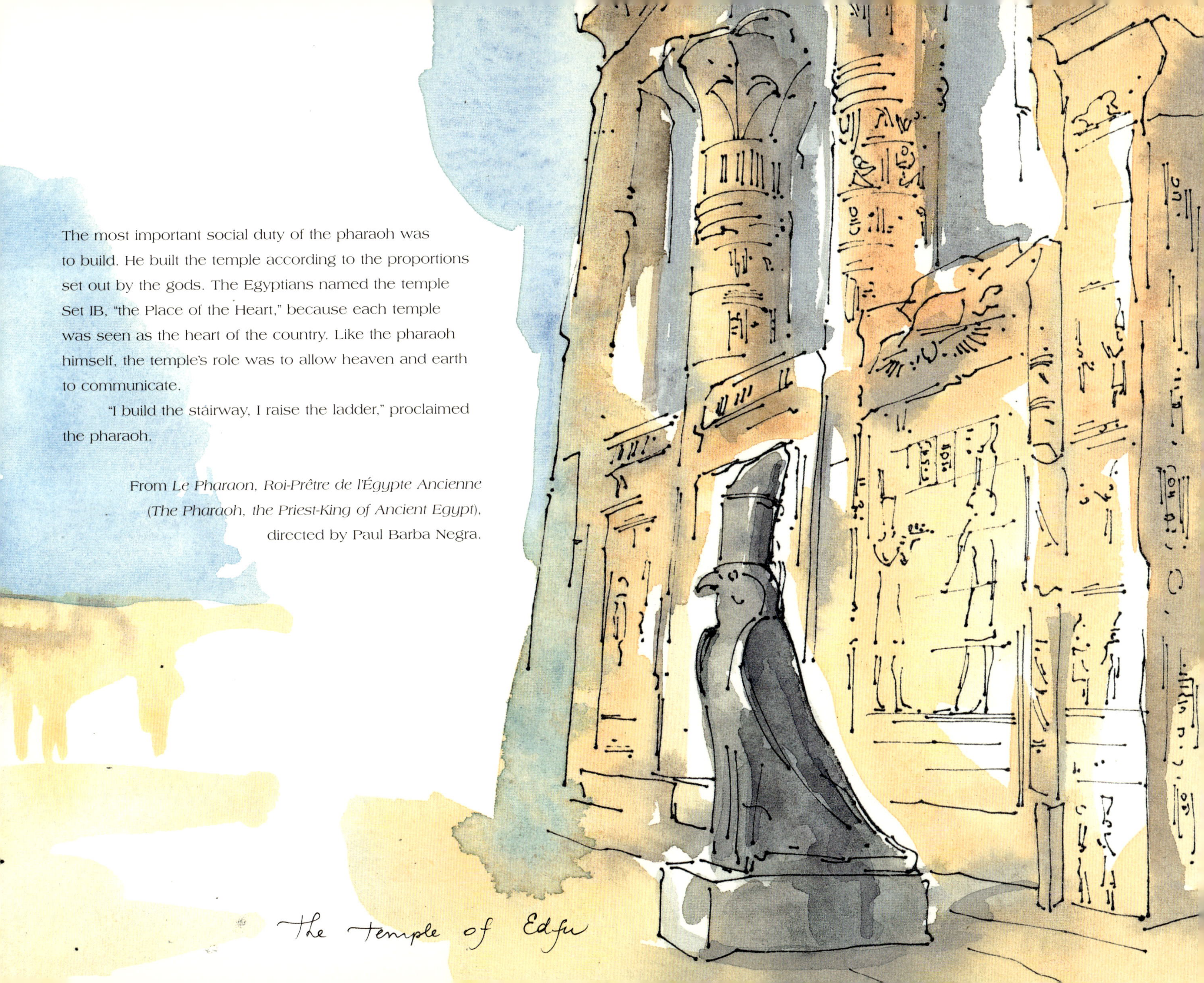

The most important social duty of the pharaoh was
to build. He built the temple according to the proportions
set out by the gods. The Egyptians named the temple
Set IB, "the Place of the Heart," because each temple
was seen as the heart of the country. Like the pharaoh
himself, the temple's role was to allow heaven and earth
to communicate.

  "I build the stairway, I raise the ladder," proclaimed
the pharaoh.

From *Le Pharaon, Roi-Prêtre de l'Égypte Ancienne*
(*The Pharaoh, the Priest-King of Ancient Egypt*),
directed by Paul Barba Negra.

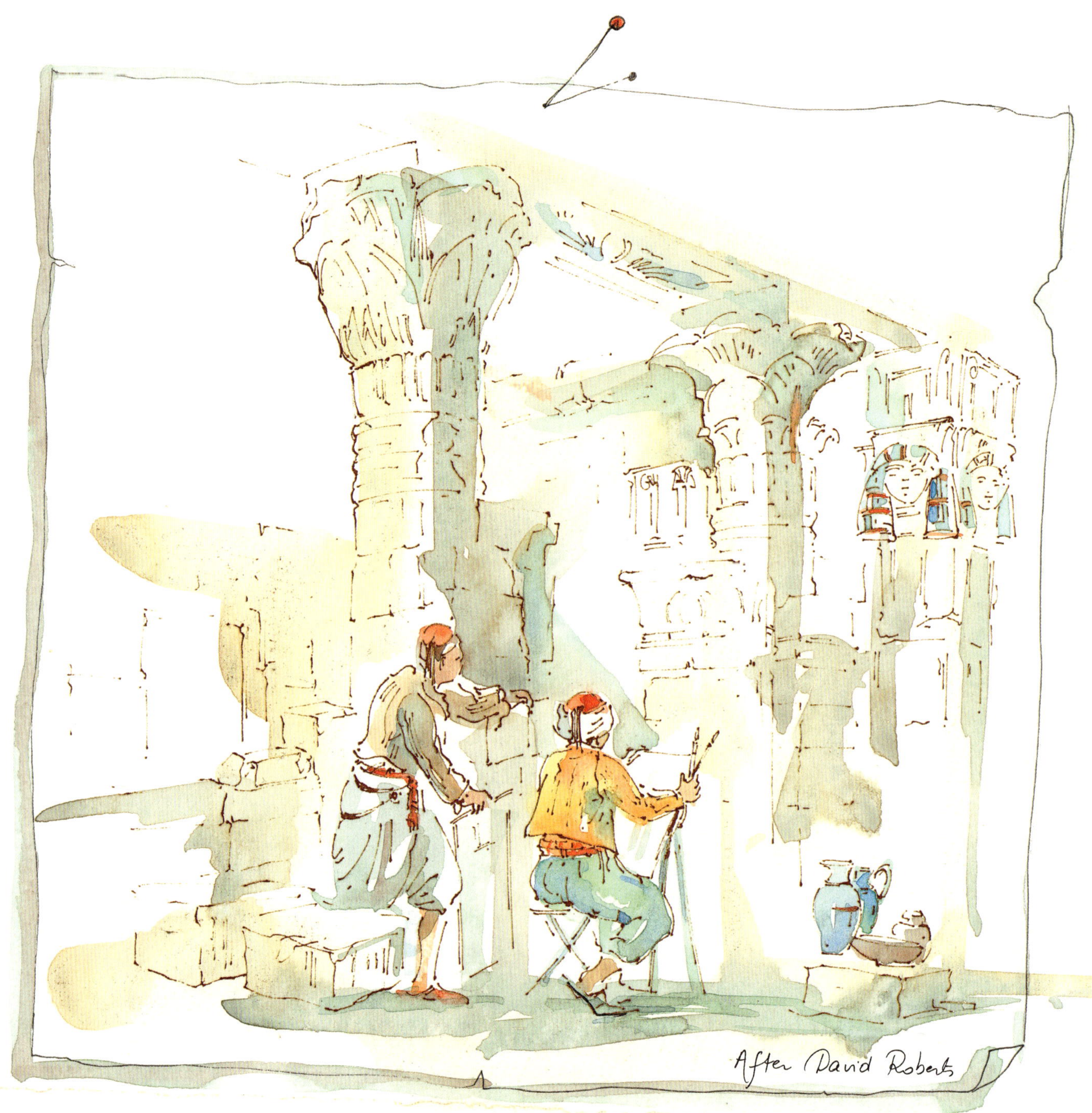

After David Roberts

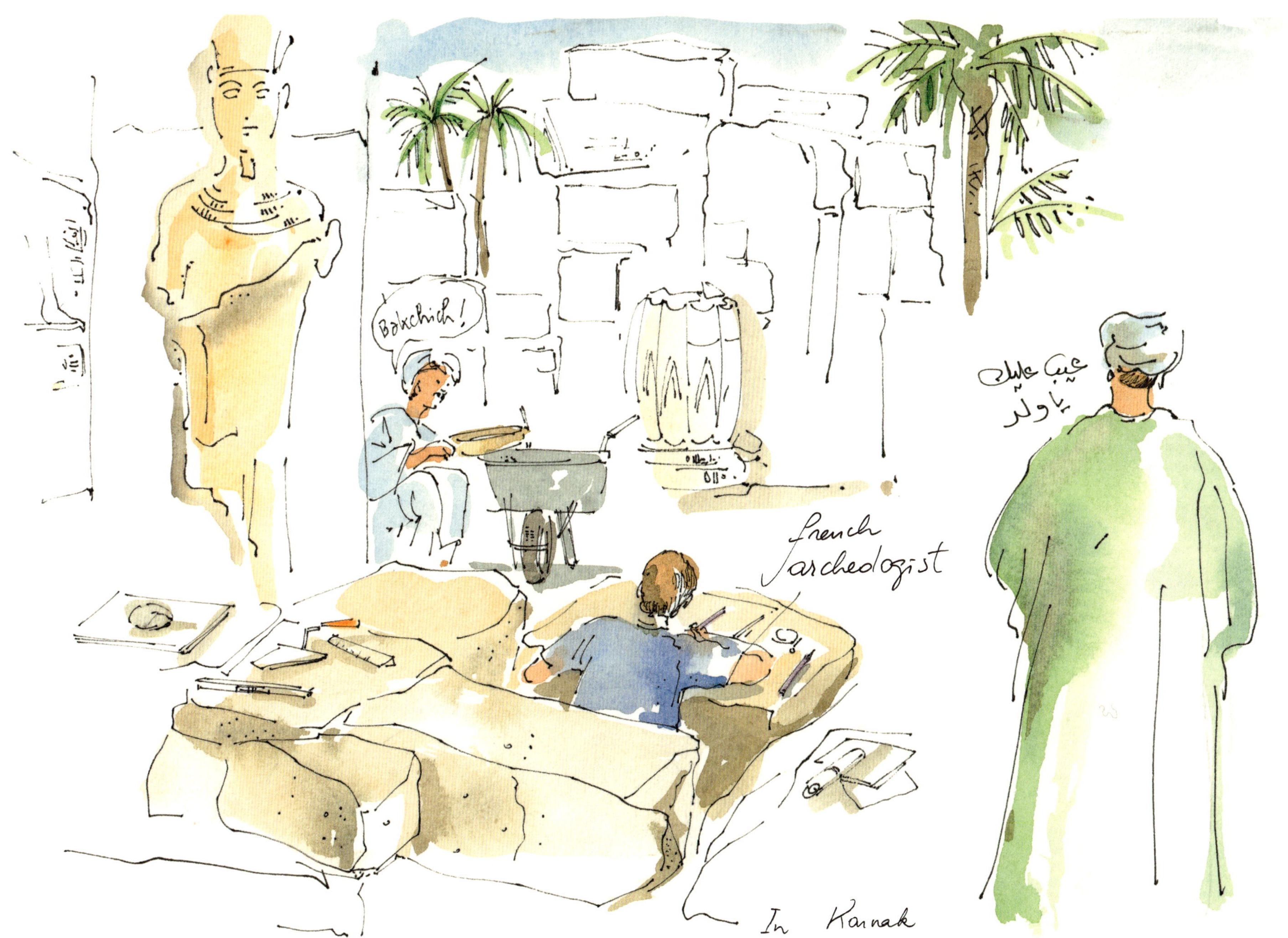
Bakchich!
French
archeologist
In Karnak
عيب عليك يا ولد

"The god Ammon created Thebes and seared it with the flame of his gaze."
Each of its temples formed a giant eye open onto the world. Along with Karnak, Luxor and the funerary temples of the western bank, the holy city of Thebes constituted "the complete eye, the eye of God." The light of the eye is "the sun" and for the Egyptian, nothing was more important in life than to be able to open one's inner eye as guided by the pharaoh, king, priest, and great builder of temples.

From *Le Pharaon, Roi-Prêtre de l'Égypte Ancienne* (*The Pharaoh, the Priest-King of Ancient Egypt*), directed by Paul Barba Negra.

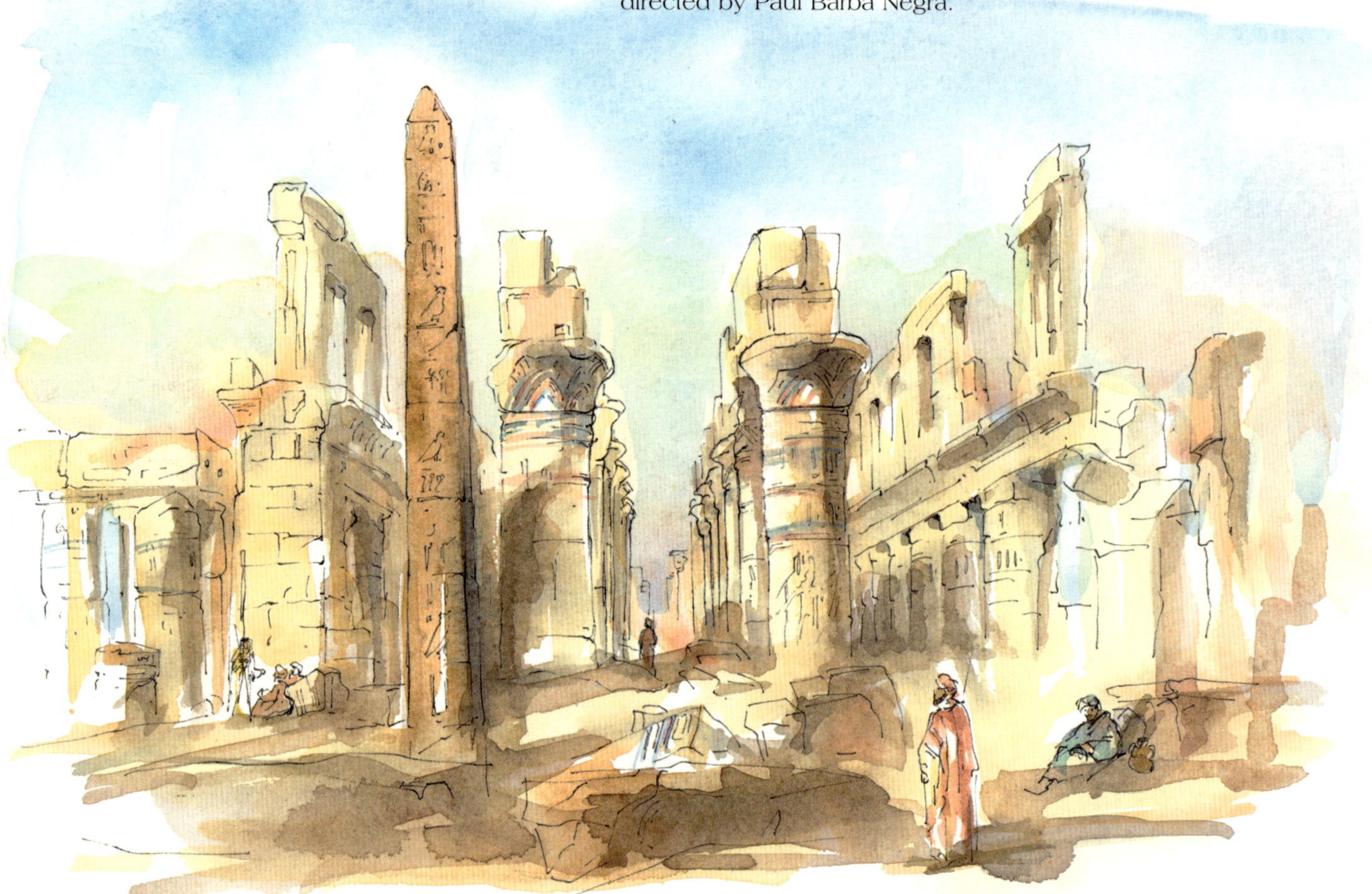

After Jacobs Jacob. "The temple of Karnak at Luxor" 1856

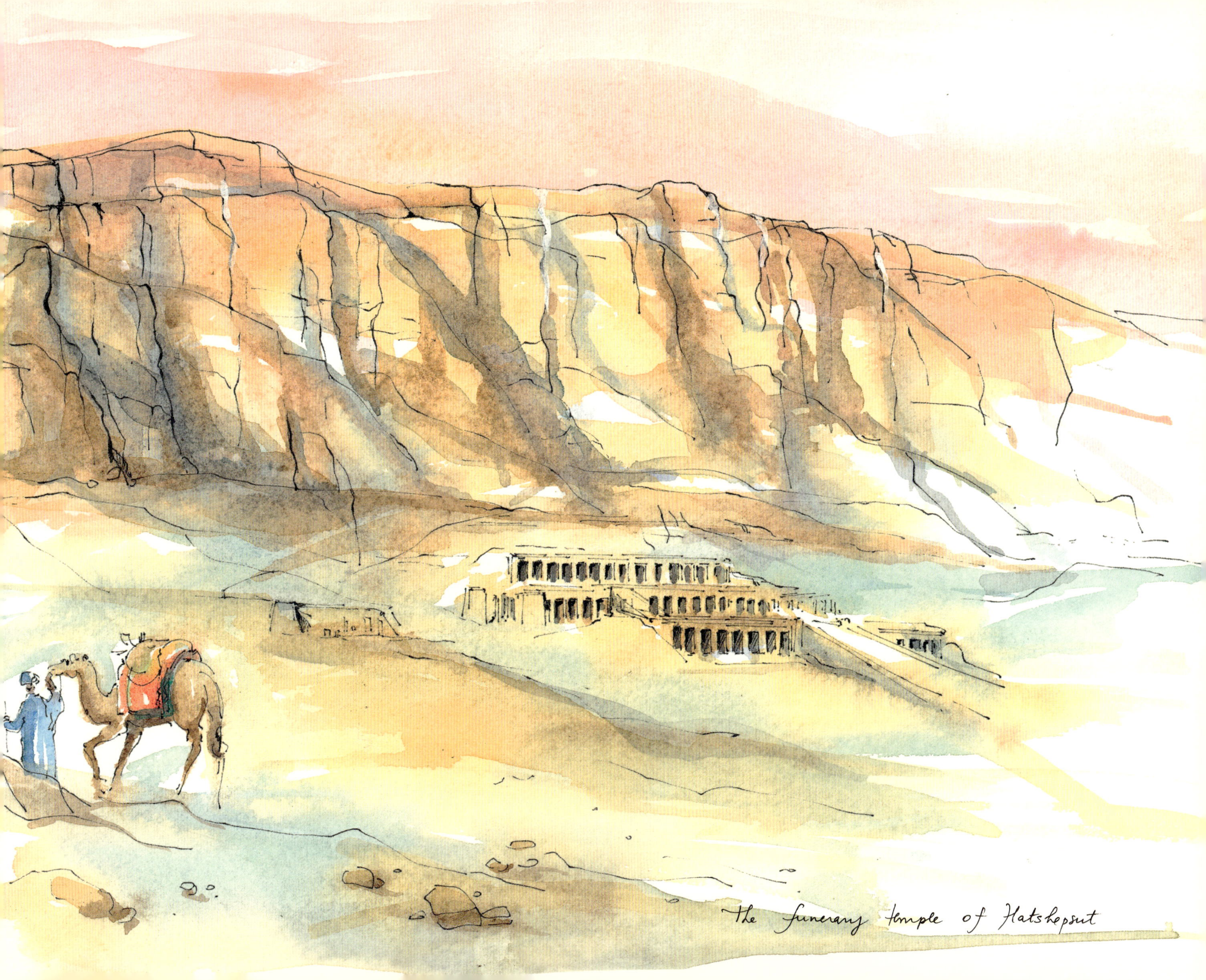

The funerary temple of Hatshepsut

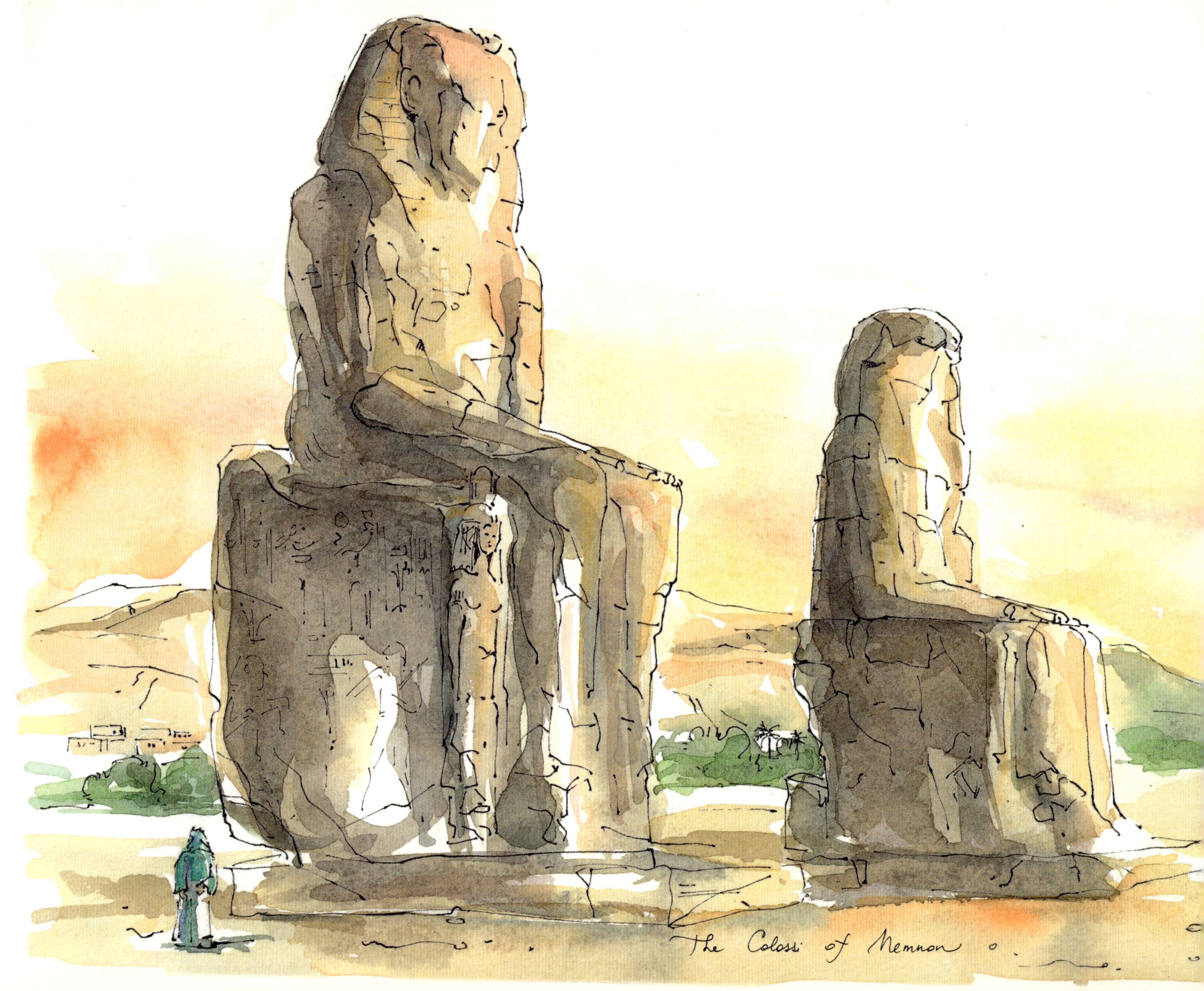

The Colossi of Memnon

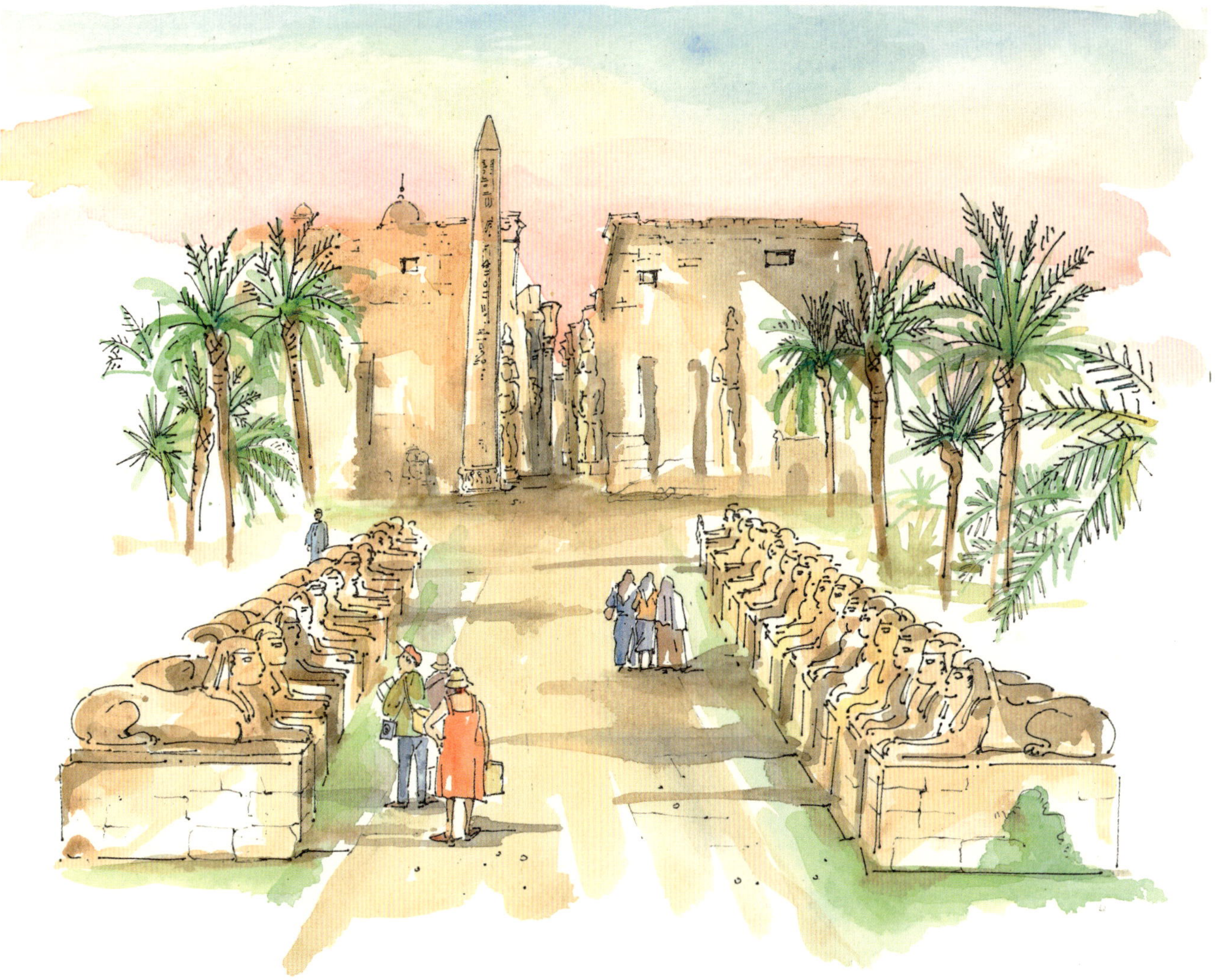

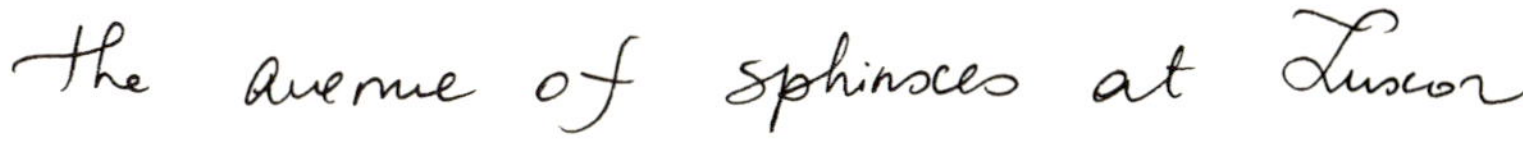

The avenue of sphinxes at Luxor

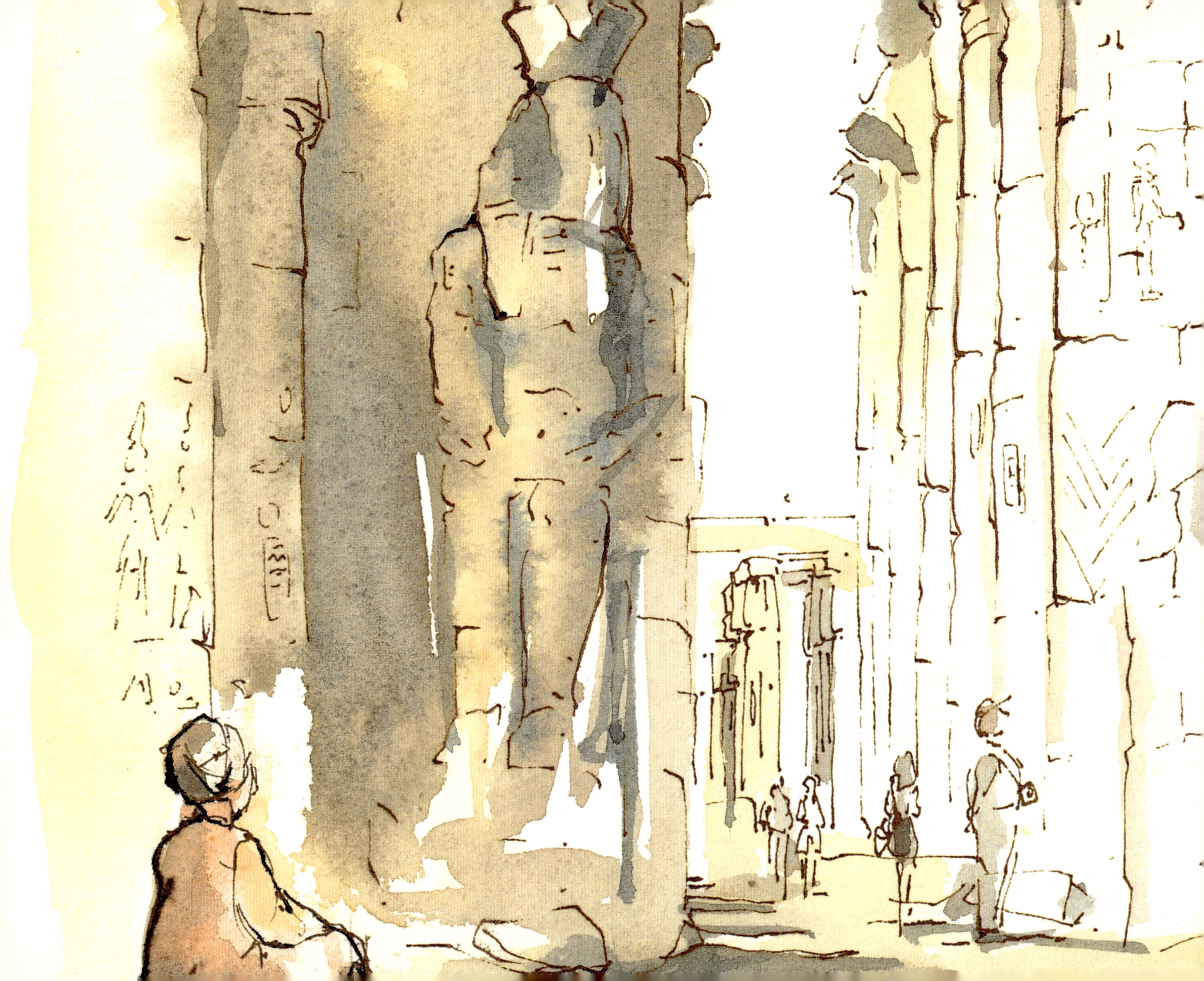

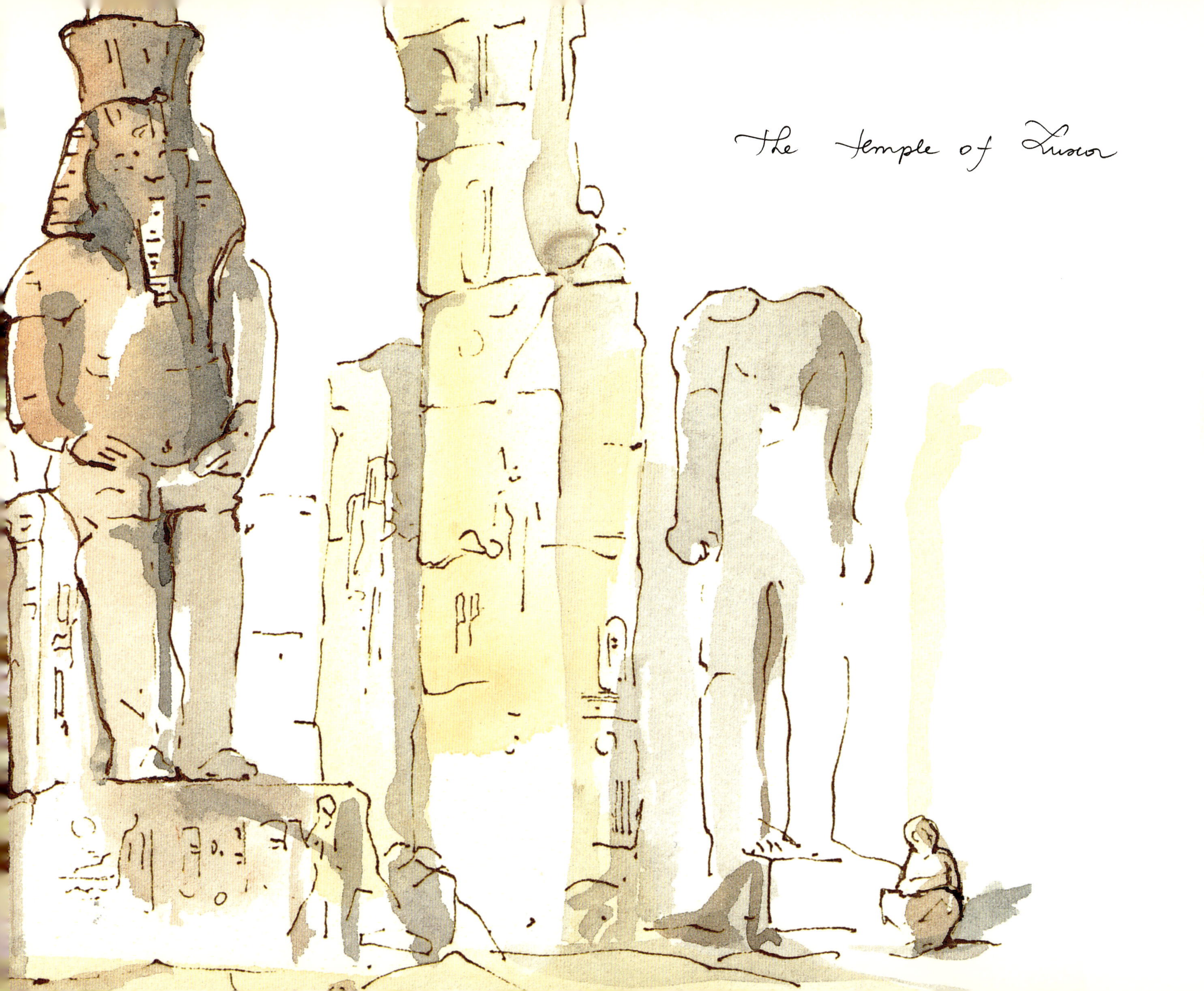
The Temple of Luxor

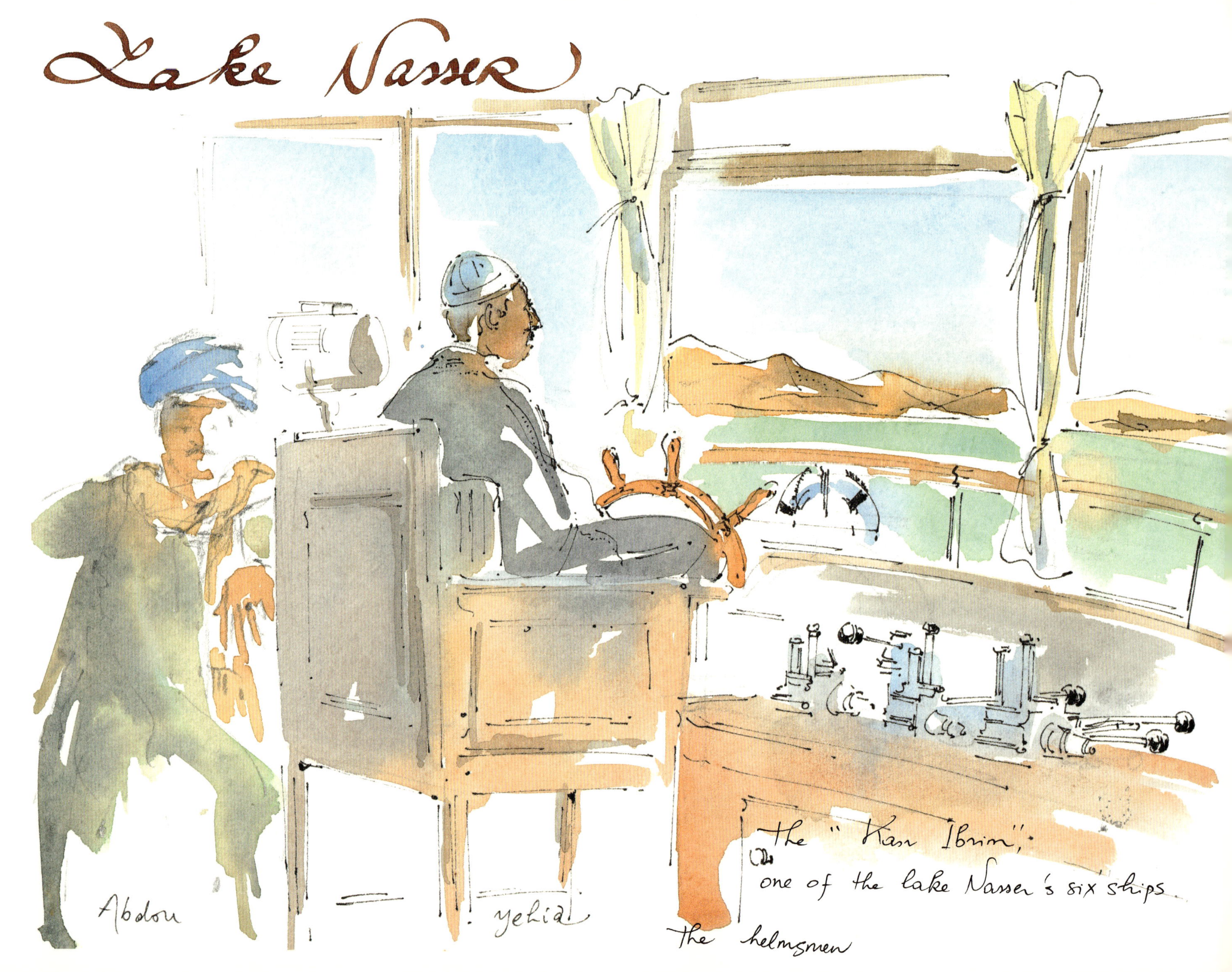

Lake Nasser
Abdou
yehia
The "Kasr Ibrim",
one of the lake Nasser's six ships
the helmsmen

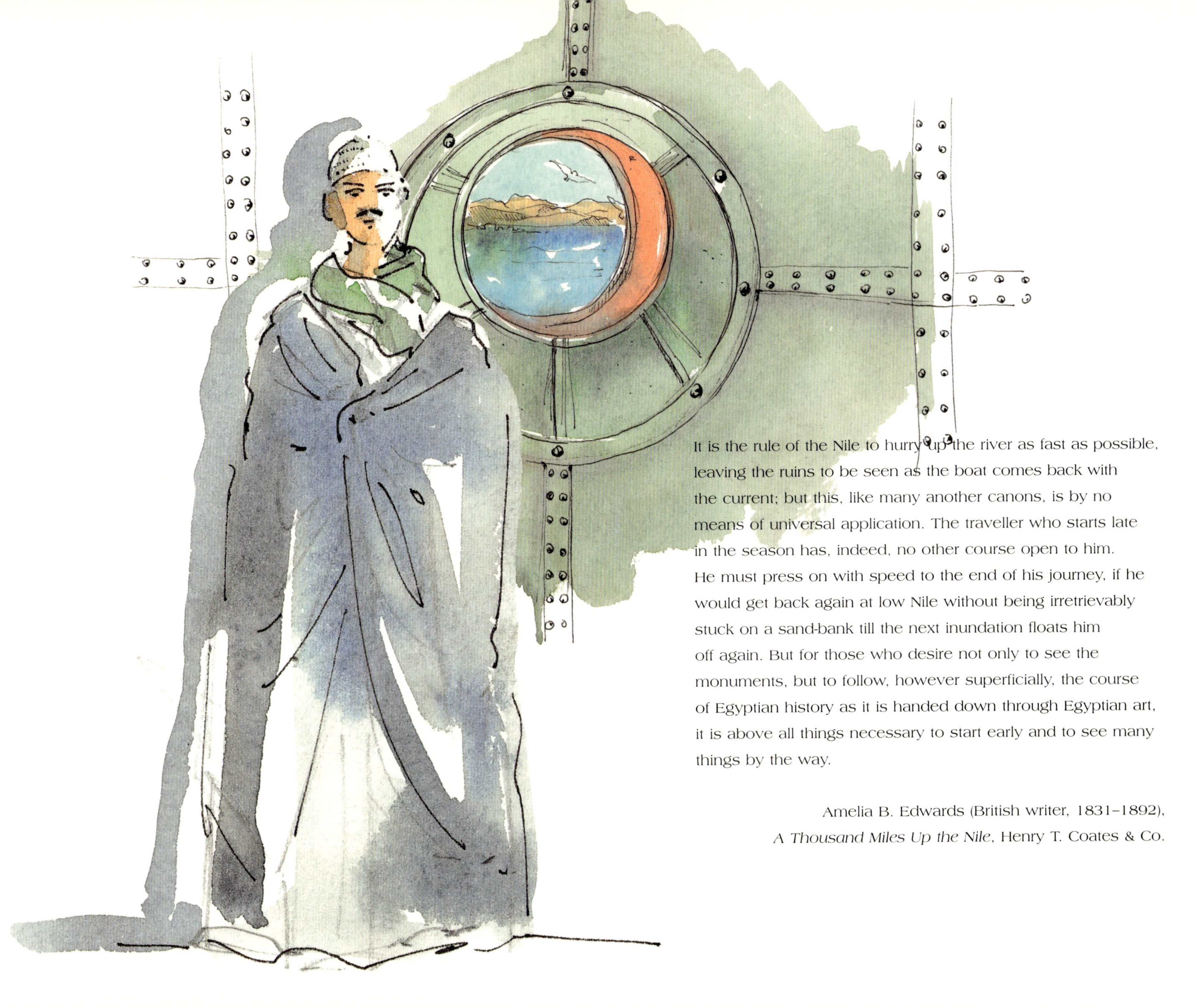

It is the rule of the Nile to hurry up the river as fast as possible, leaving the ruins to be seen as the boat comes back with the current; but this, like many another canons, is by no means of universal application. The traveller who starts late in the season has, indeed, no other course open to him. He must press on with speed to the end of his journey, if he would get back again at low Nile without being irretrievably stuck on a sand-bank till the next inundation floats him off again. But for those who desire not only to see the monuments, but to follow, however superficially, the course of Egyptian history as it is handed down through Egyptian art, it is above all things necessary to start early and to see many things by the way.

Amelia B. Edwards (British writer, 1831–1892),
A Thousand Miles Up the Nile, Henry T. Coates & Co.

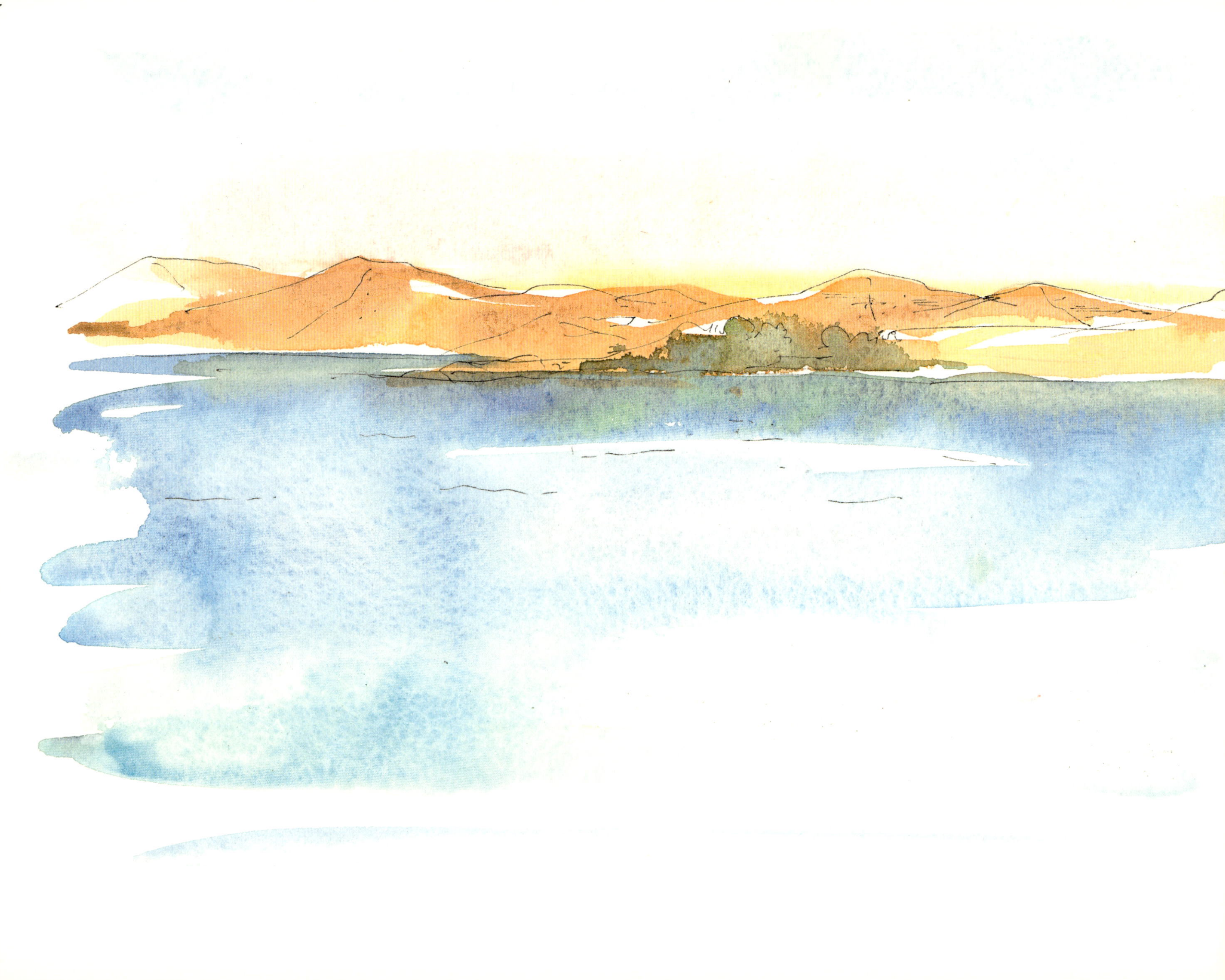

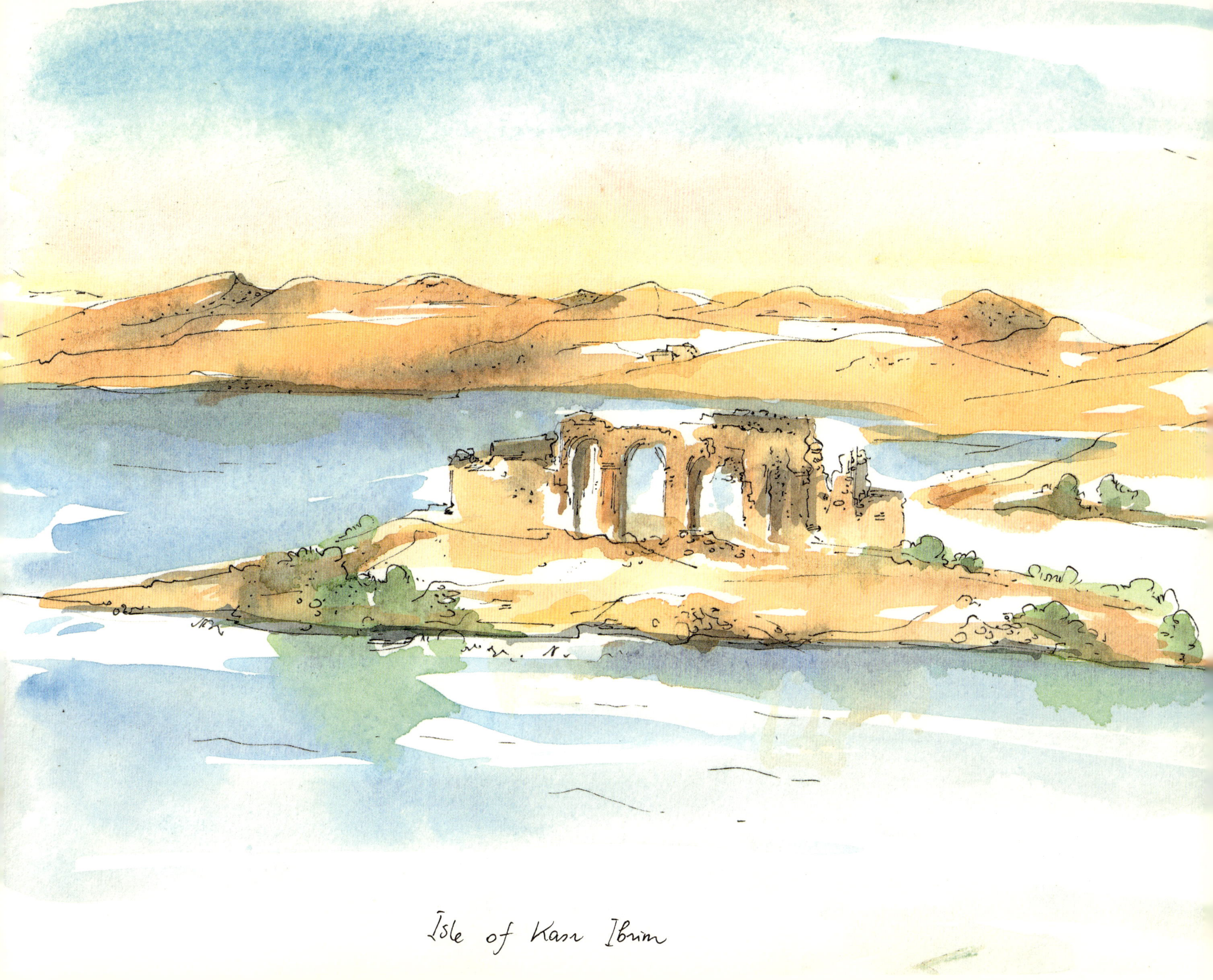

Isle of Kasr Ibrim

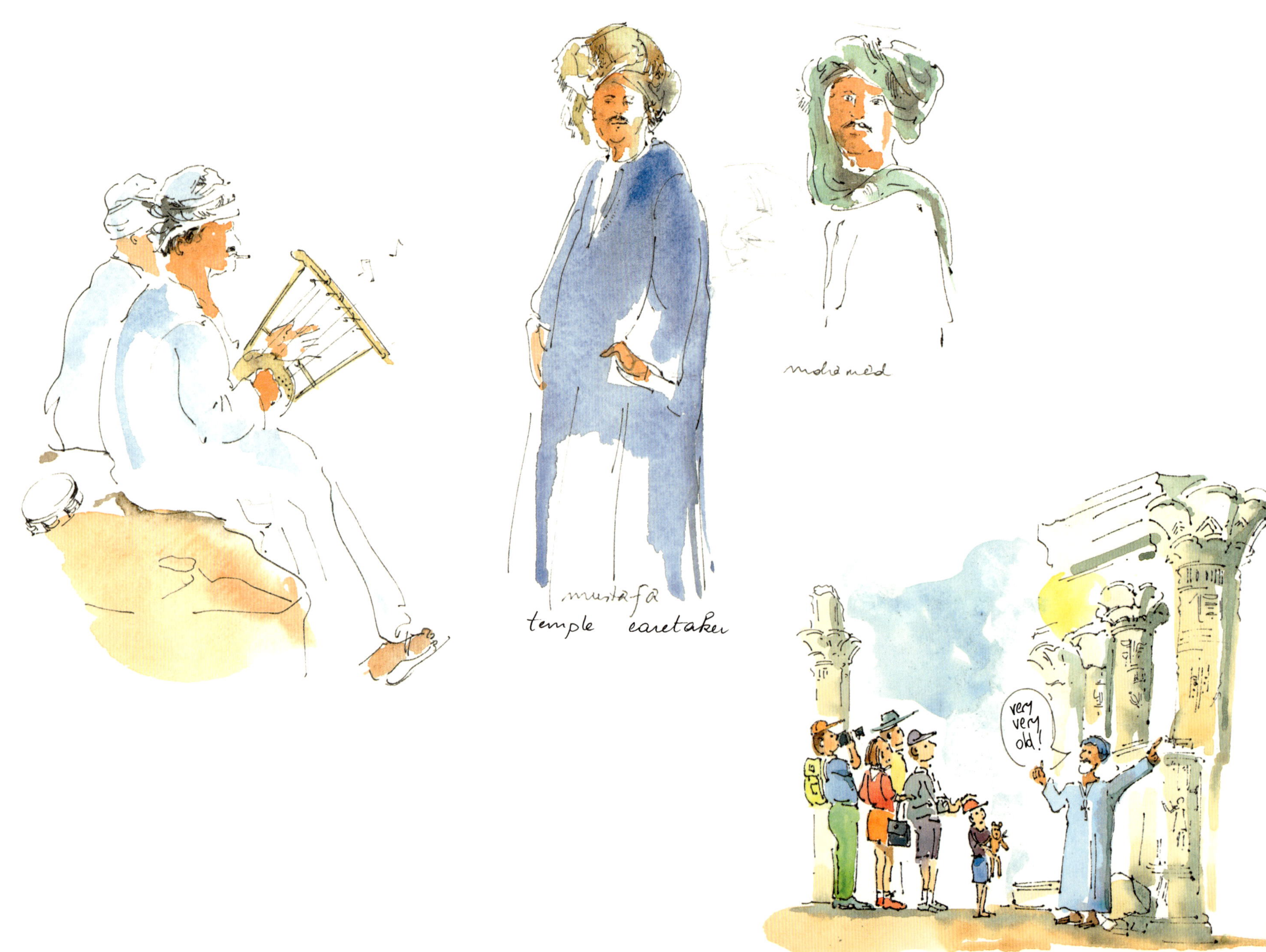

mohamed
mustafa
temple caretaker
very very old!

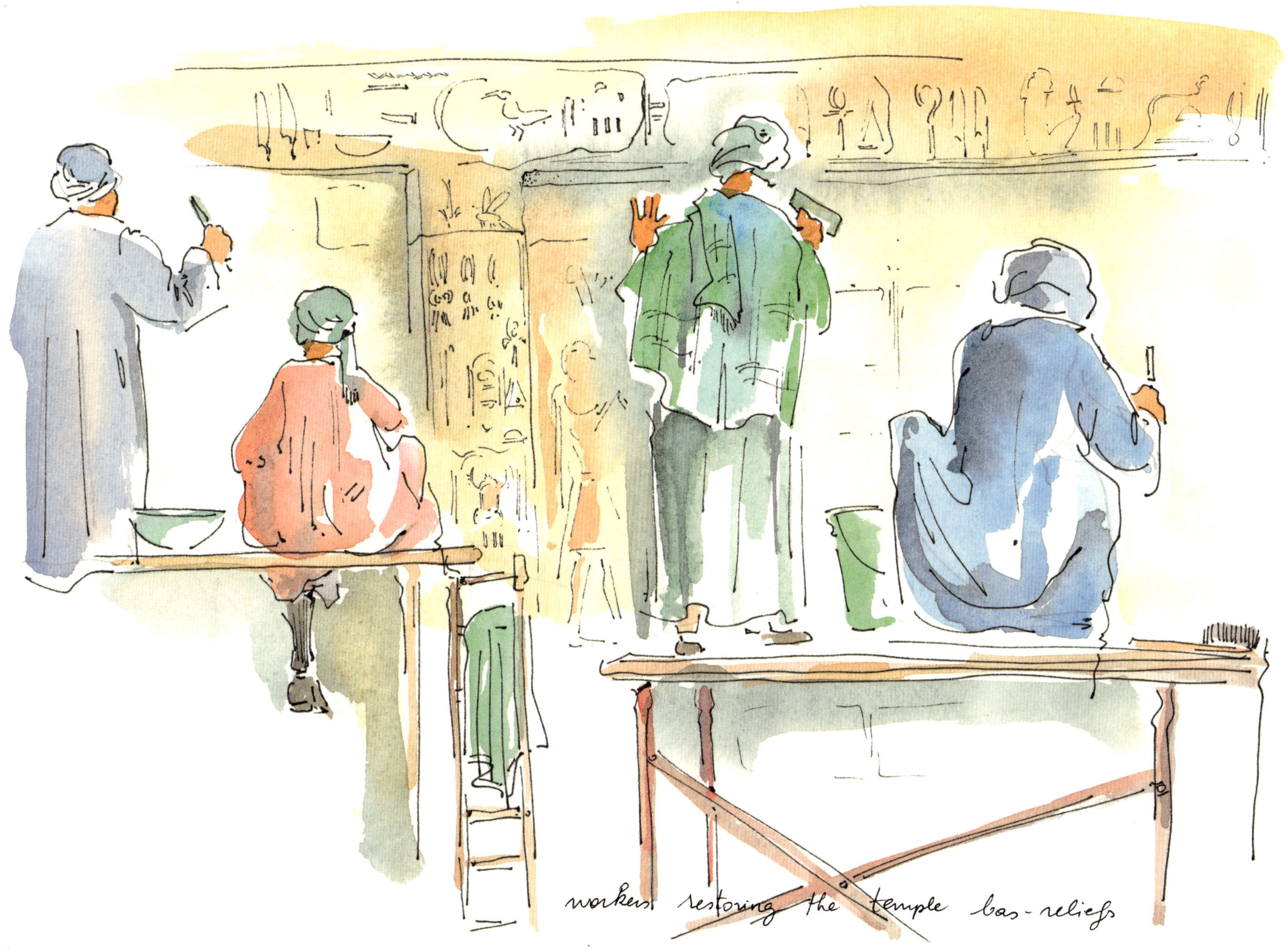

workers restoring the temple bas-reliefs

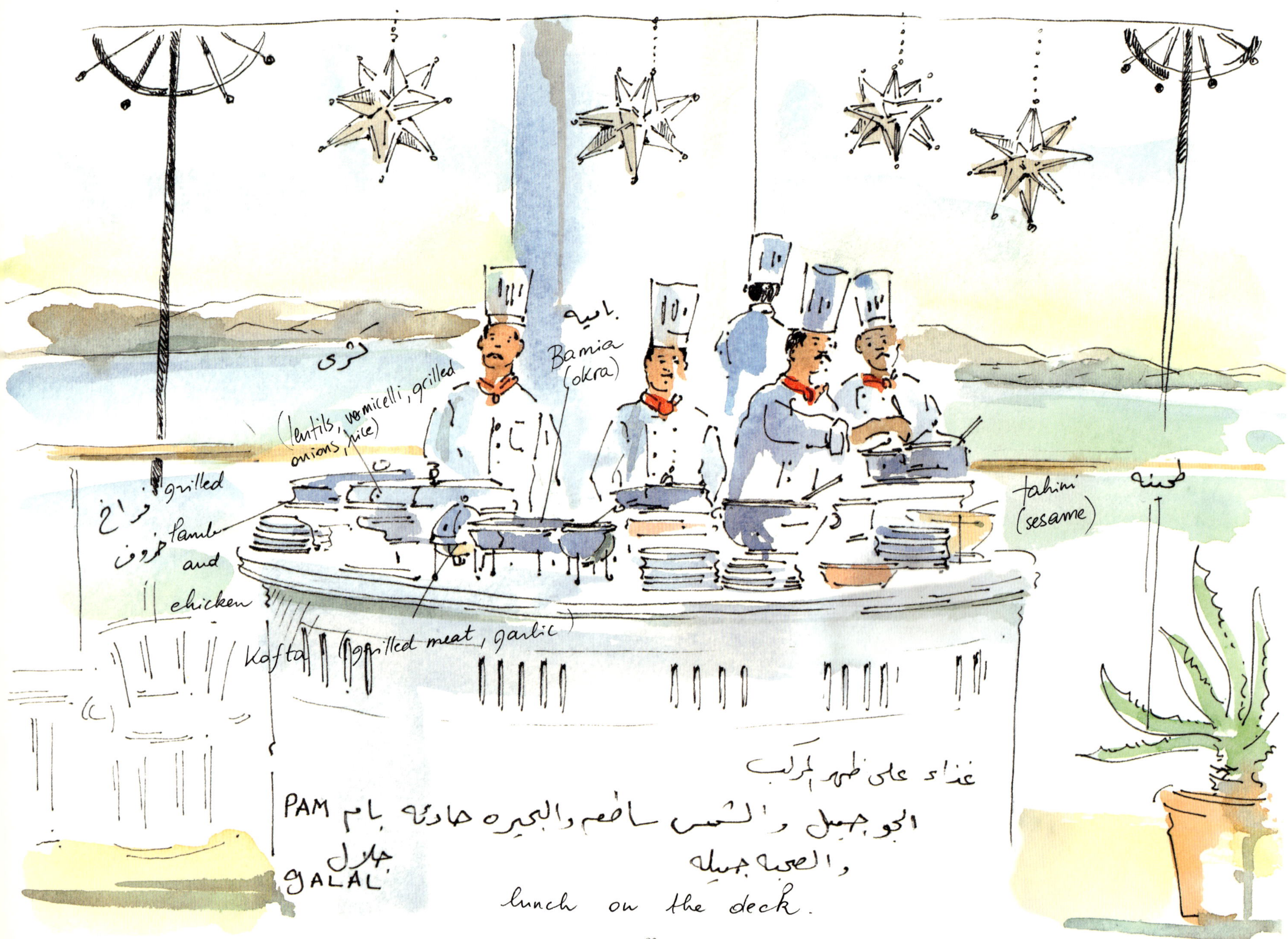

بامية
Bamia
(okra)
كشرى
(lentils, vermicelli, grilled onions, rice)
فراخ وخروف
grilled lamb and chicken
Kofta (grilled meat, garlic)
طحينة
Tahini
(sesame)
غذاء على ظهر المركب
الجو جميل والشمس ساطع والبيرة حاذقة يا
GALAL جلال
lunch on the deck.
PAM

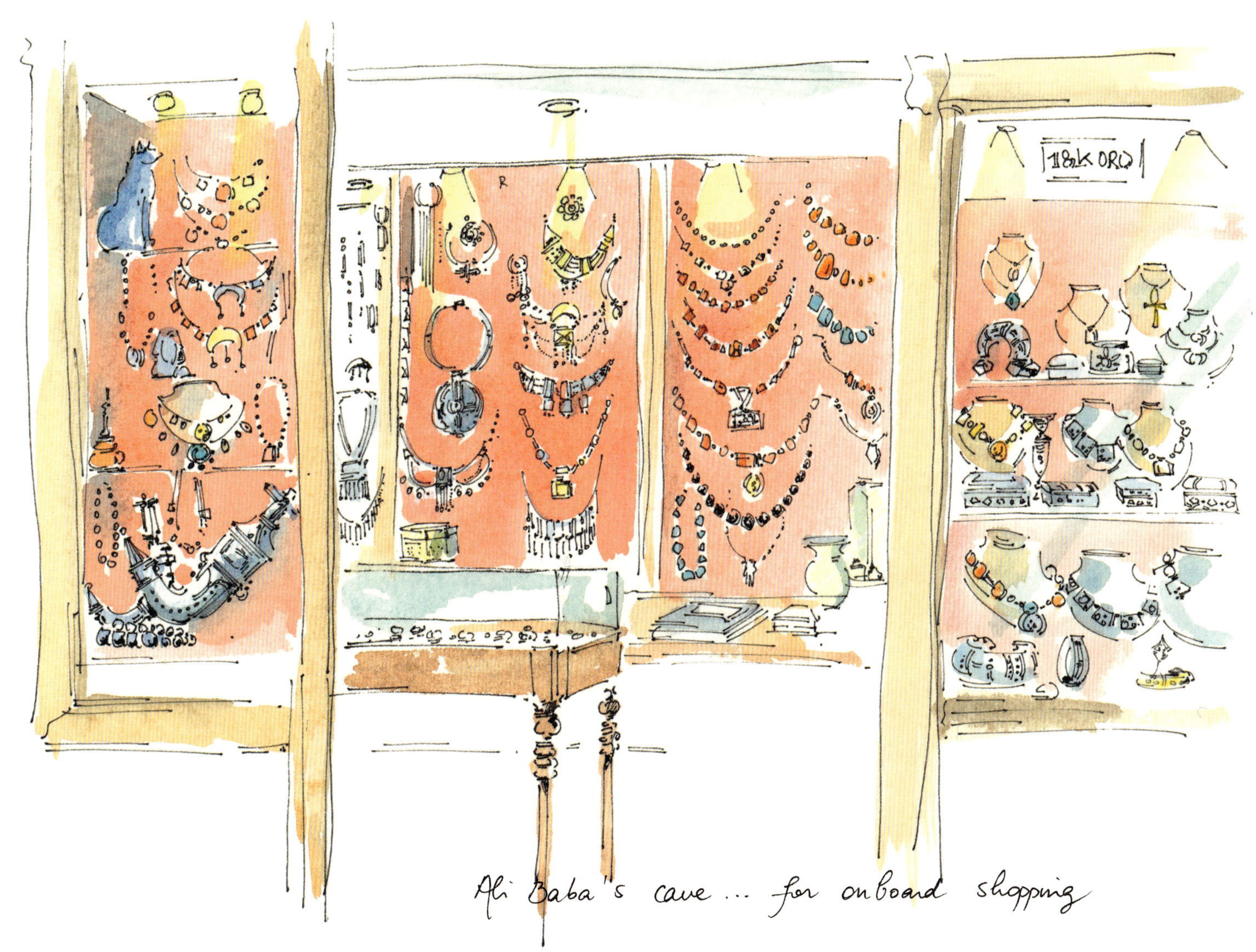

Ali Baba's cave ... for onboard shopping

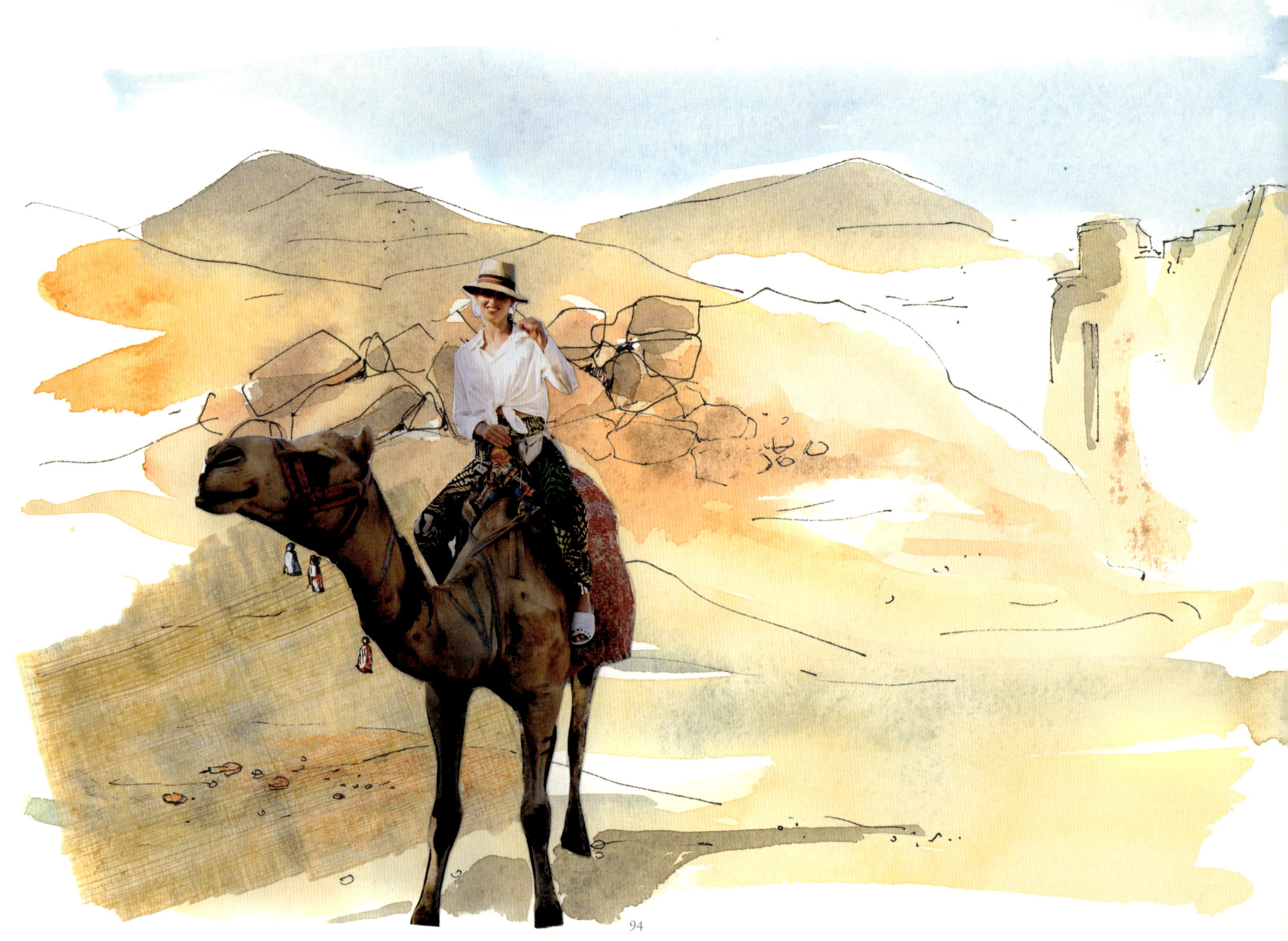

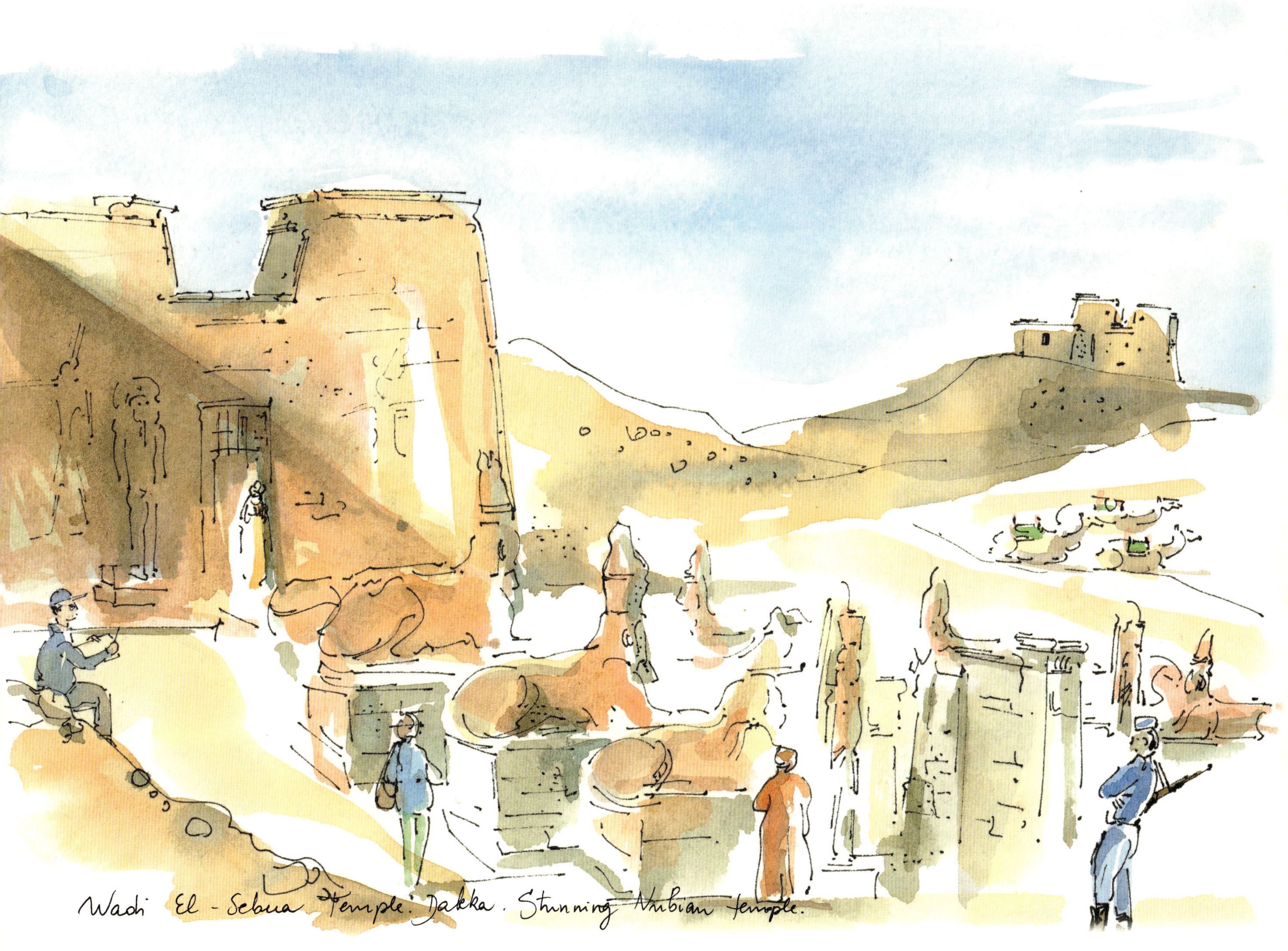

Wadi El-Sebua Temple. Dakka. Stunning Nubian temple.

The sphinx,

A creature with a human head and a lion's body, is one of the unmistakeable symbols (with obelisks, pyramids and the ubiquitous lotus plant) of ancient Egypt. Though there is equally early evidence for the monster in Asia Minor, dating to the end of the third millennium BC, Egypt is perceived to be its true birthplace. Once established in a form which was male, magnificent, threatening, representative of pharaonic power and prestige, the sphinx changed very little, except in detail, throughout the dynastic period, probably because of the essentially unchanging nature of Egyptian civilization during which fixed forms in art were upheld, the view being that having created something so pleasing in the first place, it was impossible to improve it by much. Even when the human head was replaced by that of an animal or bird, such as the ram sacred to the god Amun (a criosphinx) or the falcon sacred to Horus (a hierosphinx), the general impression remained very much the same.

Whatever its context, the role of the sphinx has always been the same: to inject an authentic aura of antiquity into its surroundings. And whatever antiquity suggested at the time, the sphinx was endlessly adaptable: threatening, mystic, morbid, decorative, amusing, exotic, even erotic. Regardless of where it found itself, the sphinx retained its integrity, its dignity and its power; with its archaic charm, its formal elegance and ambiguous sexuality, it is the brooding enigma of the most remote and perennial past.

Henrietta MacCall, *Mythical Beasts*, British Museum Press, 1995.

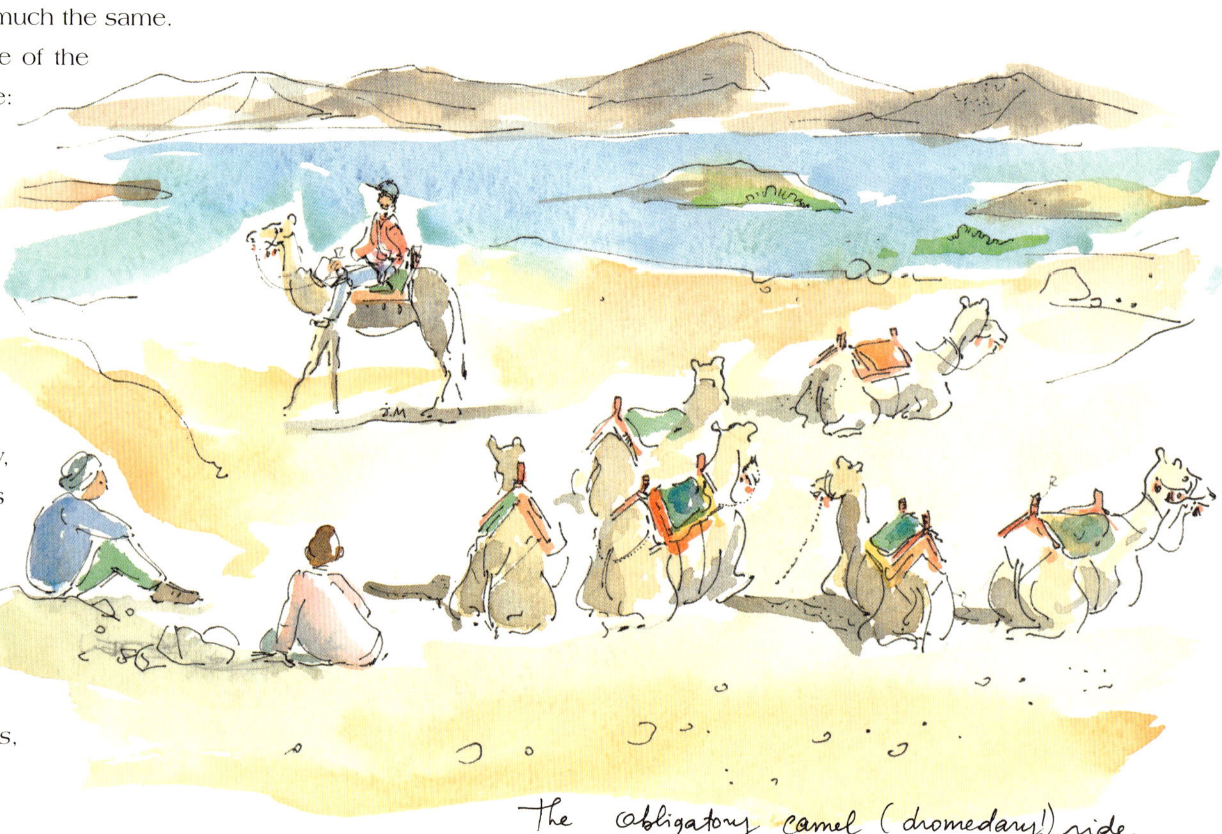

The obligatory camel (dromedary!) ride.

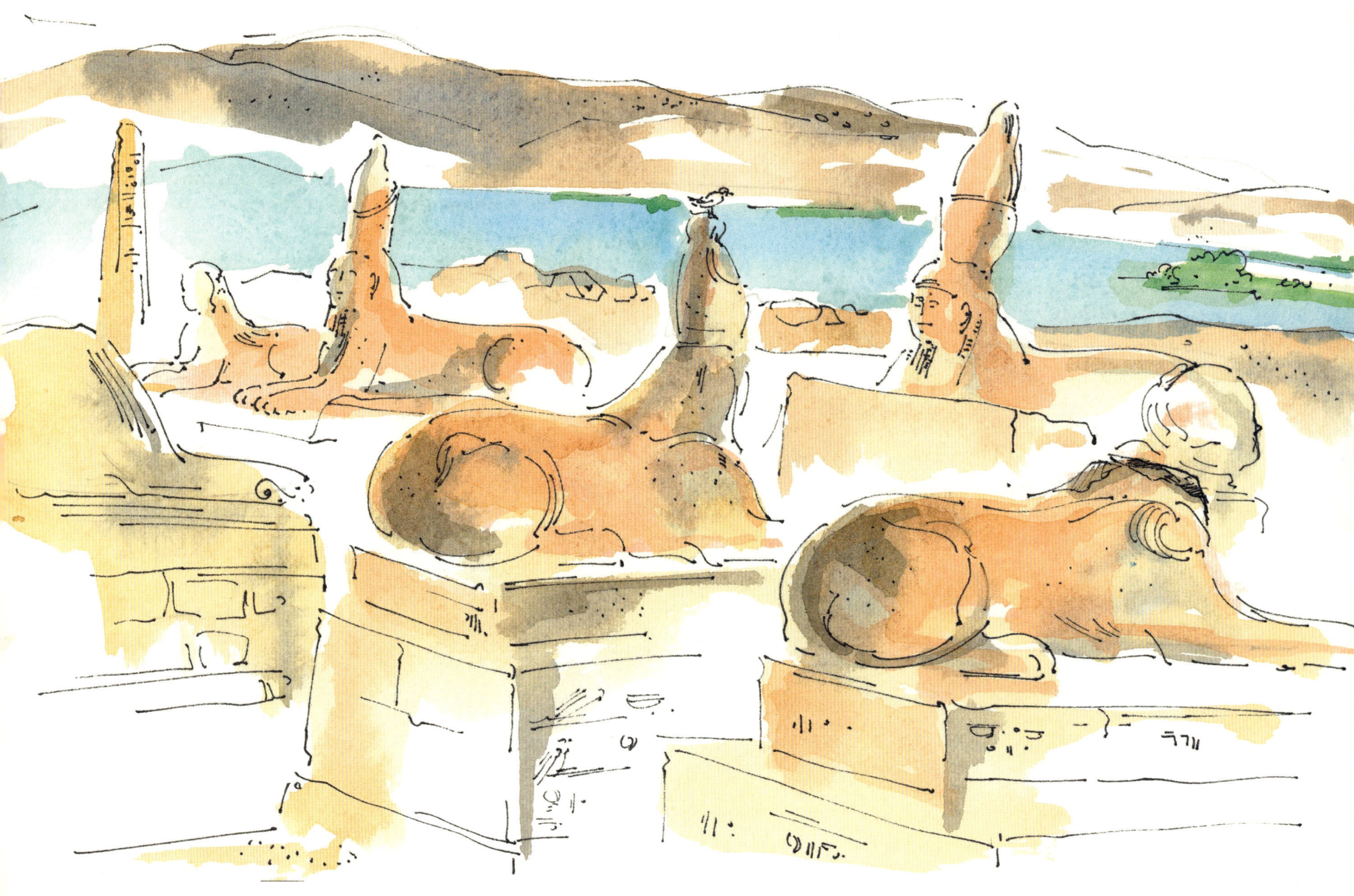

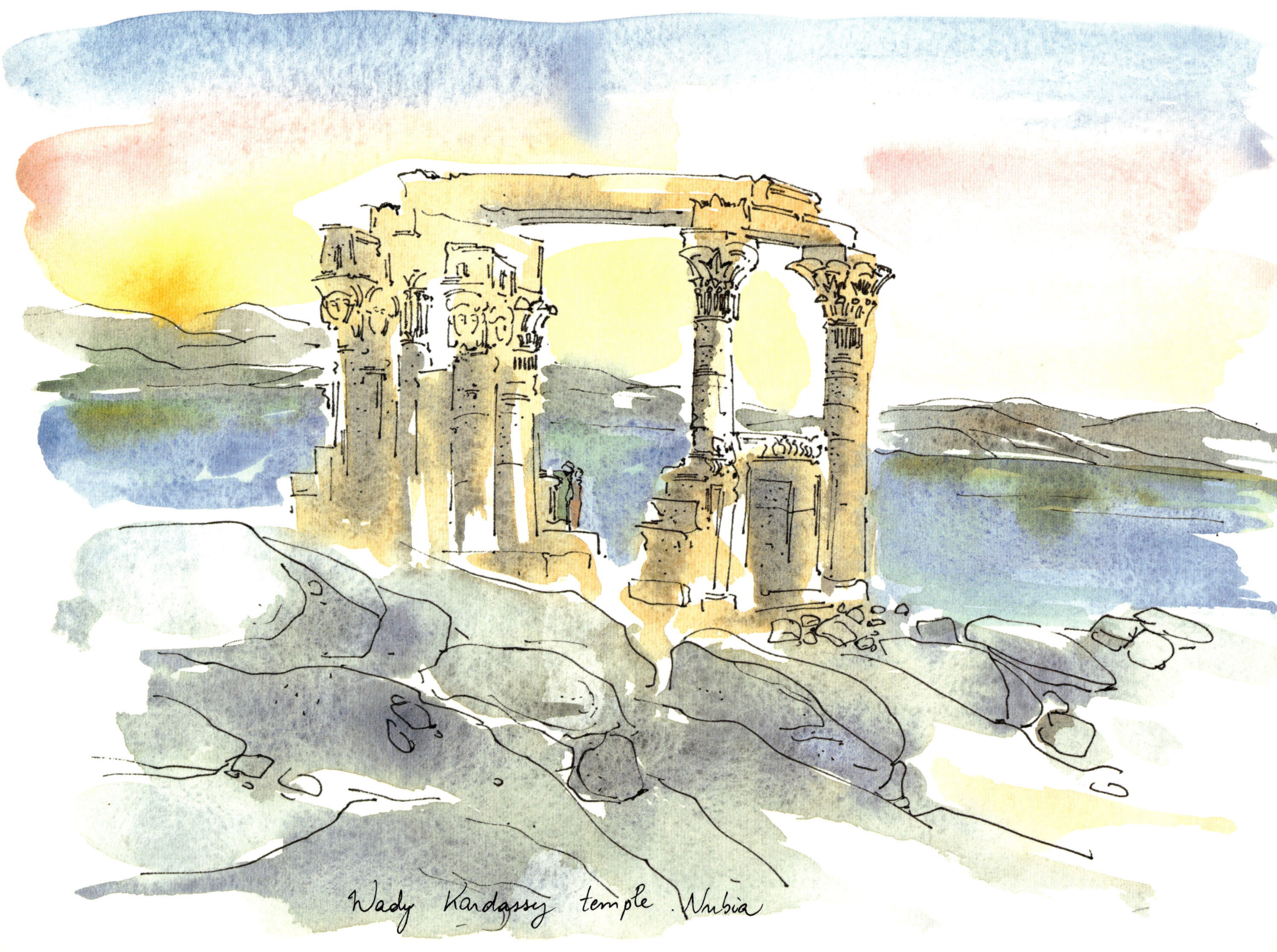

Wady Kardassy temple . Nubia

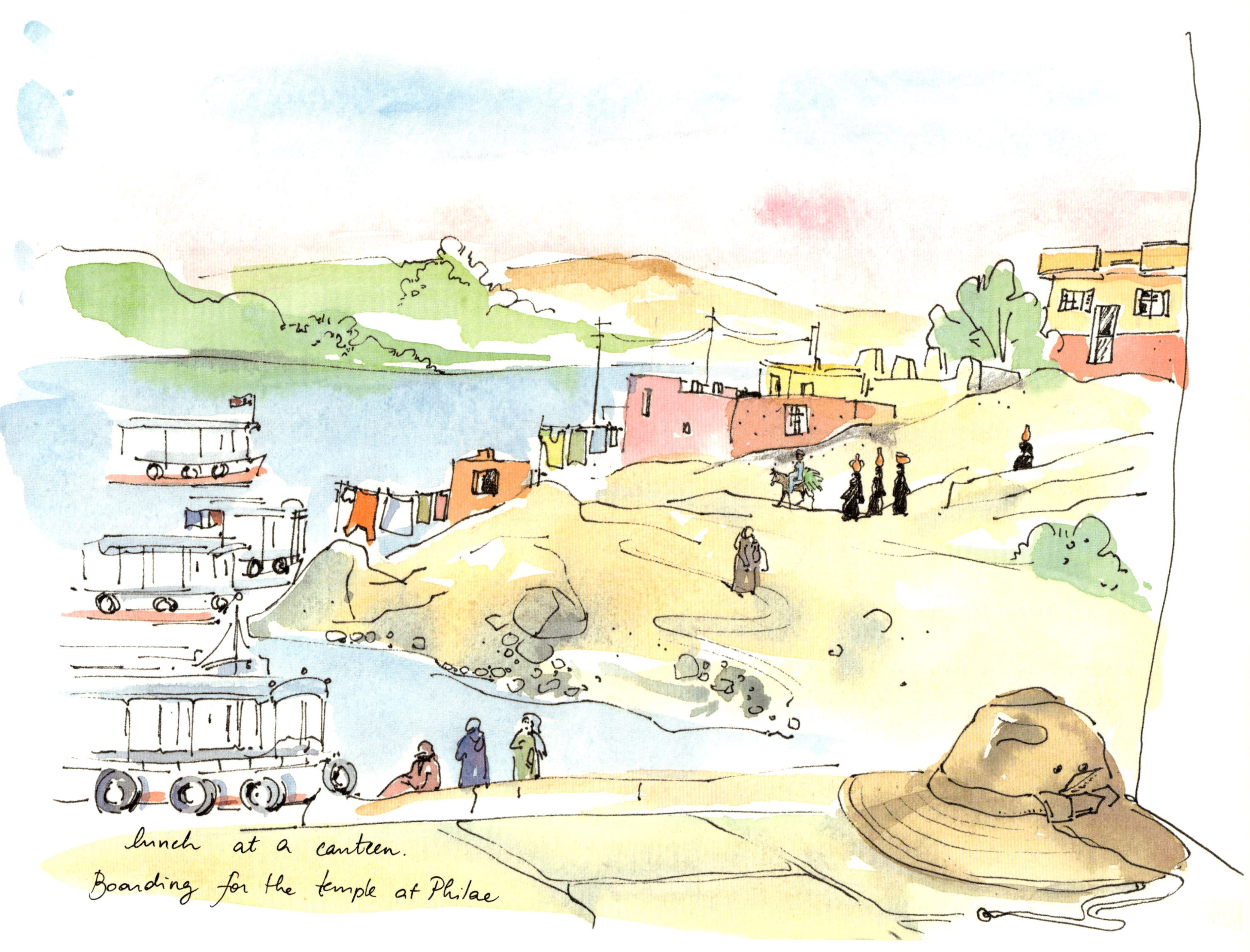

lunch at a canteen.
Boarding for the temple at Philae

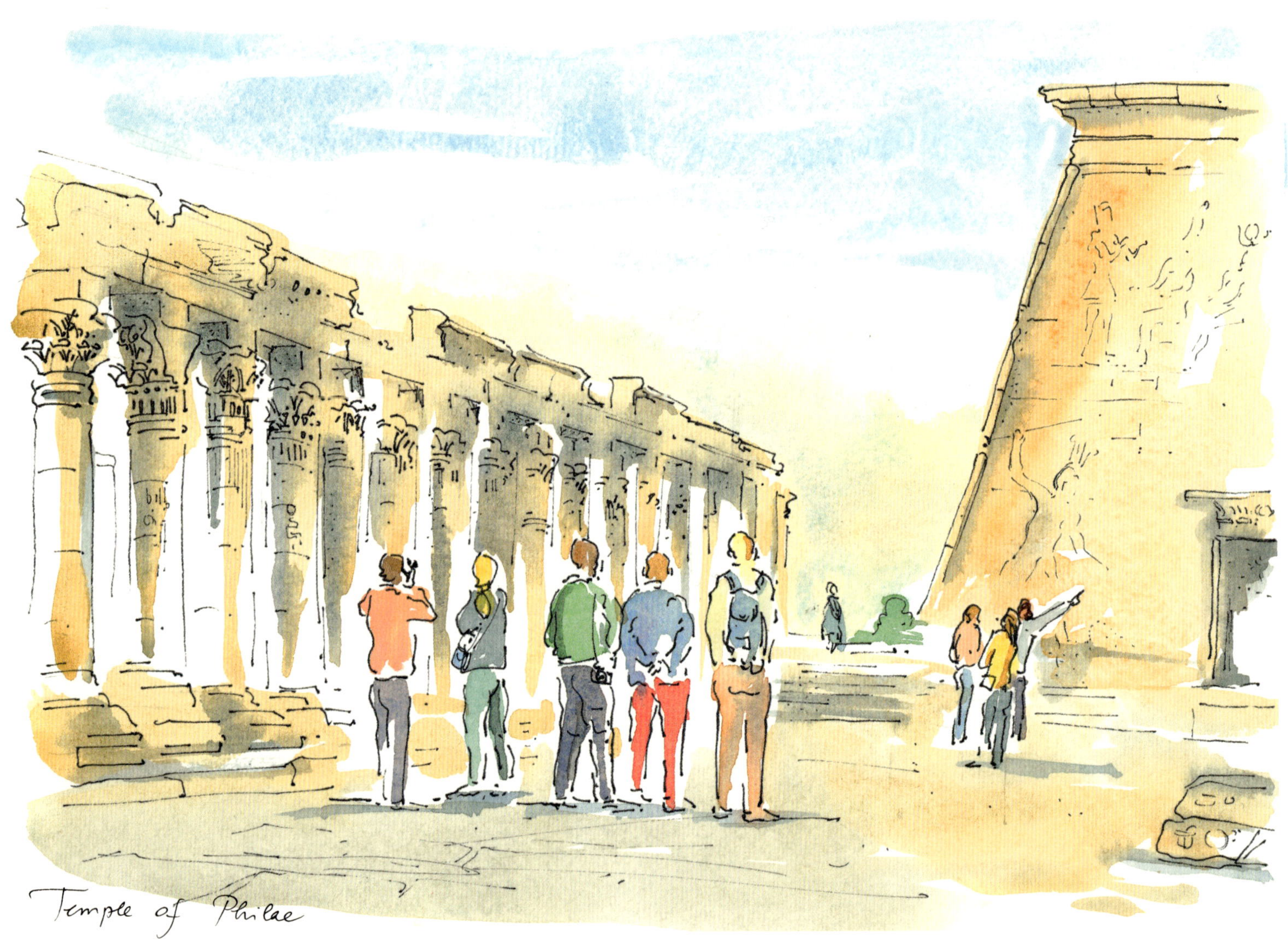

Temple of Philae

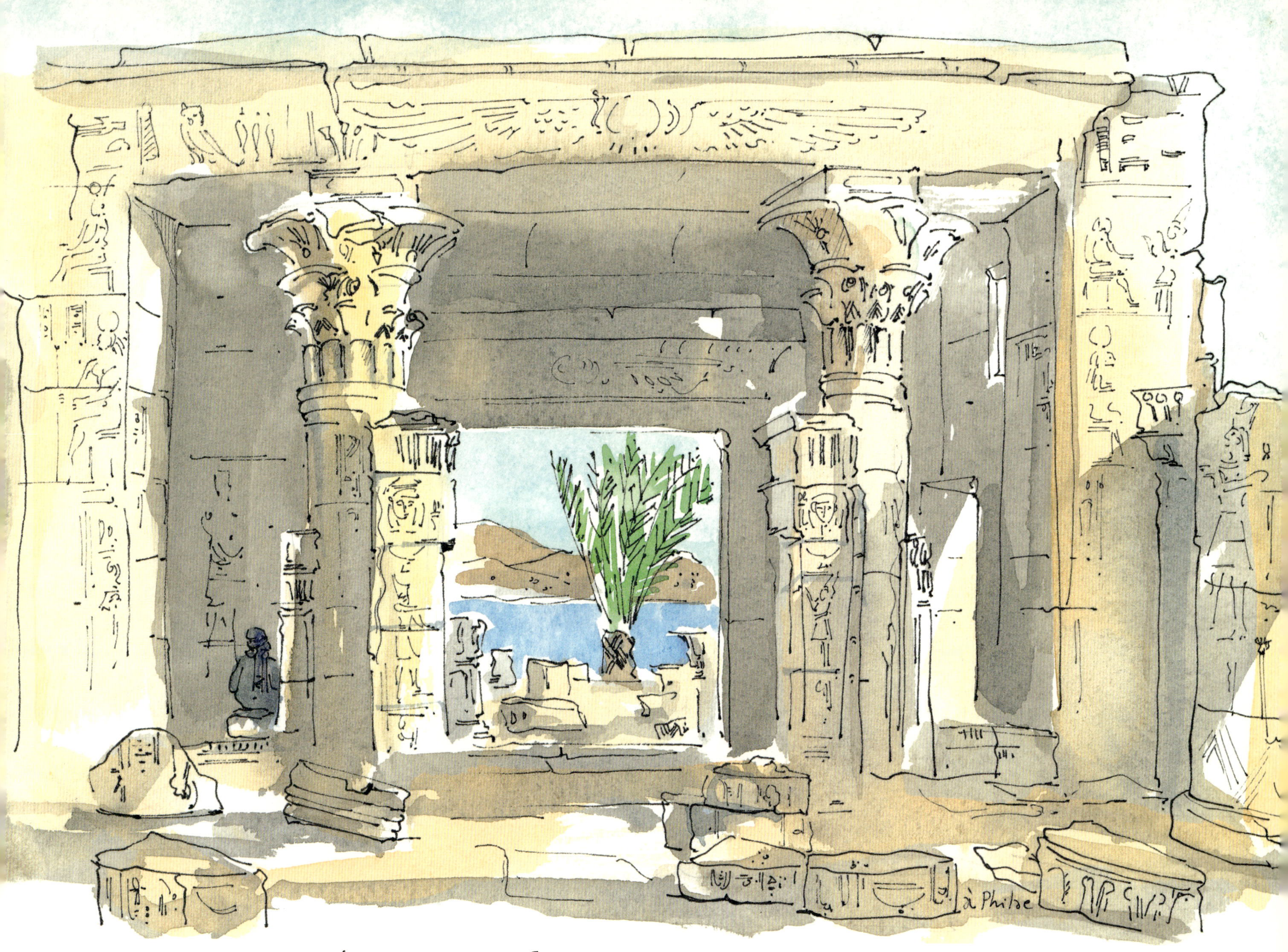

a temple in Philae

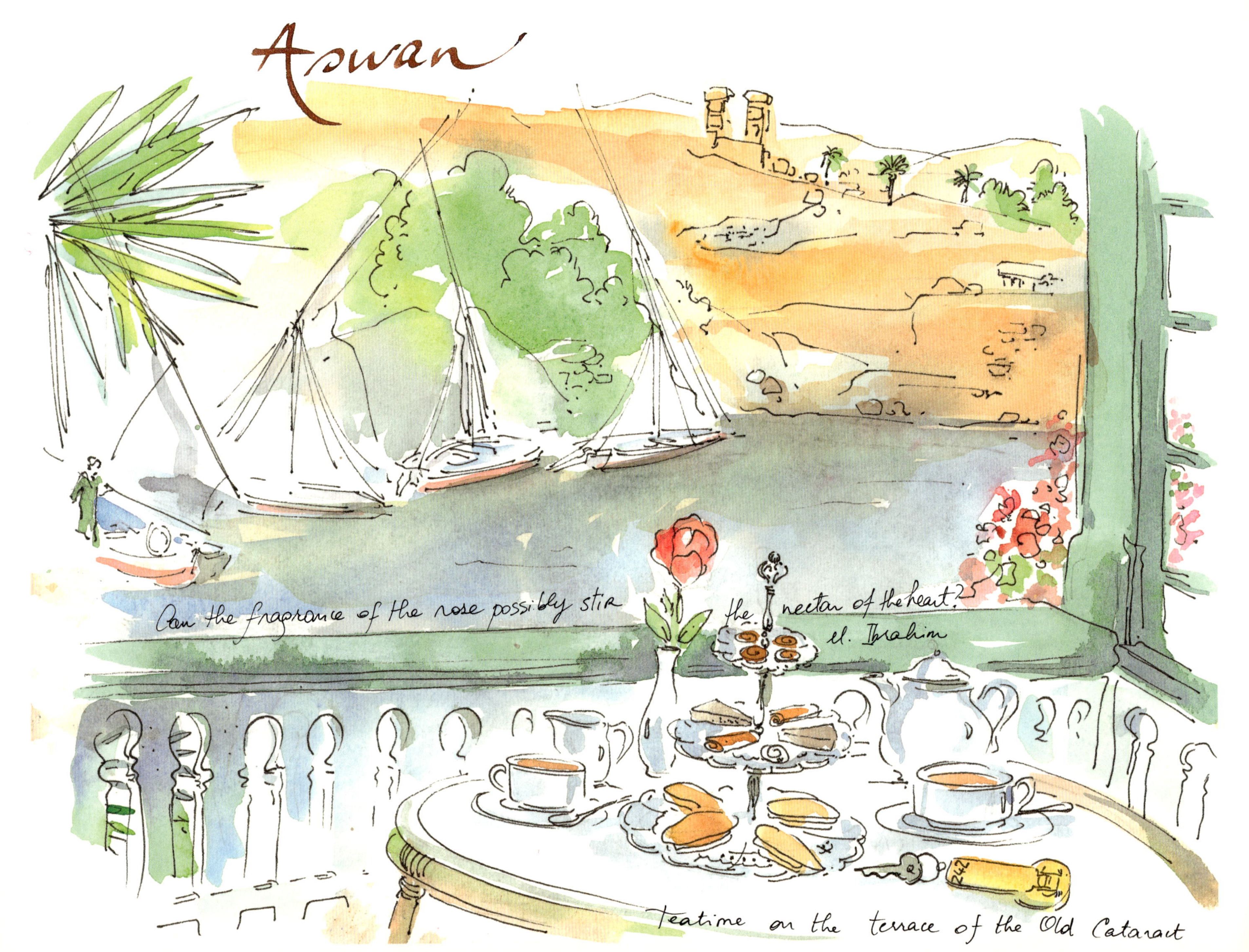

Aswan
Can the fragrance of the rose possibly stir the nectar of the heart?
El. Ibrahim
Teatime on the terrace of the Old Cataract

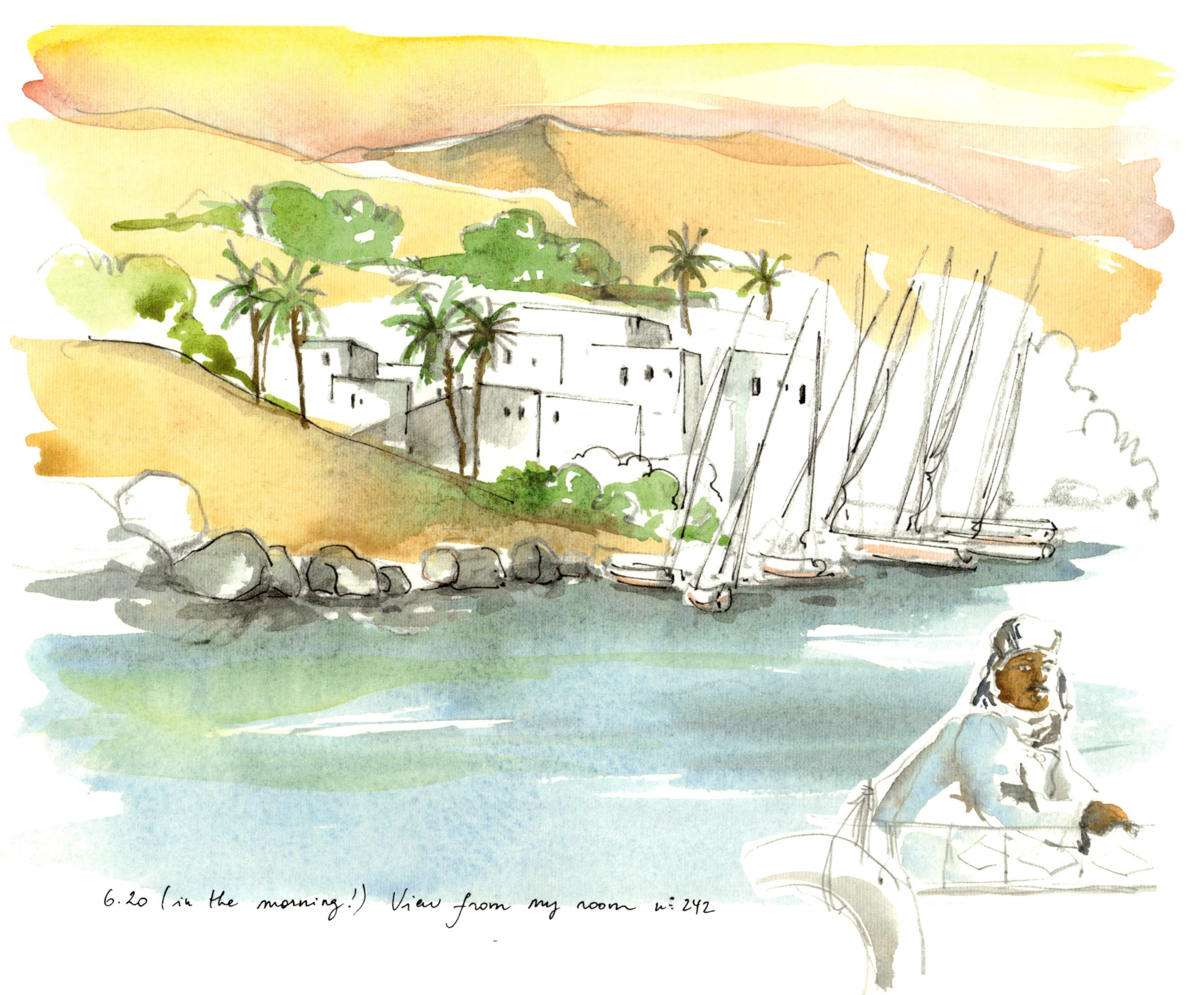

6.20 (in the morning!) View from my room n: 242

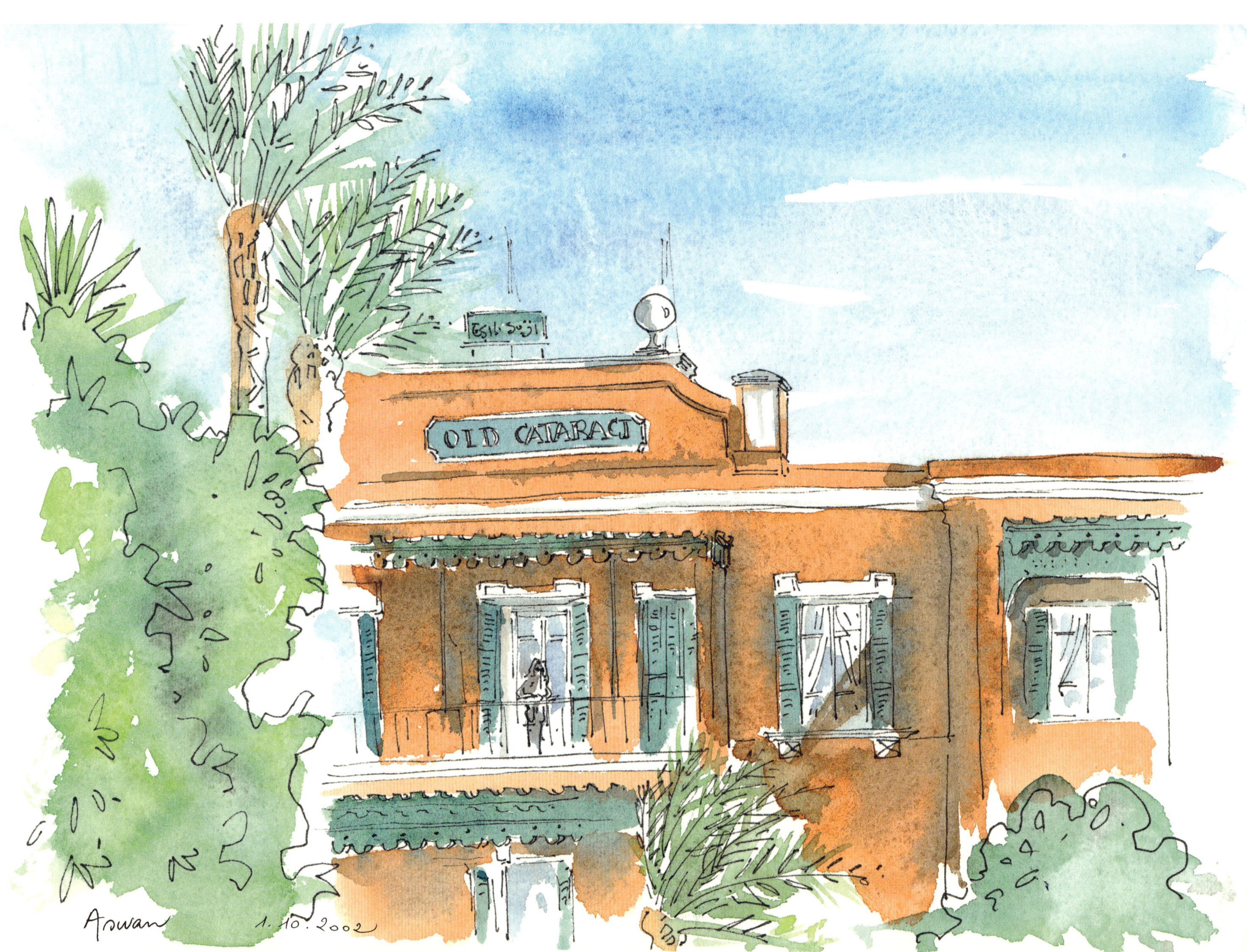
الأقصر الكتراكت
OLD CATARACT
Aswan   1. 10. 2002

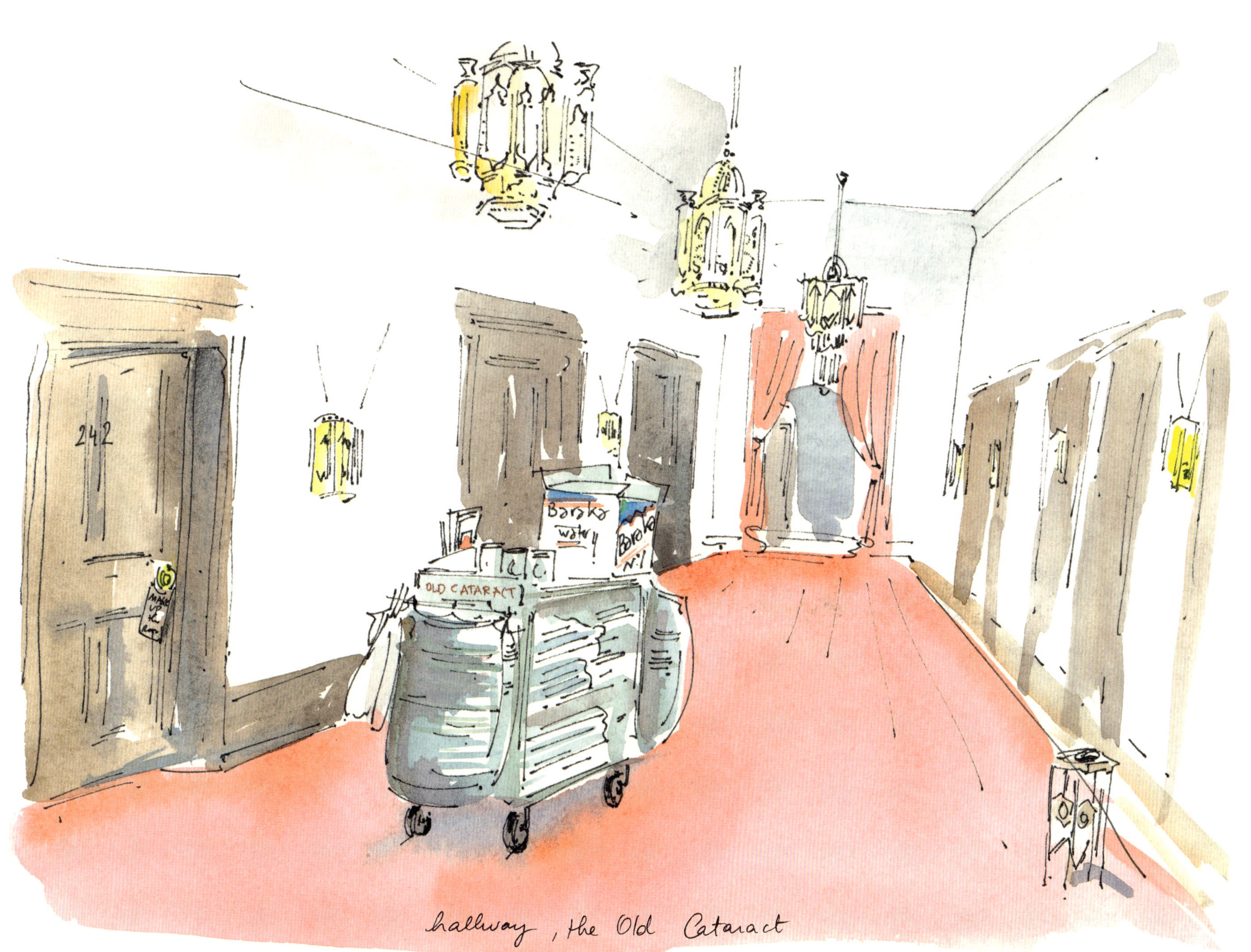

hallway, the Old Cataract

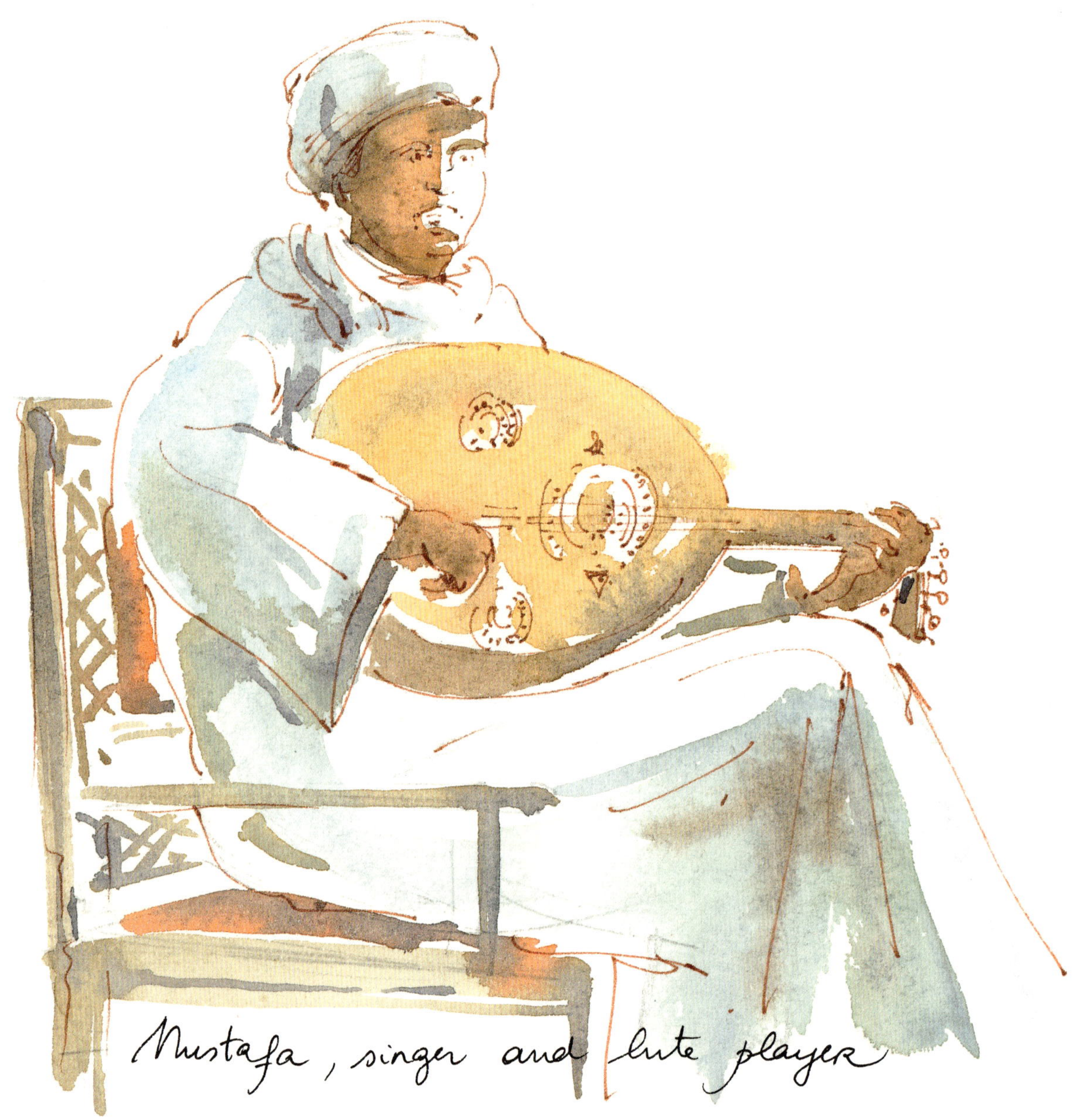

Mustafa, singer and lute player

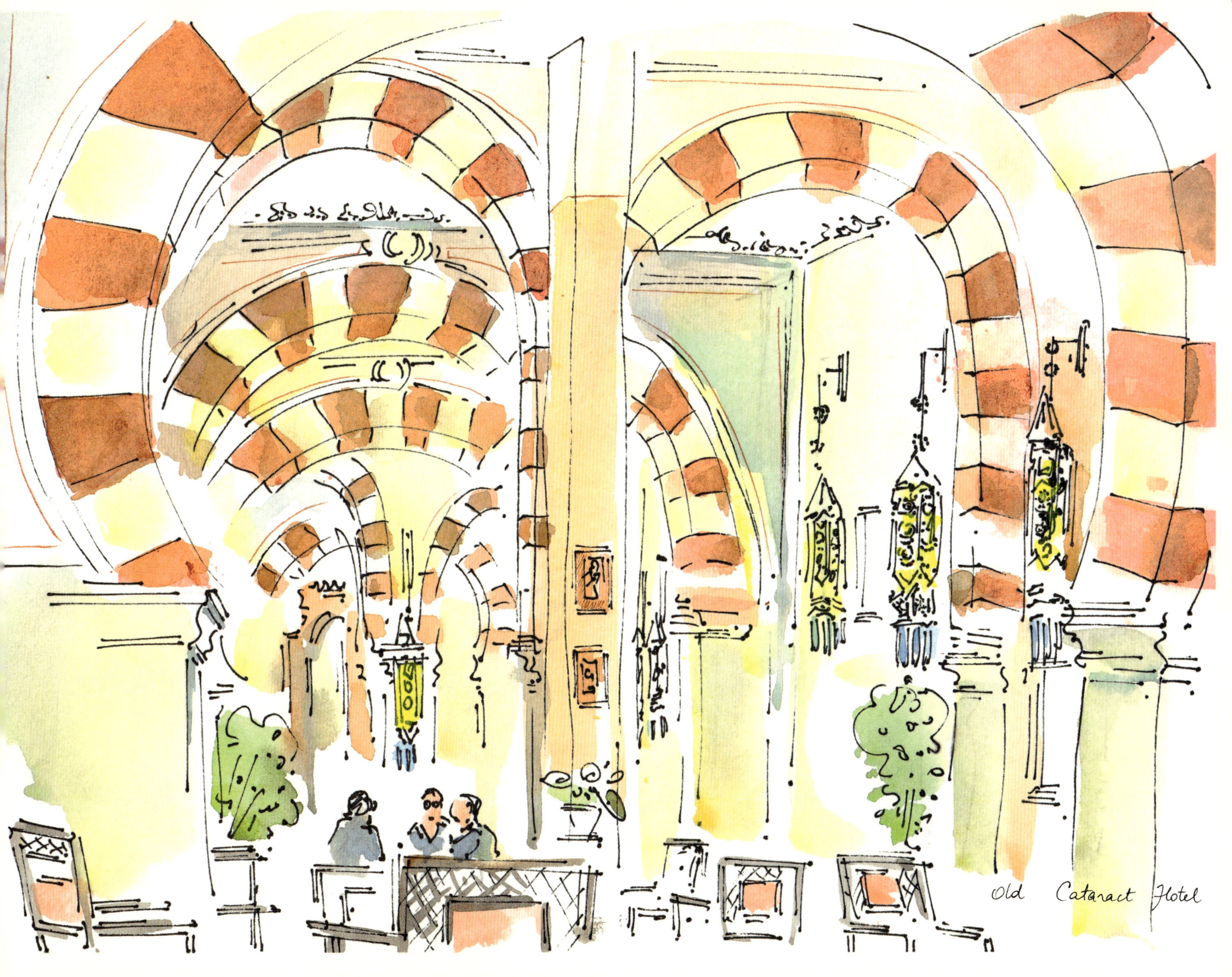

Old Cataract Hotel

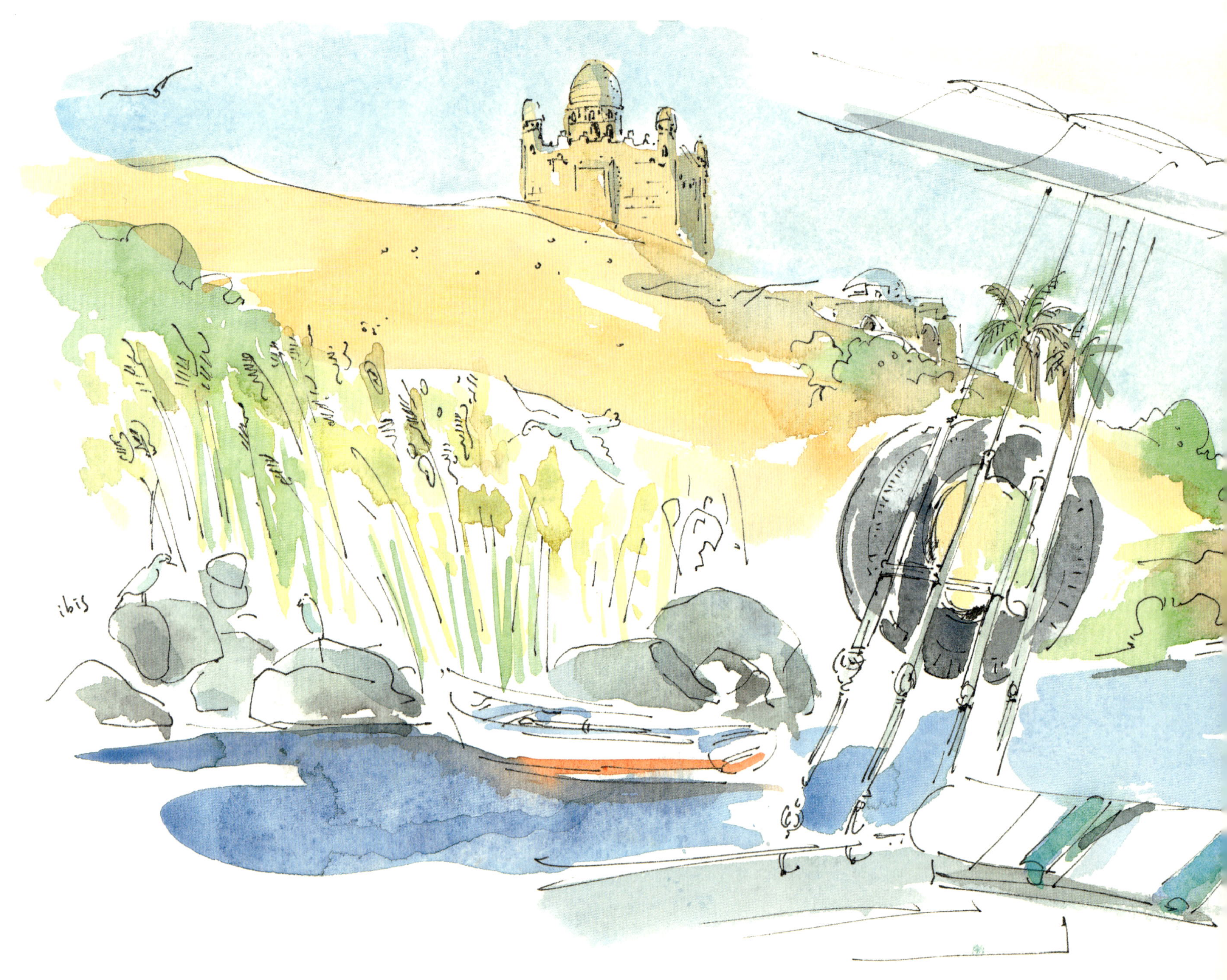
ibis

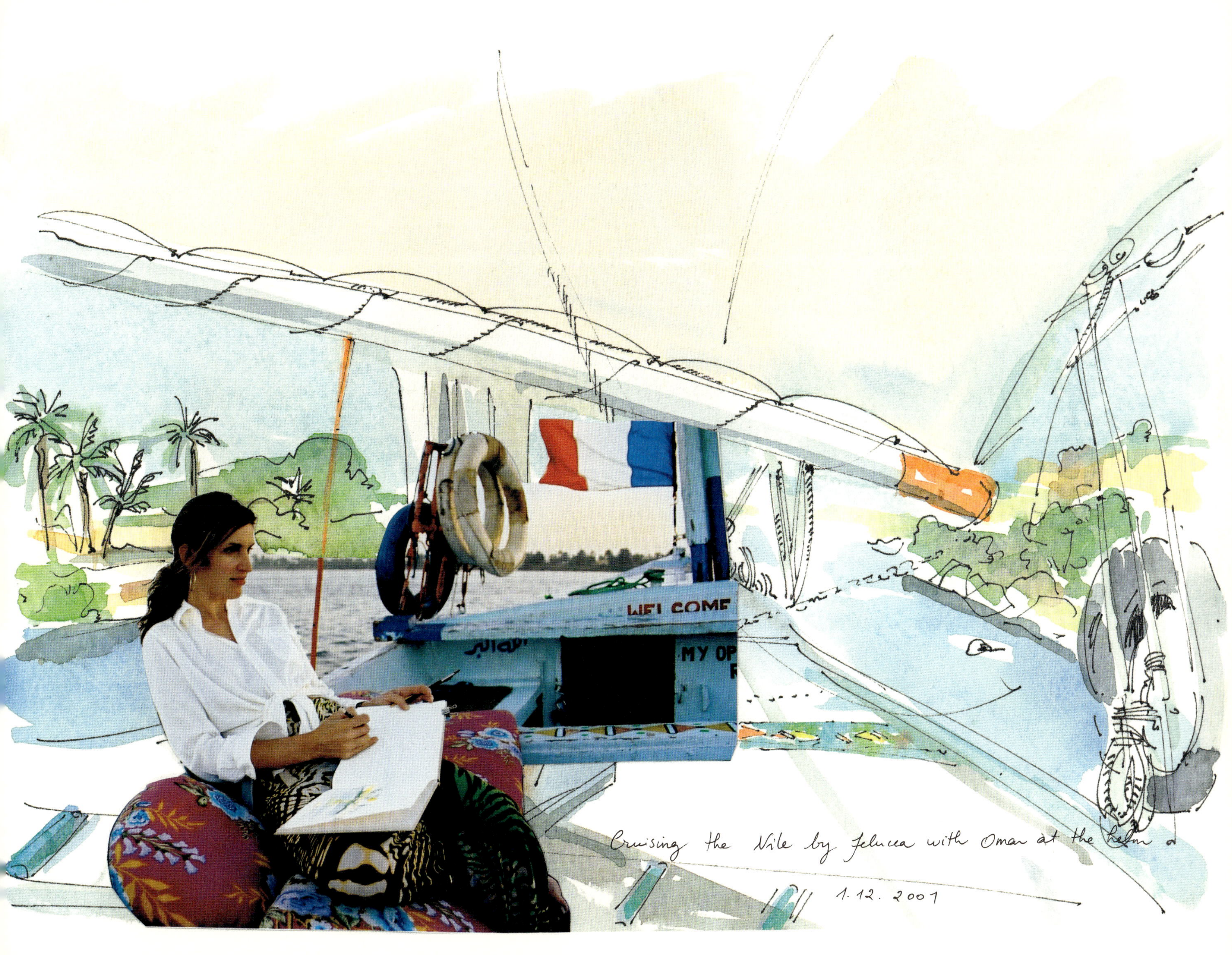

Cruising the Nile by Felucca with Omar at the helm
1.12.2001

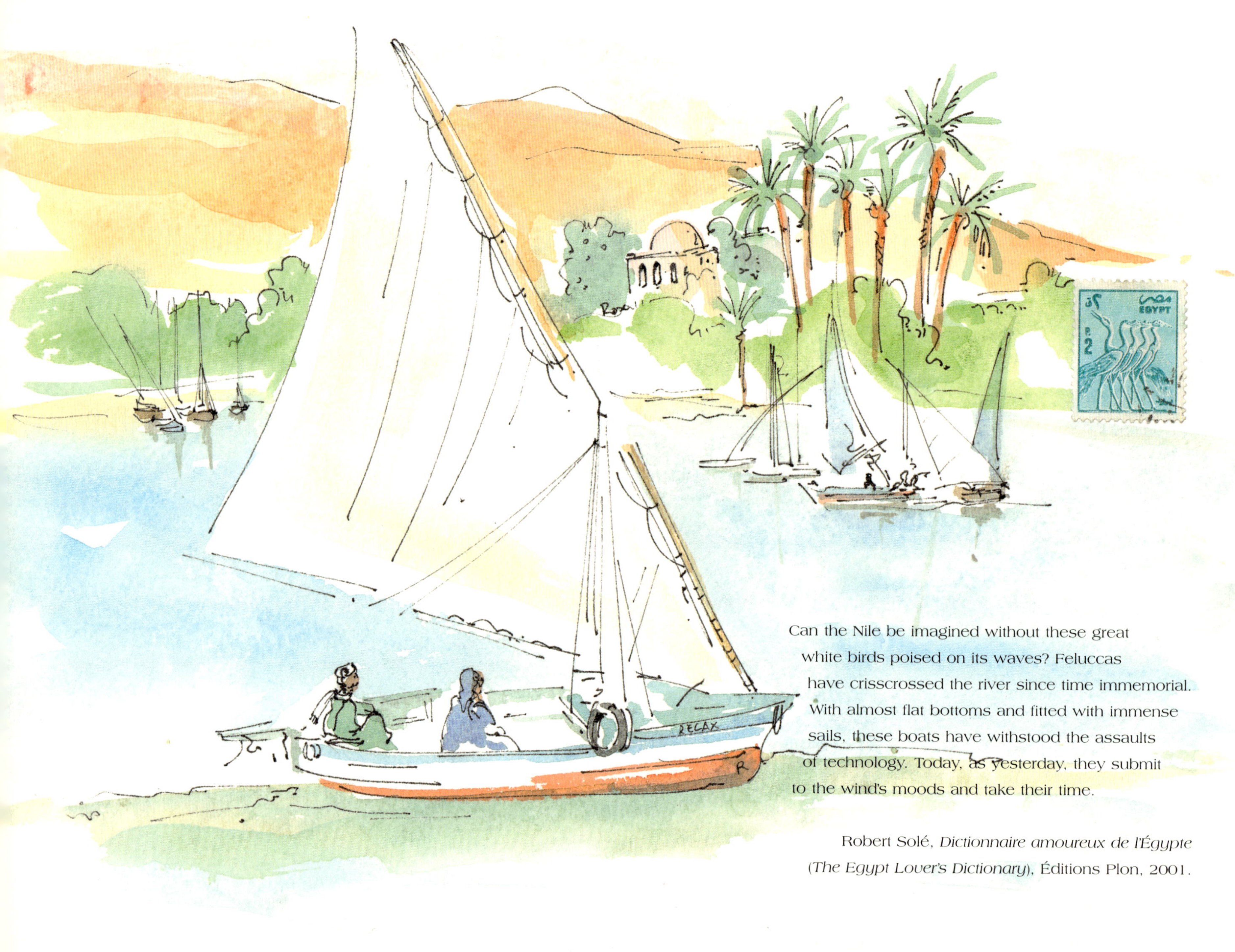

Can the Nile be imagined without these great white birds poised on its waves? Feluccas have crisscrossed the river since time immemorial. With almost flat bottoms and fitted with immense sails, these boats have withstood the assaults of technology. Today, as yesterday, they submit to the wind's moods and take their time.

Robert Solé, *Dictionnaire amoureux de l'Égypte* (*The Egypt Lover's Dictionary*), Éditions Plon, 2001.

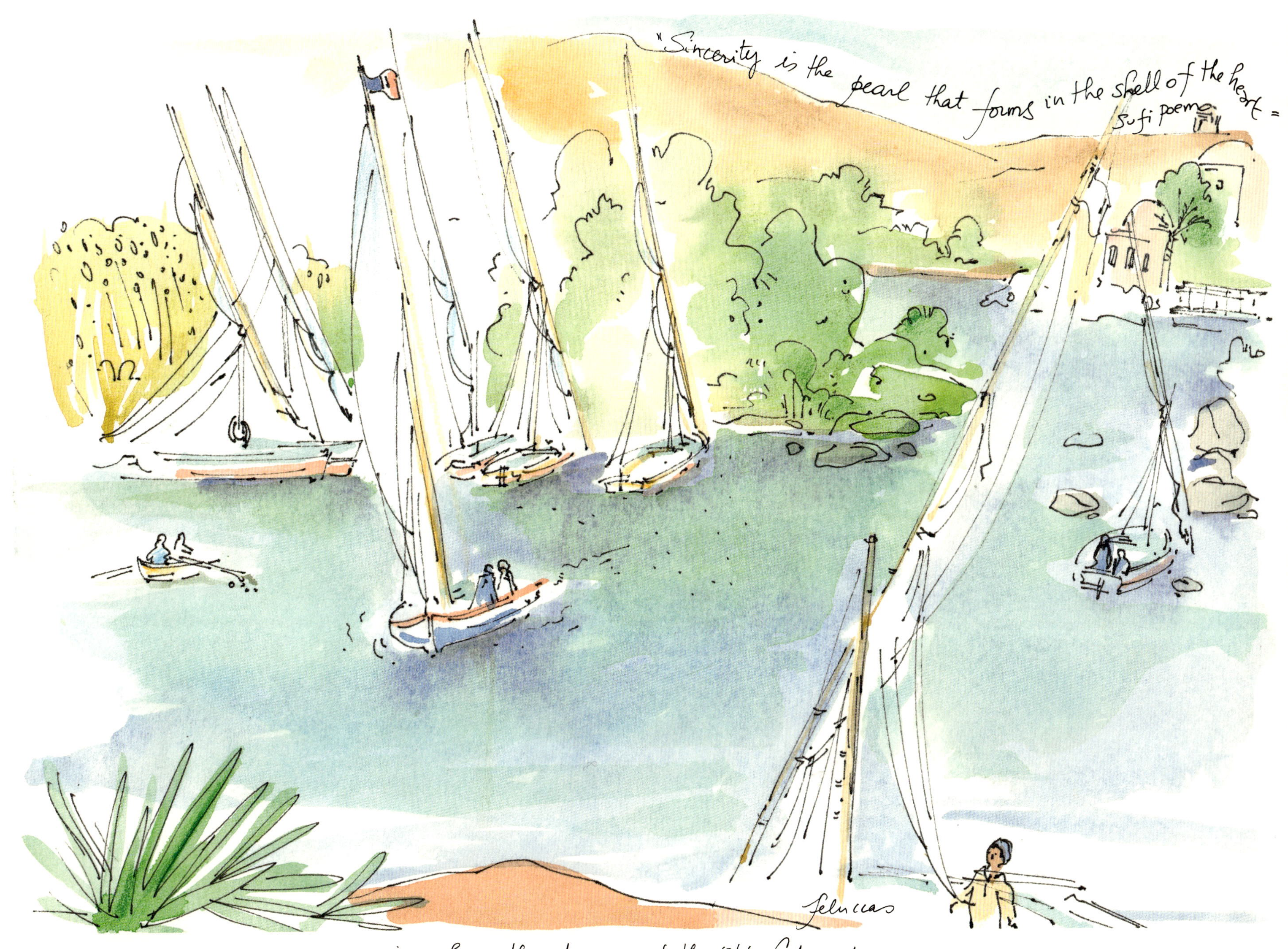
"Sincerity is the pearl that forms in the shell of the heart = sufi poem =
feluccas
view from the terrace of the Old Cataract

Abu Simbel

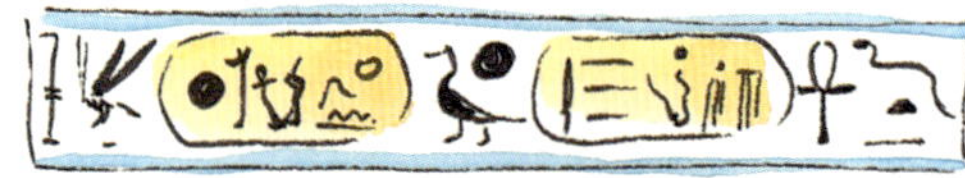

Thanks to its temples, Egypt retained the capacity
to reconcile everyday life with the highest
principles of divine life throughout the millennia.
A land of initiation into and transmission
of knowledge, it attracted the elite of
neighboring countries, including Greece –
from Pythagoras to Plato, via Solon,
Thales and many others.
In Egypt, there is no clearly defined
boundary between what we call "life"
and what we call "death."

From *Le Pharaon, Roi-Prêtre
de l'Égypte Ancienne* (*The Pharaoh,
the Priest-King of Ancient Egypt*),
directed by Paul Barba Negra.

Ramses II (19th dynasty)

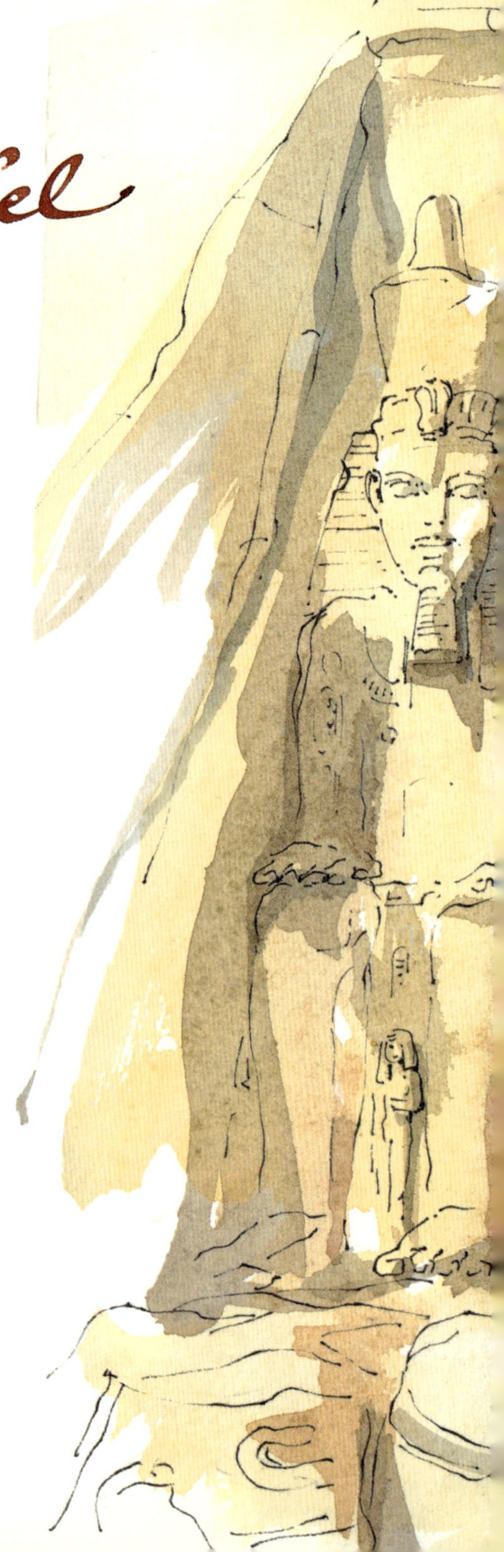

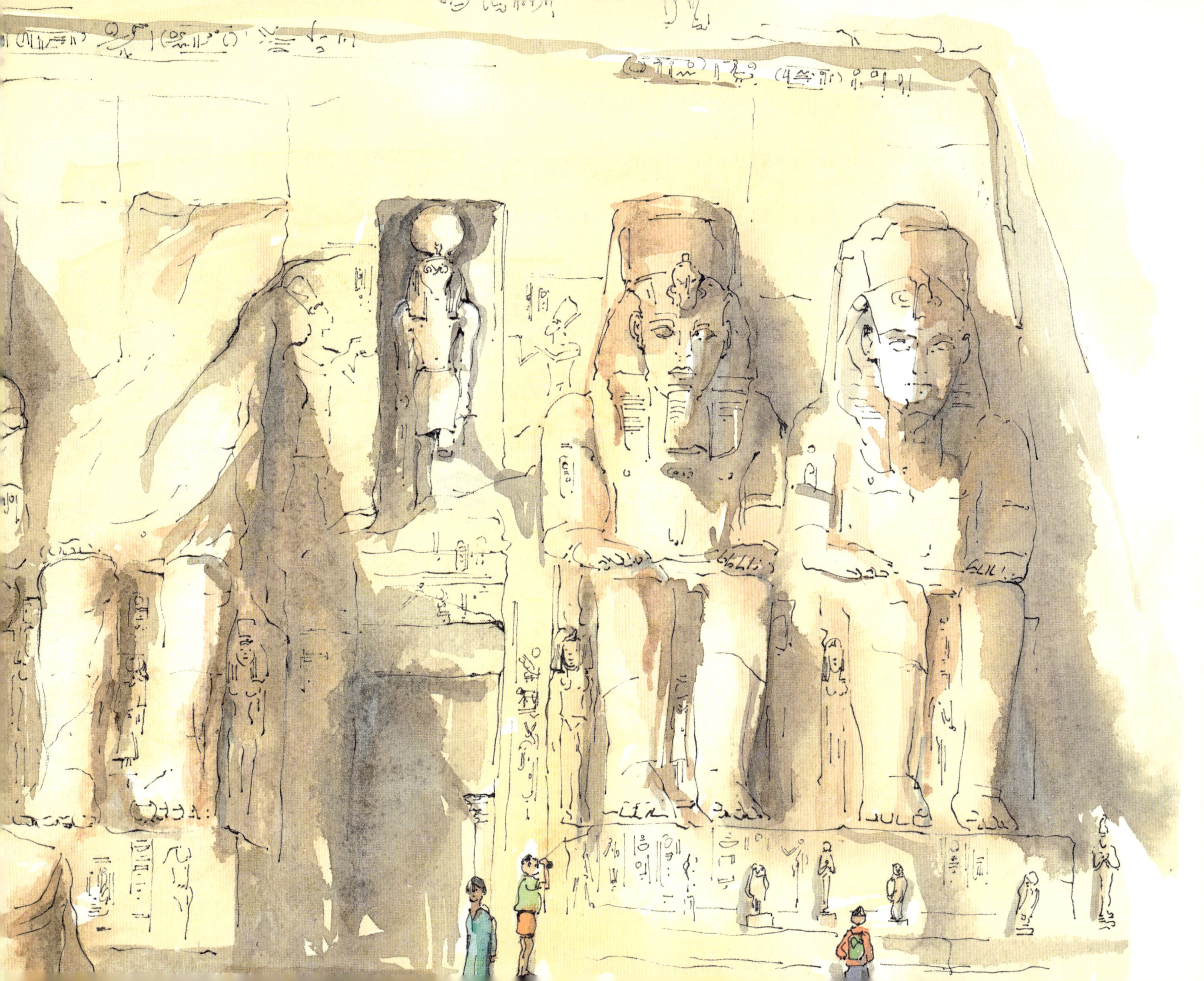

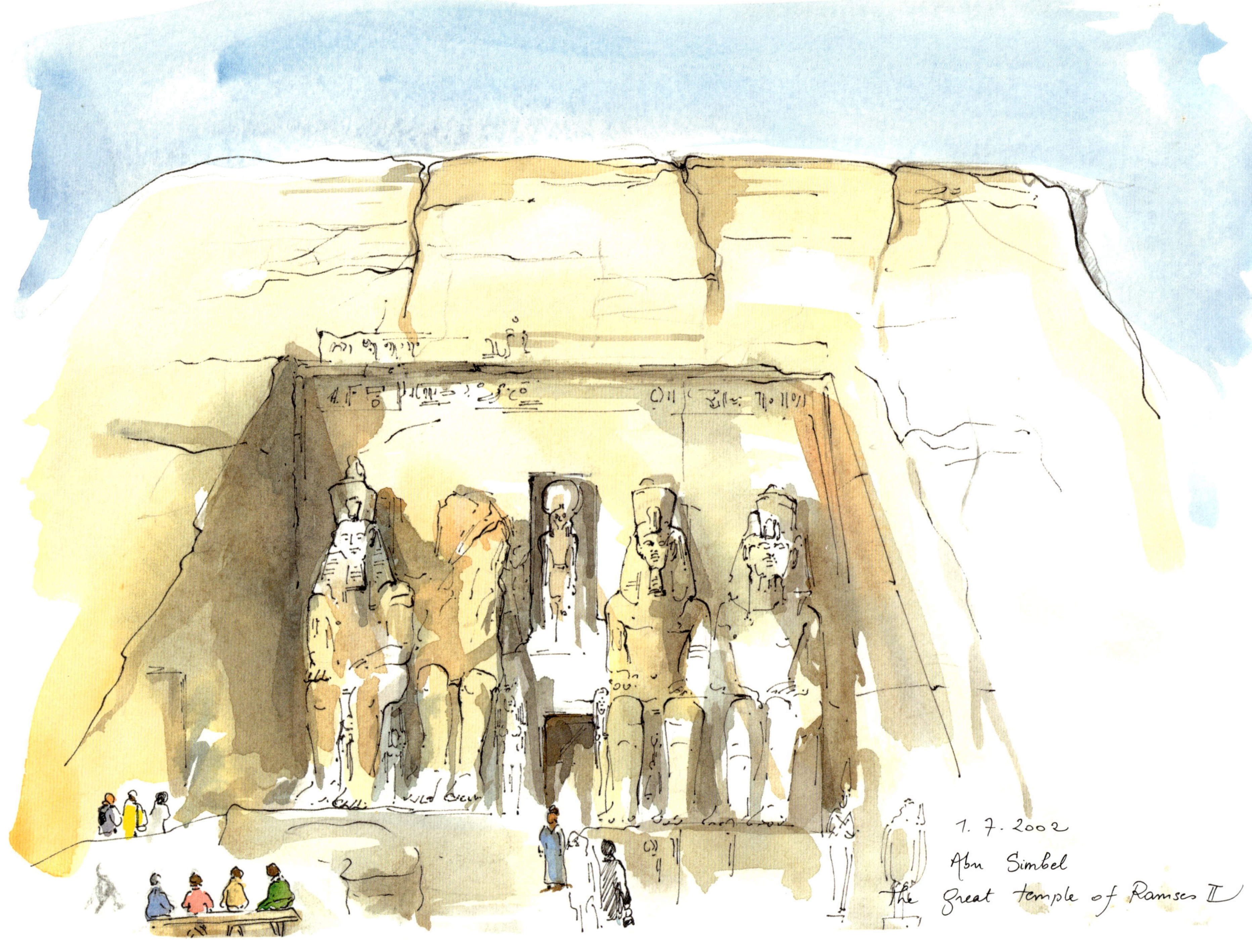

1. 7. 2002
Abu Simbel
The Great temple of Ramses II

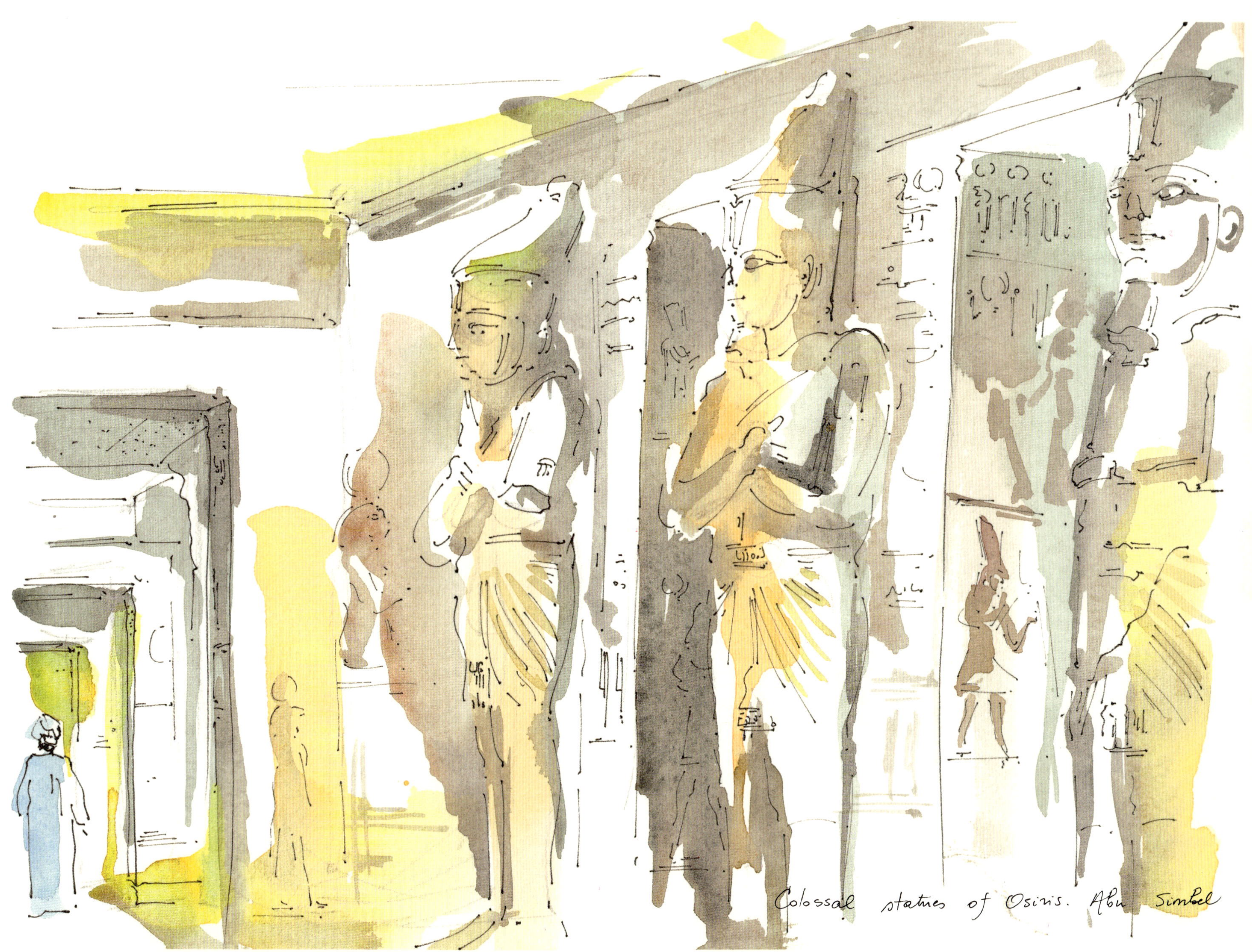

Colossal statues of Osiris. Abu Simbel

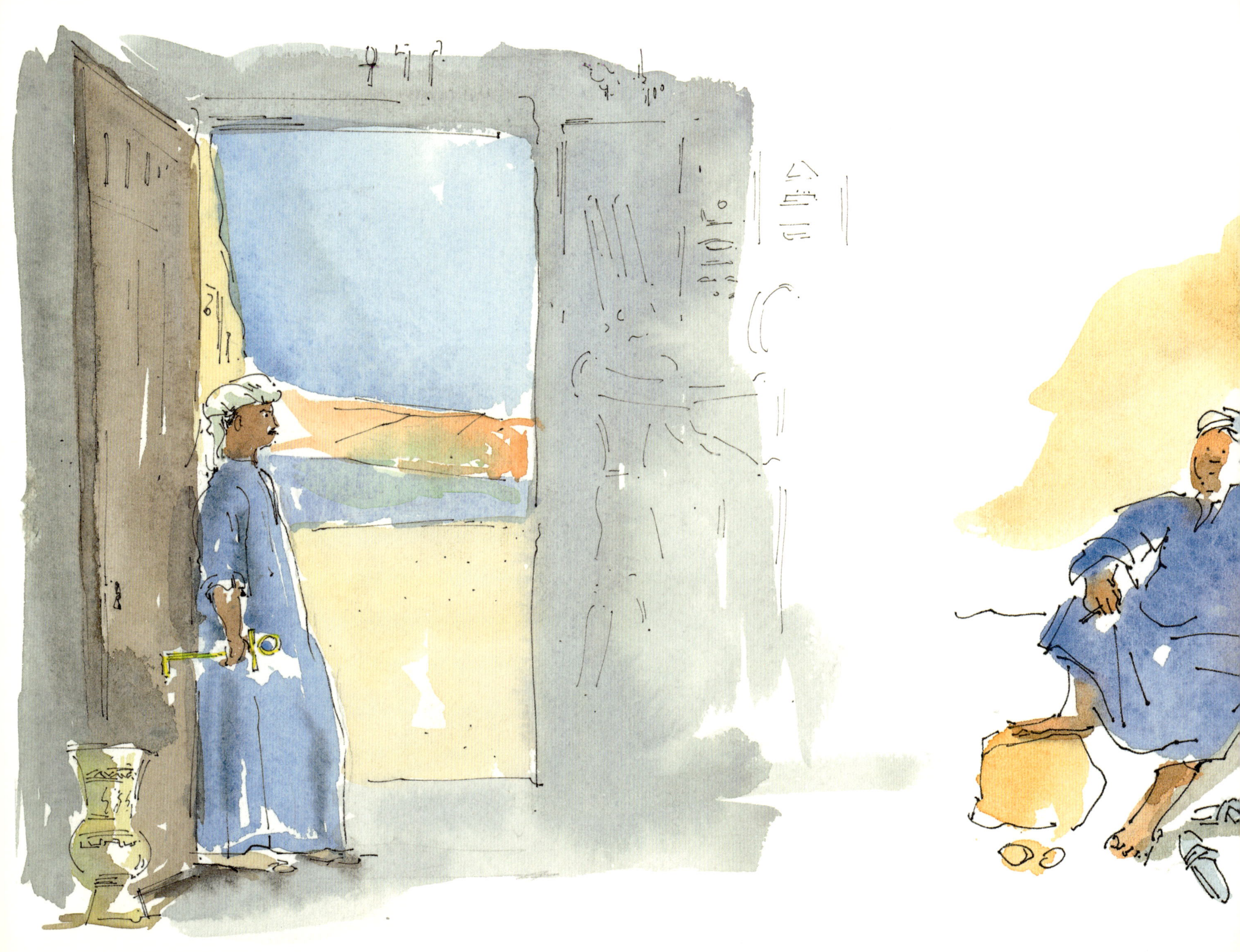

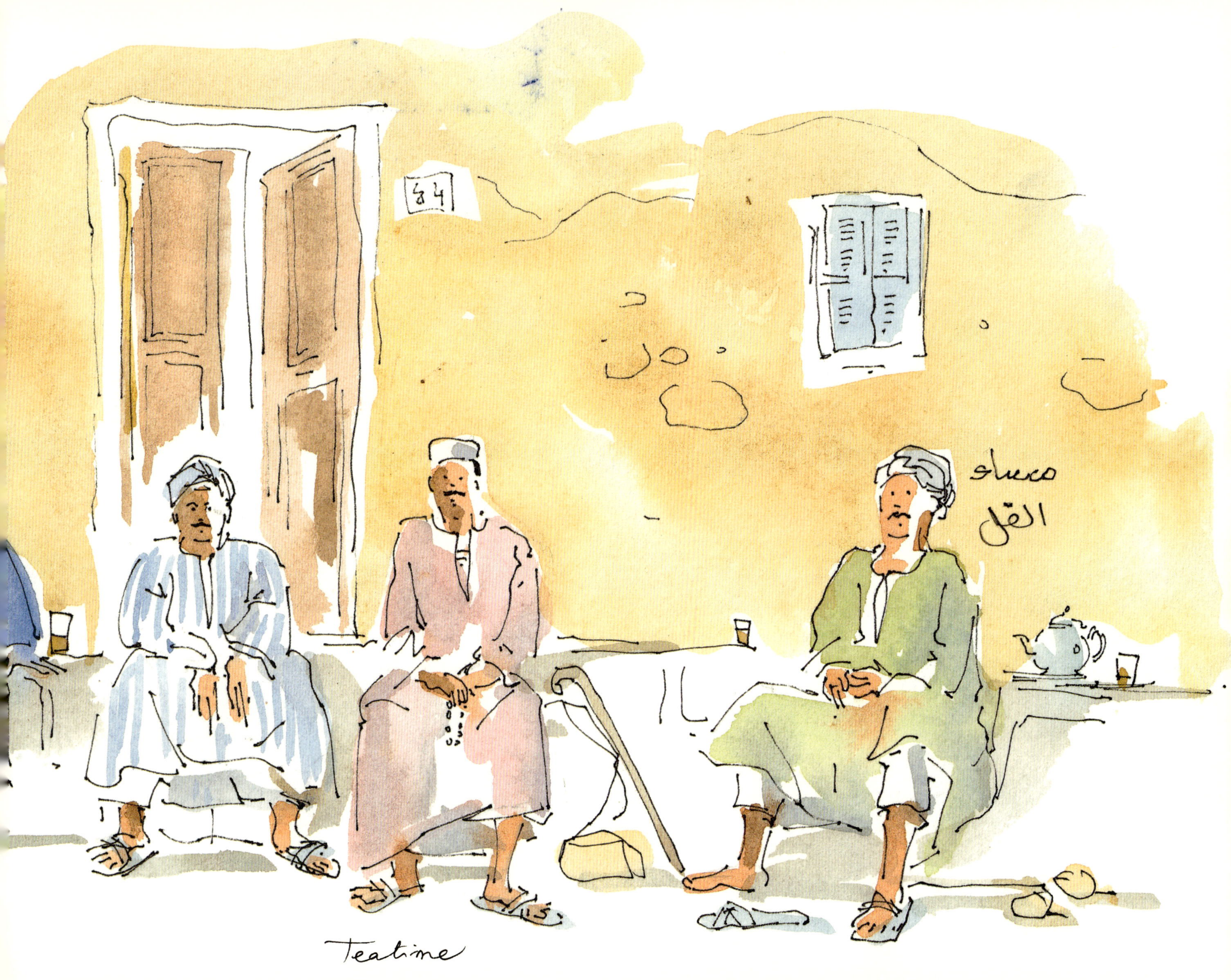
84
stucco
القل
Teatime

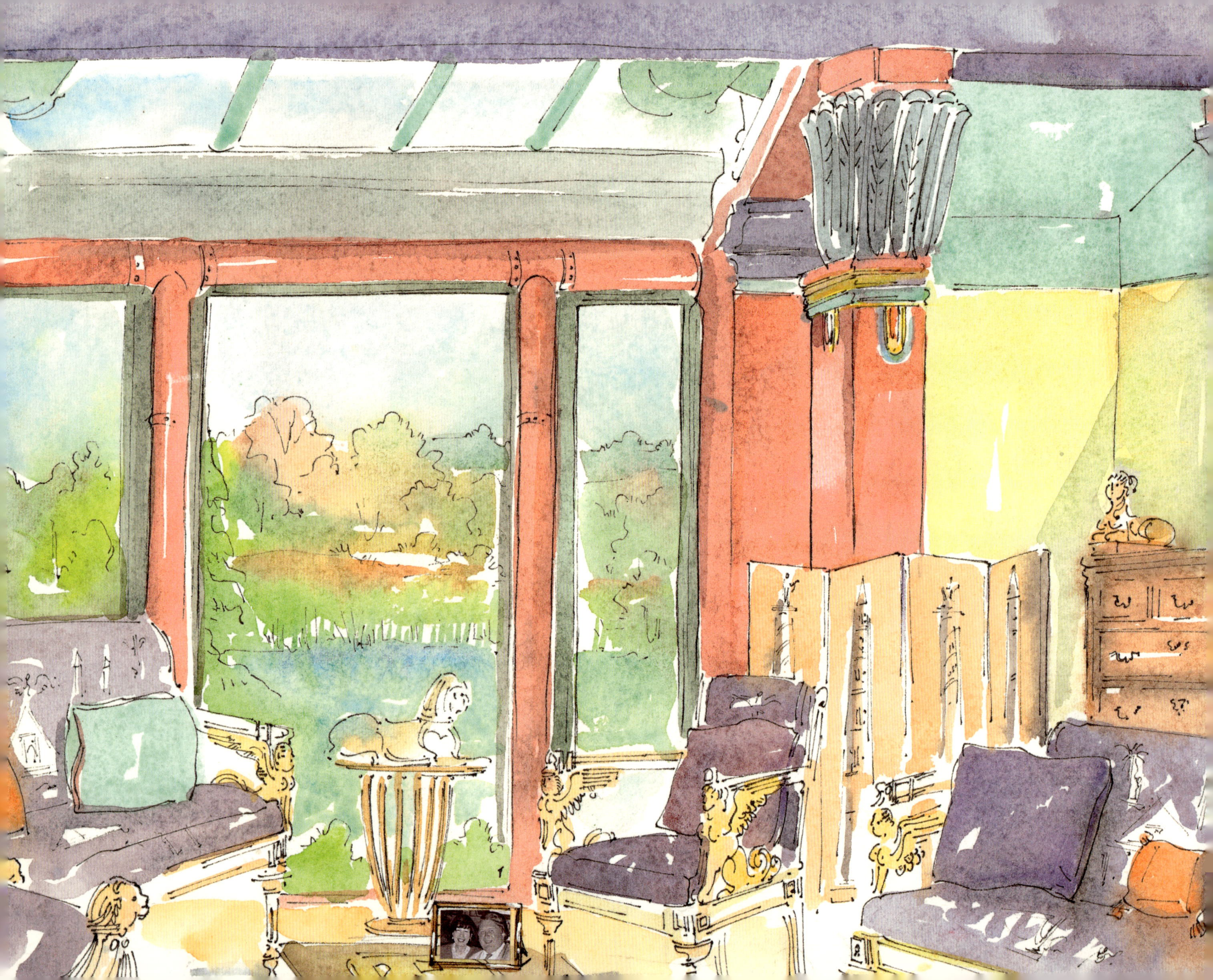

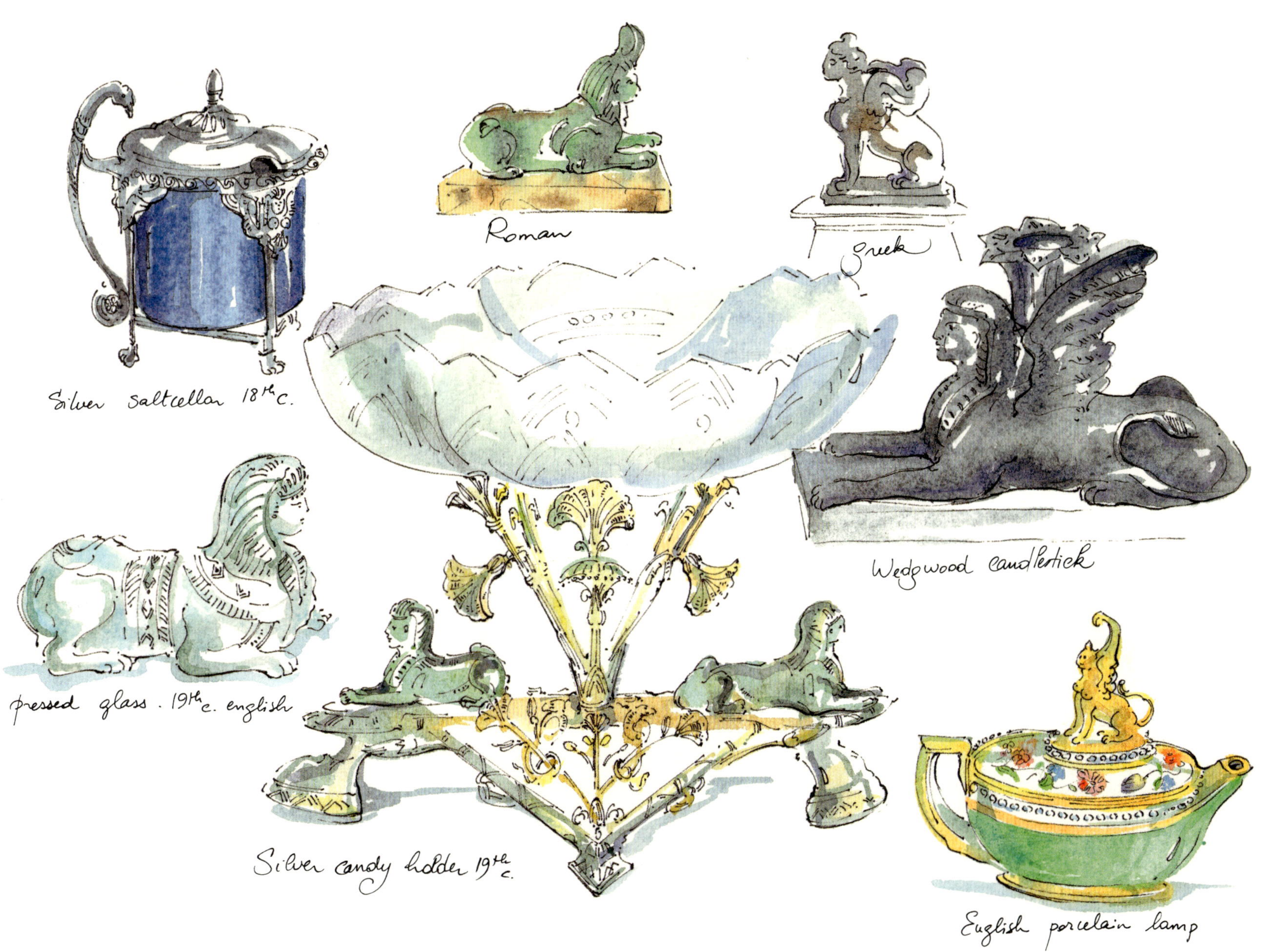

Roman
Greek
Silver saltcellar 18th c.
Wedgwood candlestick
pressed glass. 19th c. english
Silver candy holder 19th c.
English porcelain lamp
Egypt lover's house near Oxford.
Private collection

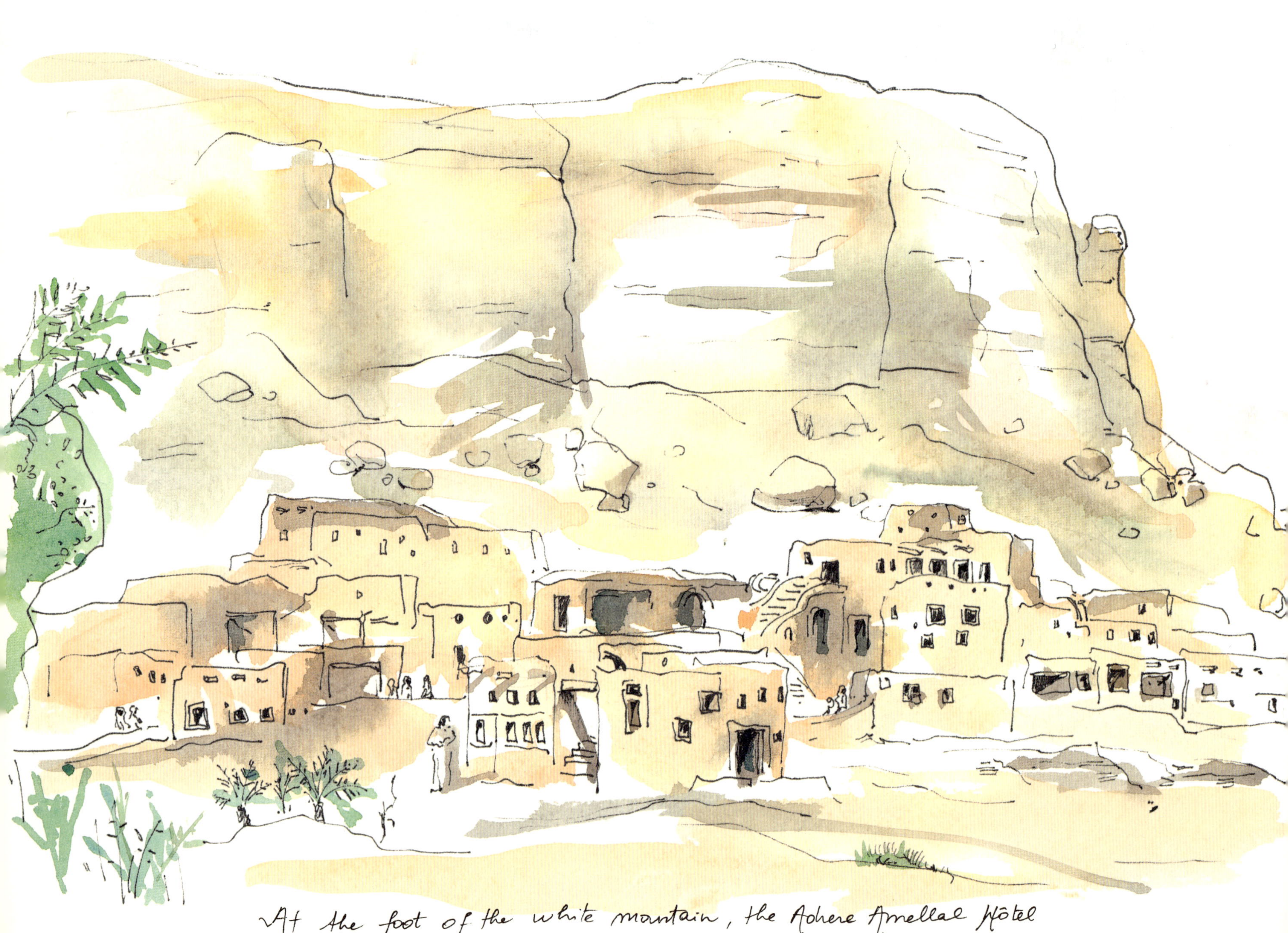

At the foot of the white mountain, the Adrere Amellal Hôtel

Siwa

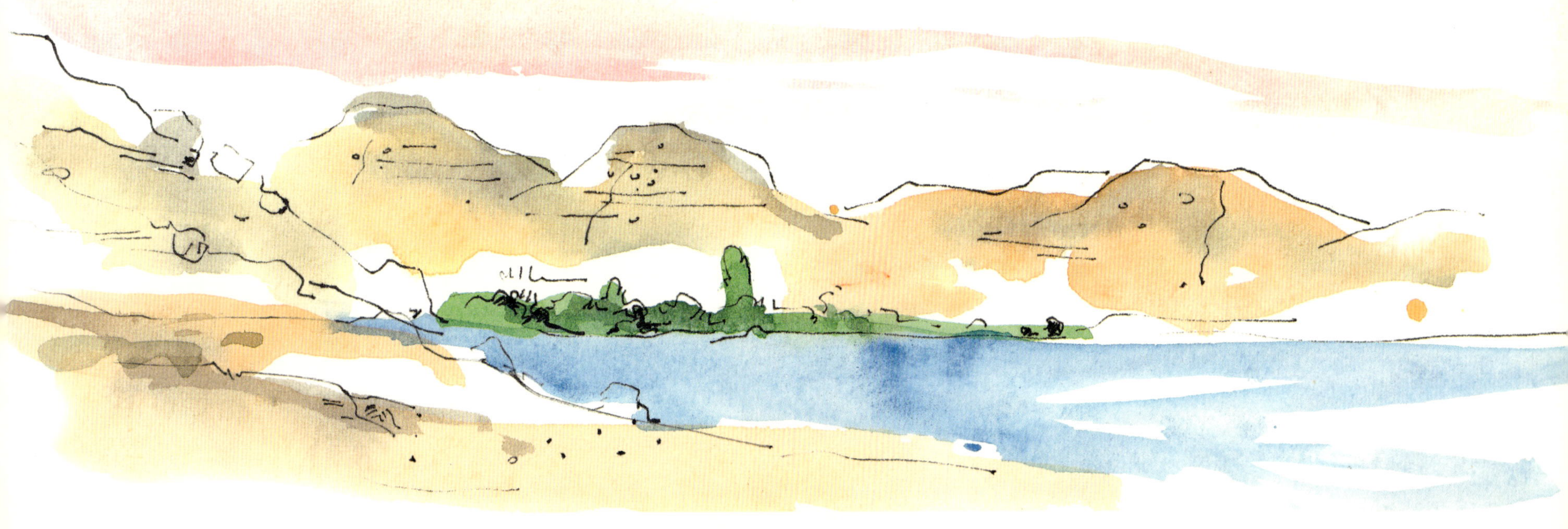

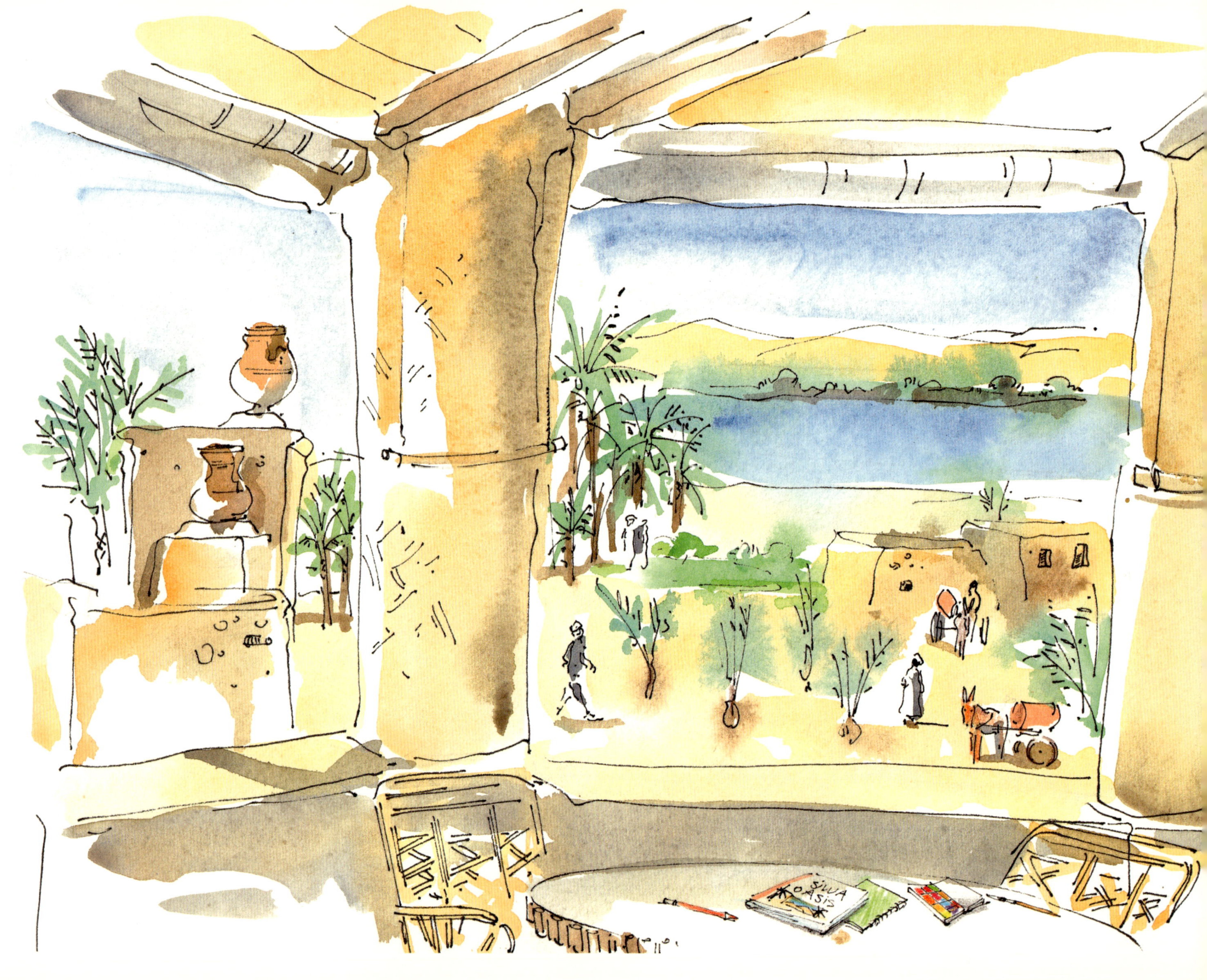

SIWA
OASIS

It is eight hours by car from Cairo to Siwa, the most mysterious of the Libyan Desert oases of north-western Egypt. Here, nestled against a white mountain, the superb Adrere Amellal Hotel emerges from its backdrop like a rock-cut temple. A veritable clay fortress constructed on the site of a Berber village, the Adrere Amellal is surrounded by a salt-water lake in the heart of a vast palm grove. This magical place owes its existence to Mounir Neamatalla, its owner and designer, as well as to his sister Leyla, in charge of the decoration. They wanted to recreate a simple yet elegant traditional dwelling—telephones and electricity have no place in the thirty-four rooms spread out over eight buildings. "I salvaged what I could by respecting traditional architectural techniques: cob for the structure and palm leaves for the roof," explains Mounir, an ecologist and environmental activist. All the rooms are unique. They are lit by beeswax candles reflected by the thousands of little white shells covering the walls. At night, the atmos-phere is magical: men in the traditional dress of Siwa light hundreds of torches, which like illuminated paths guide the guests to the vari-ous dining rooms where succulent morsels await them. Each day, the gifted chef Atef uses organic garden vegetables in traditional recipes using clay dishes and a wood fire: beet leaves stuffed with cilantro, date soufflé, and chicken and pomegranate *tagine* (stew), to name but a few.

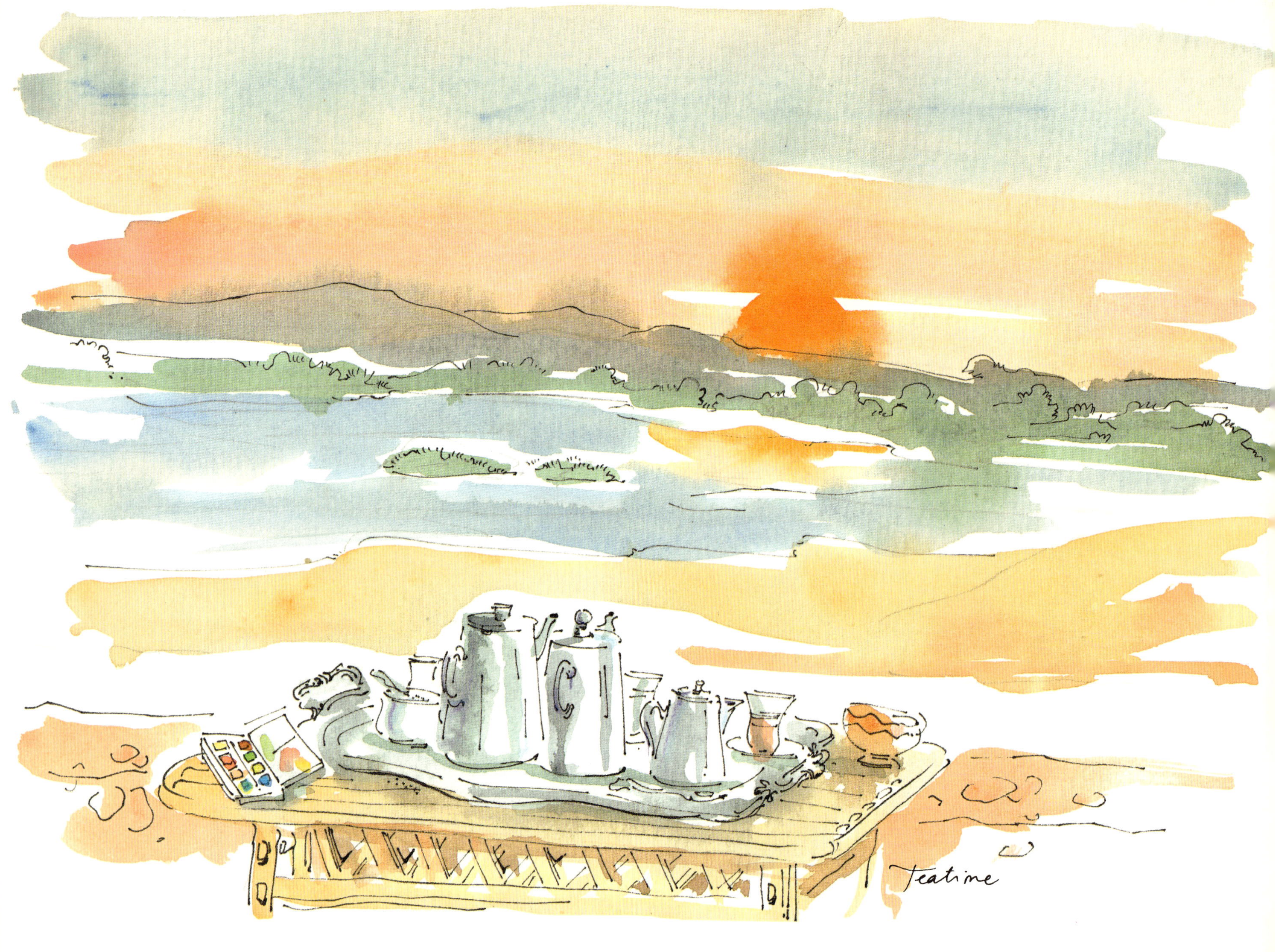
Teatime

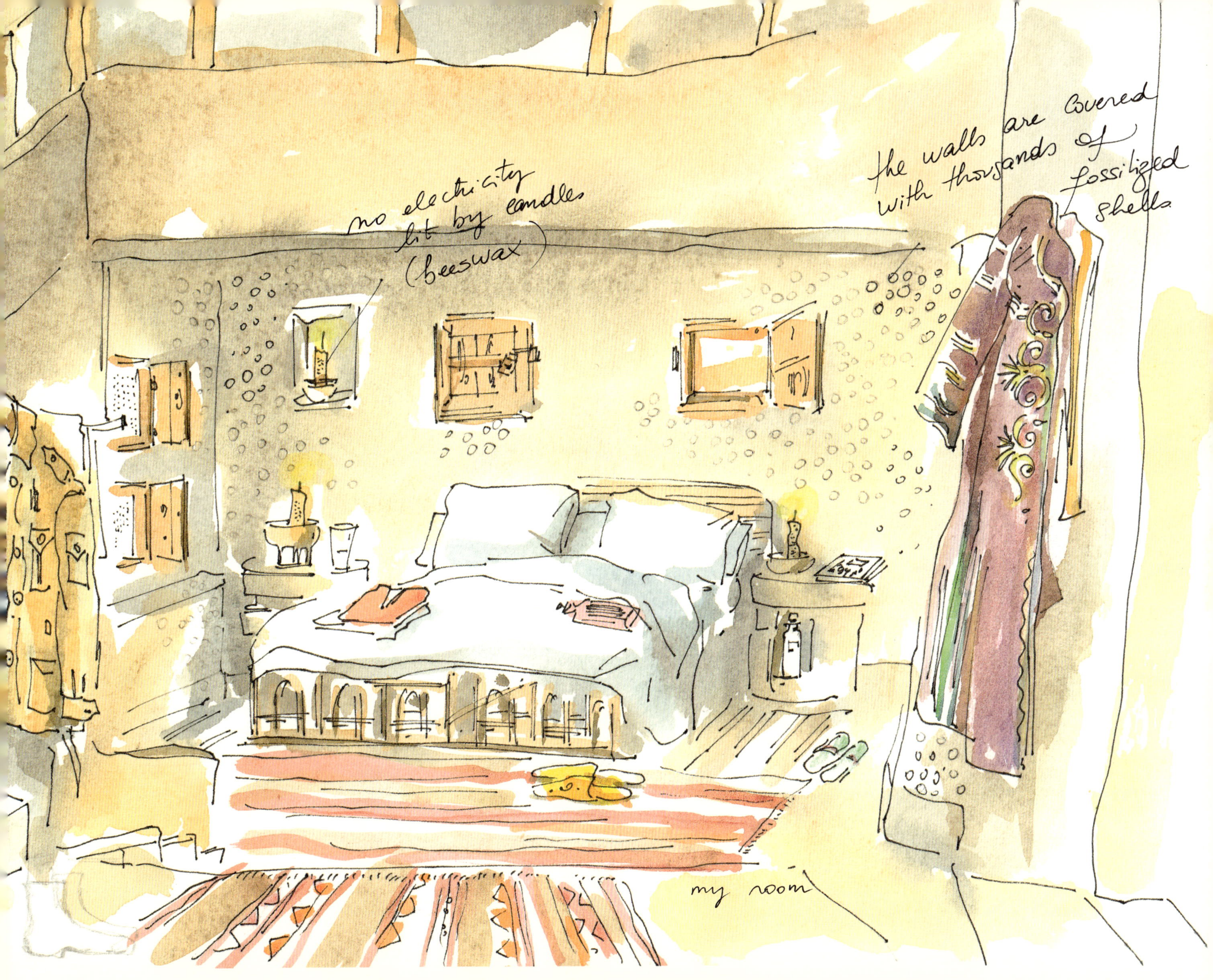

no electricity
lit by candles
(beeswax)
the walls are covered
with thousands of
fossilized
shells
my room

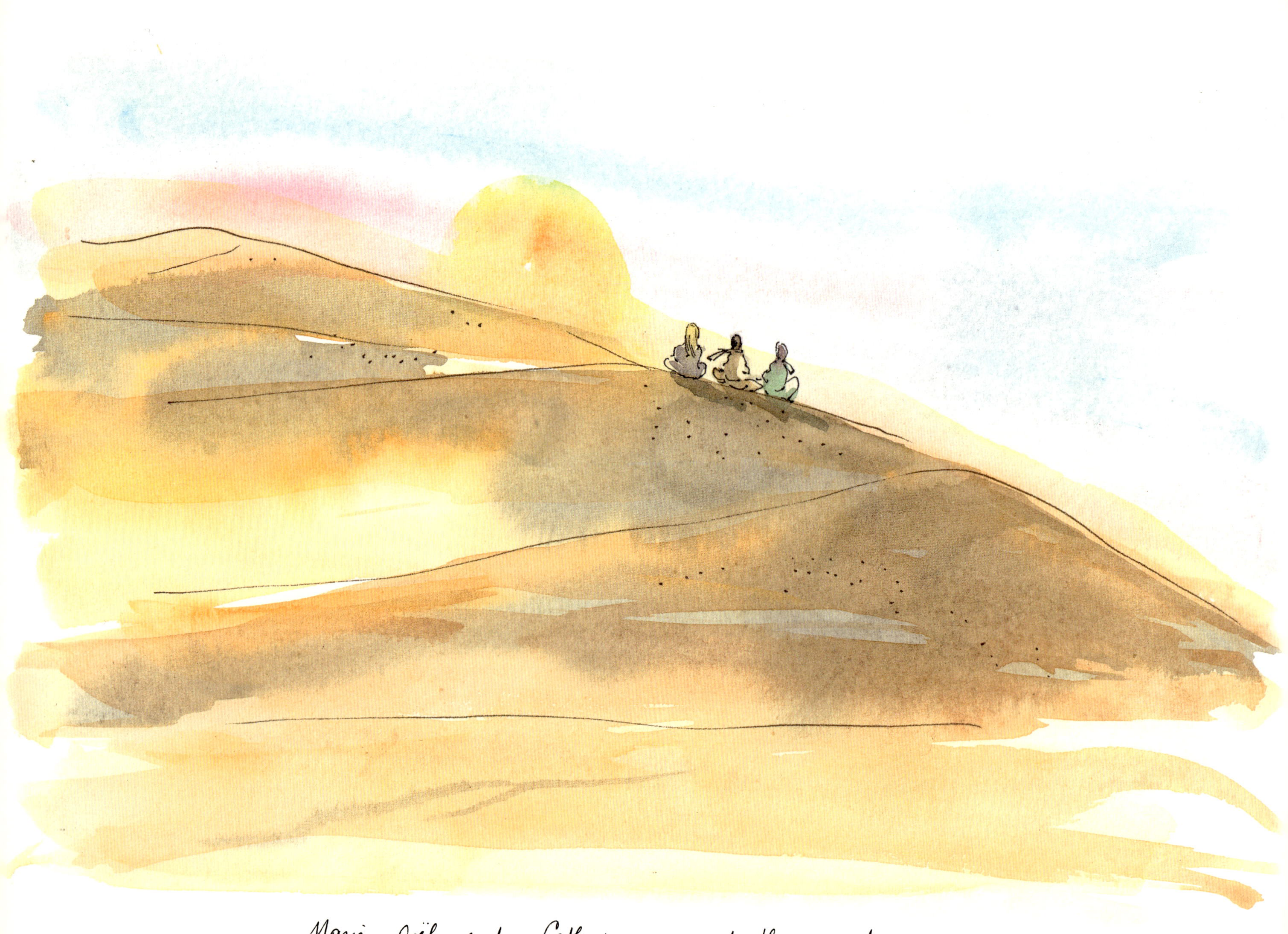

Marie, Joël, and Catherine gaze at the sunset

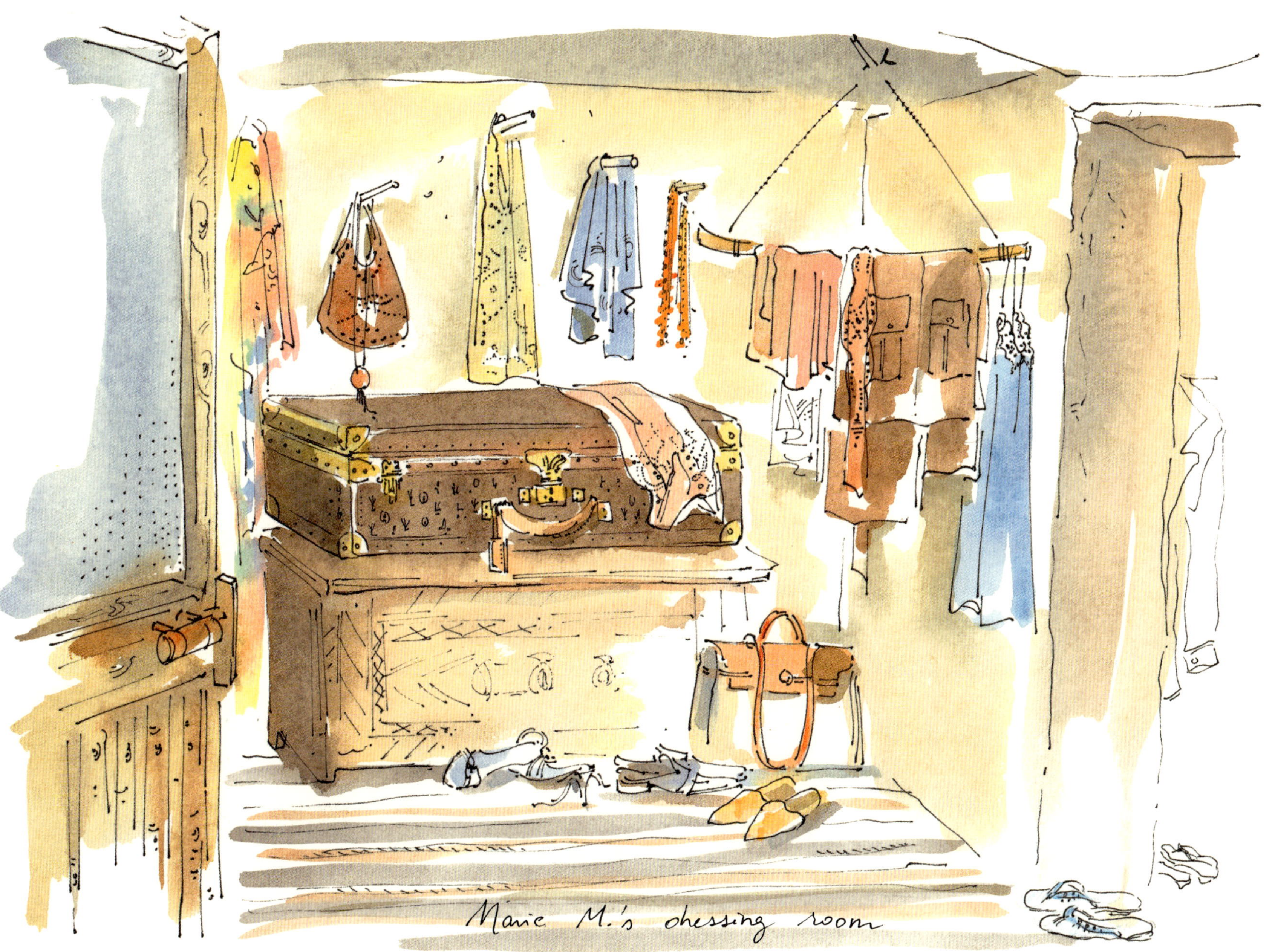

Marie M.'s dressing room

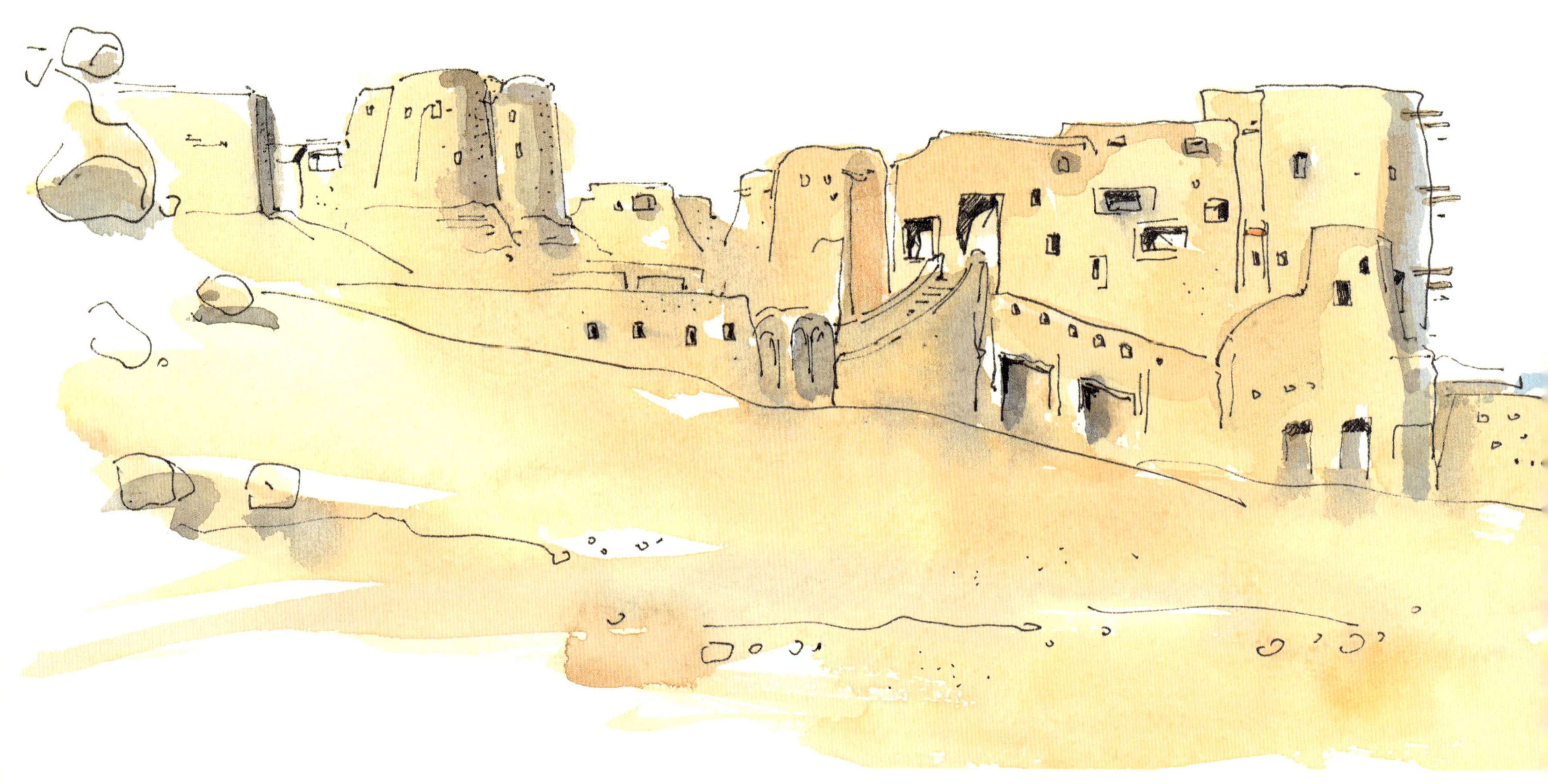

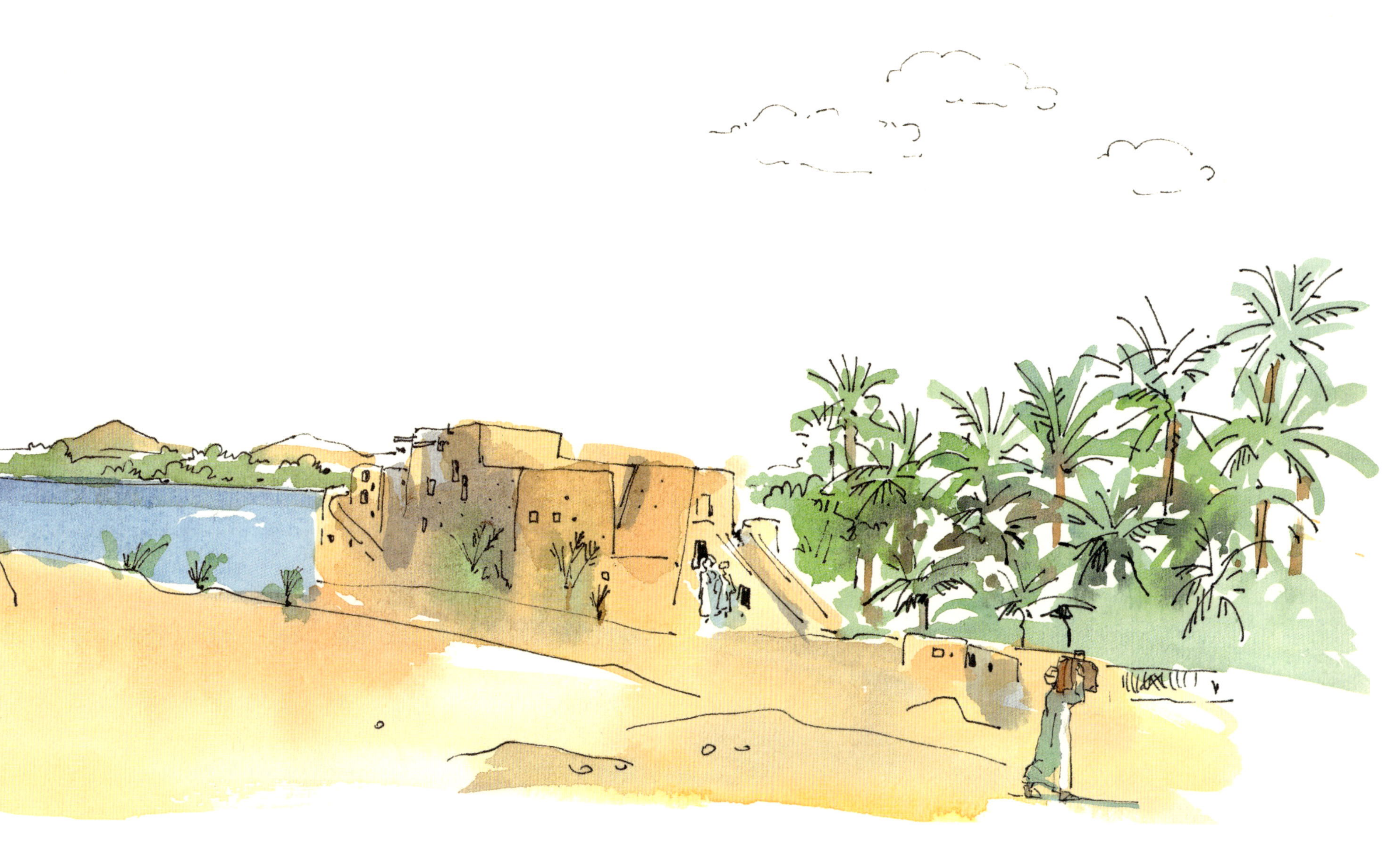

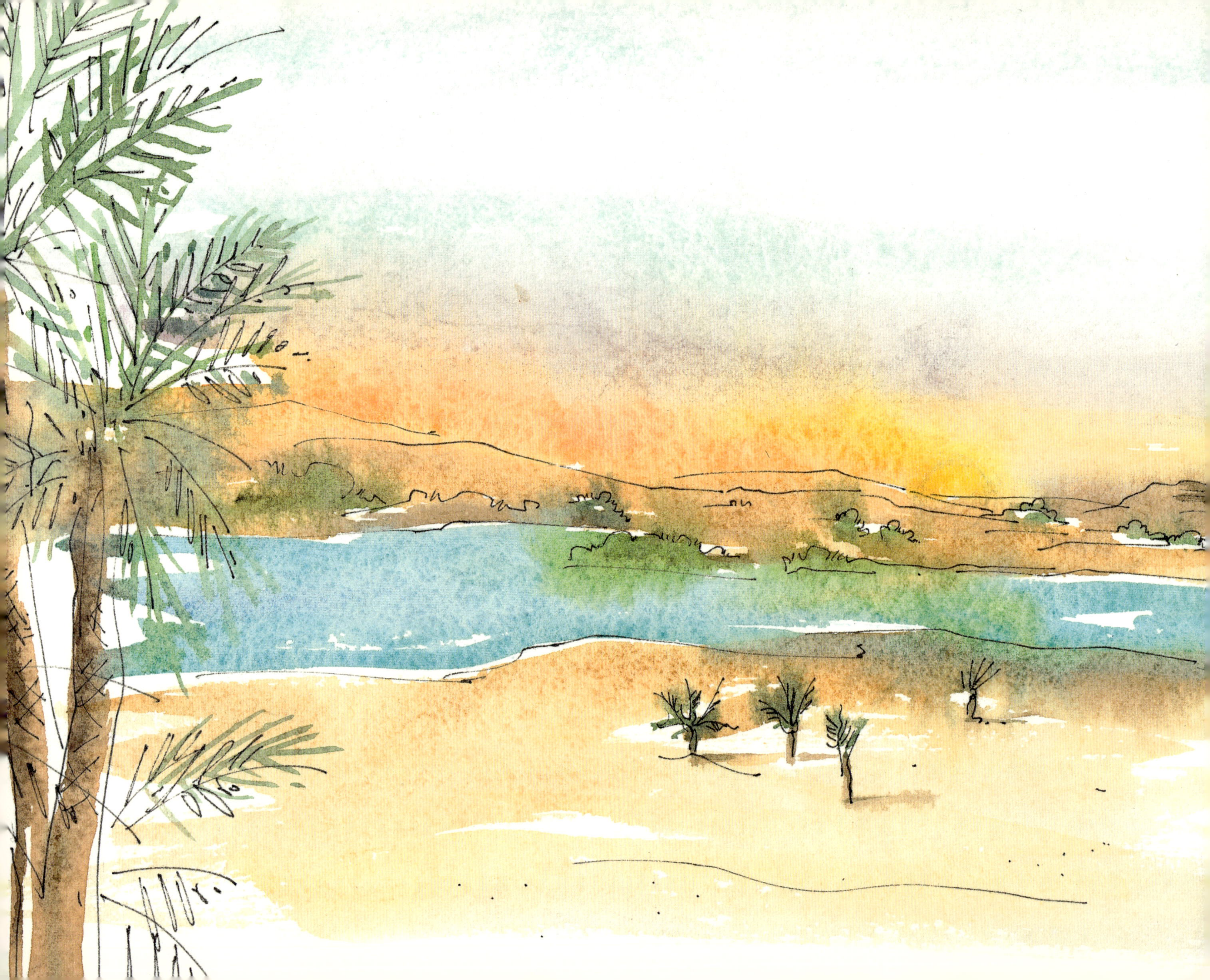

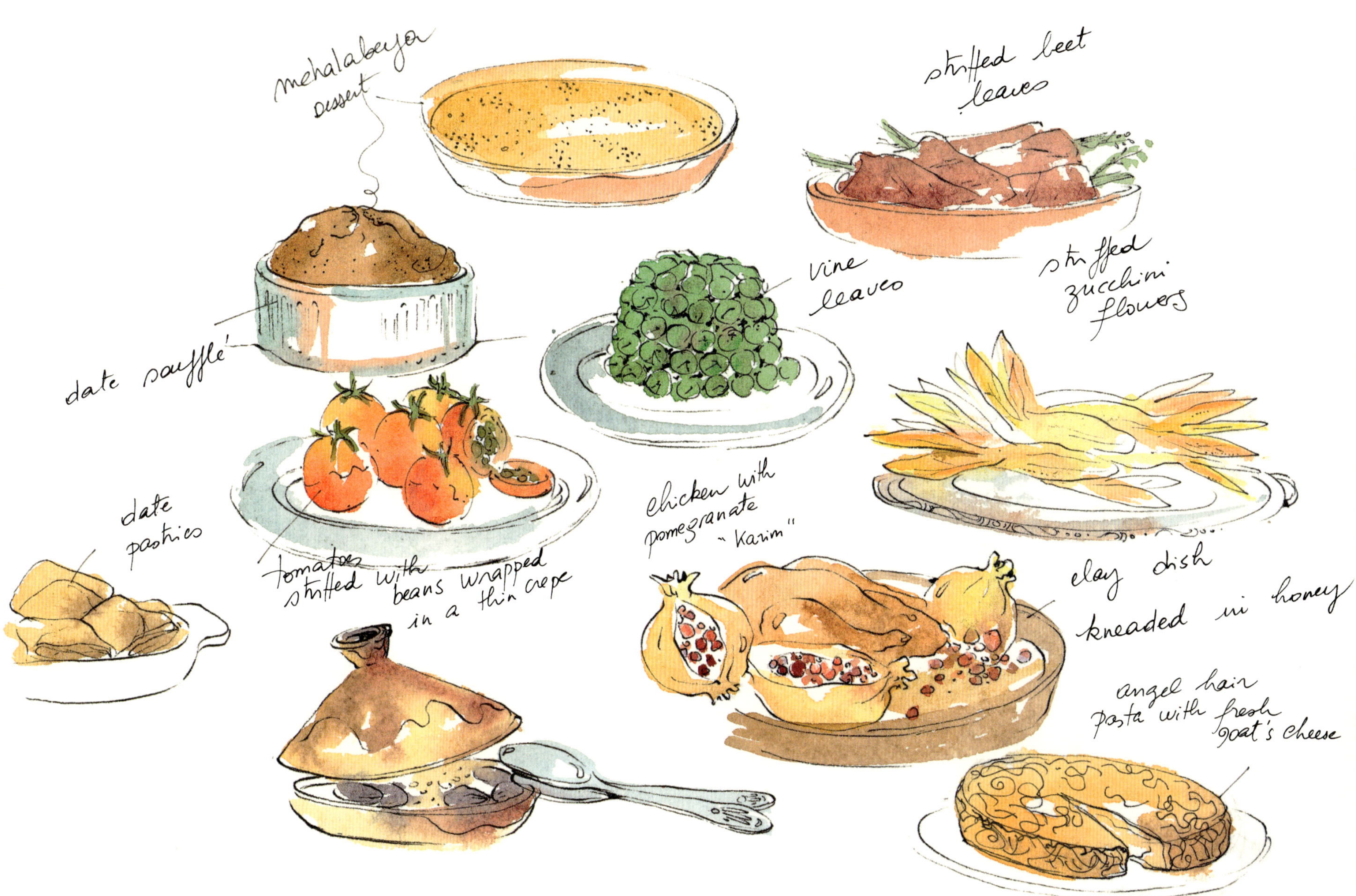

mehalabeya
dessert
stuffed beet
leaves
date soufflé
vine
leaves
stuffed
zucchini
flowers
date
pastries
tomatoes
stuffed with
beans wrapped
in a thin crepe
chicken with
pomegranate
"Karim"
clay dish
kneaded in honey
angel hair
pasta with fresh
goat's cheese

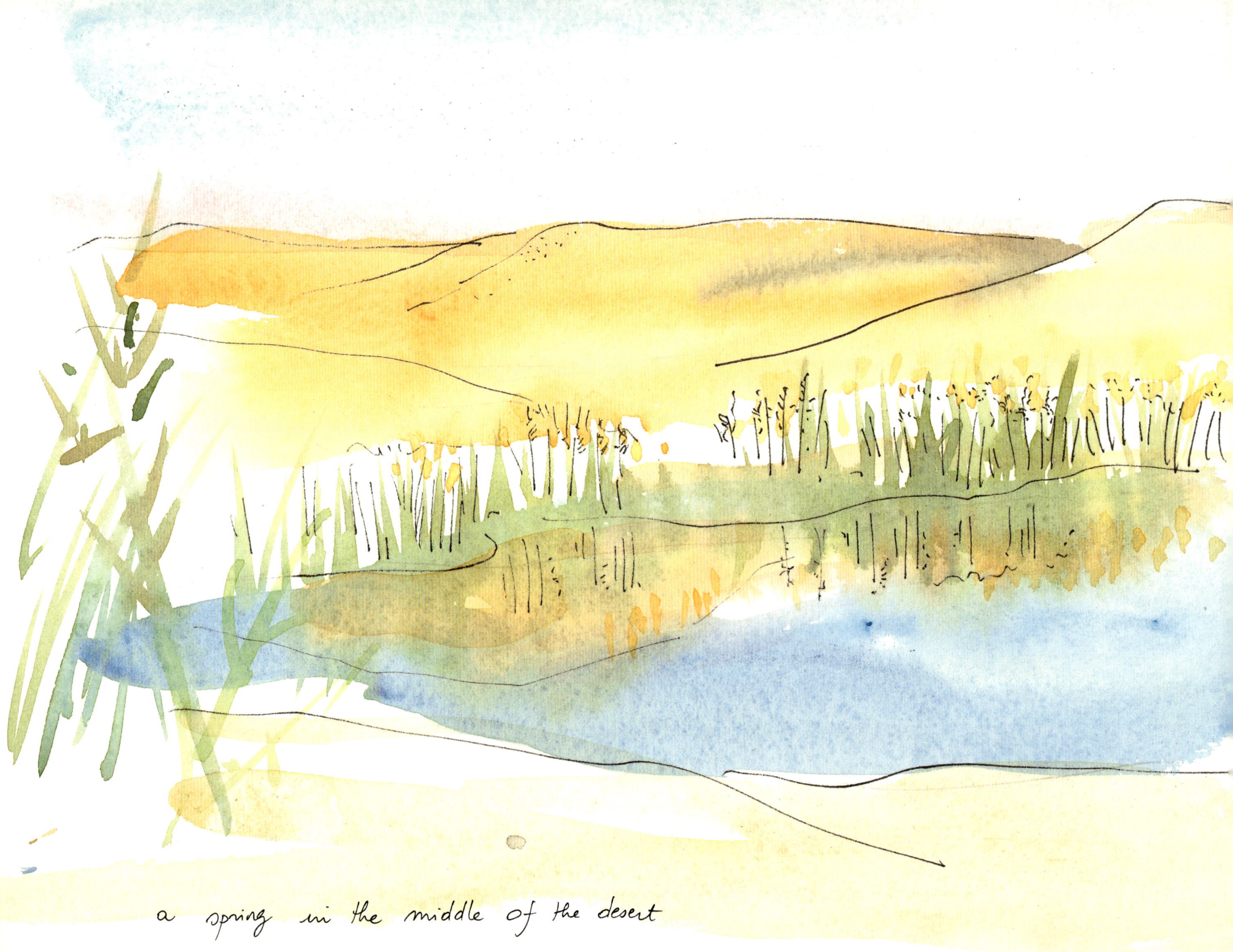

a spring in the middle of the desert

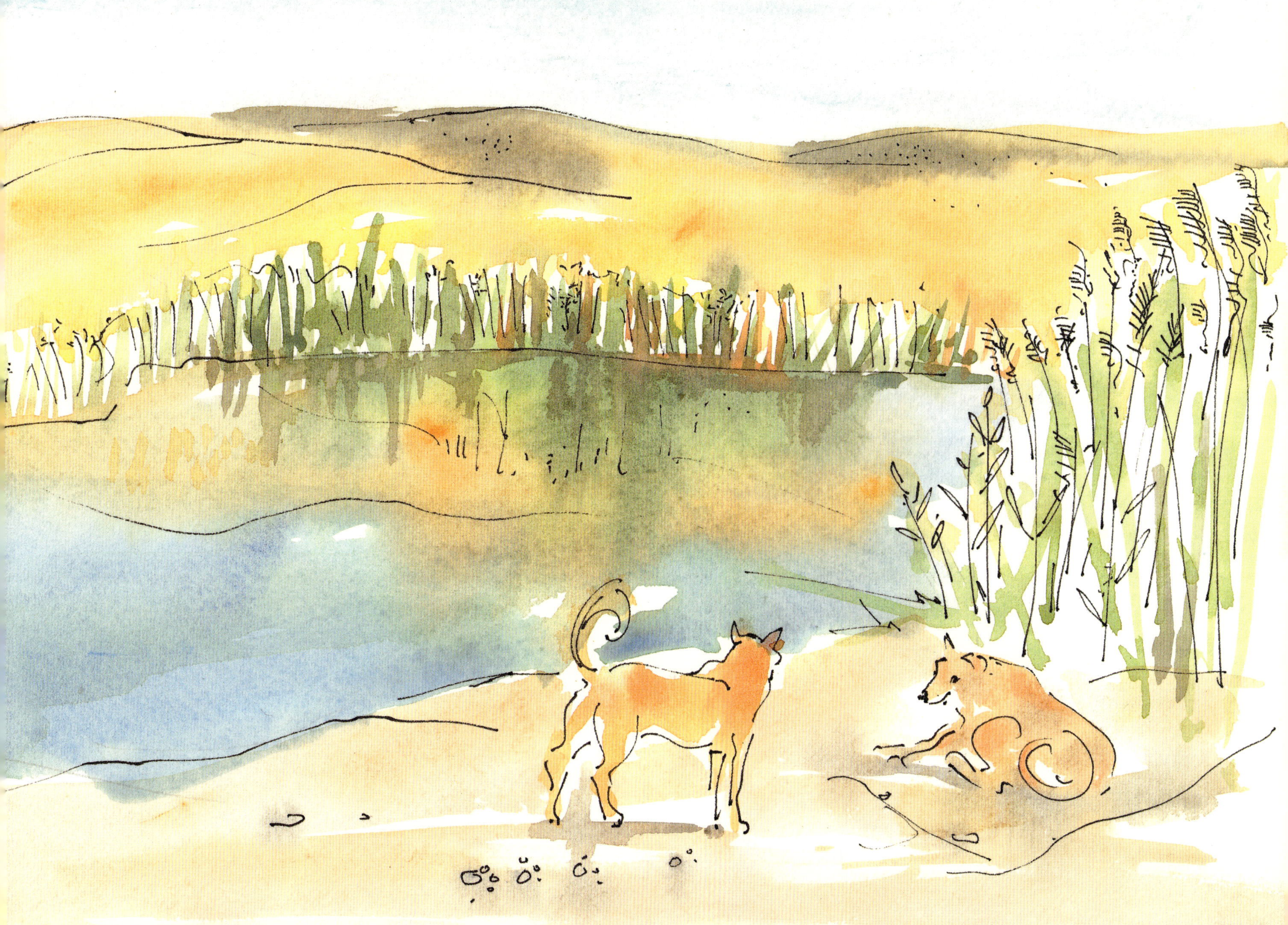

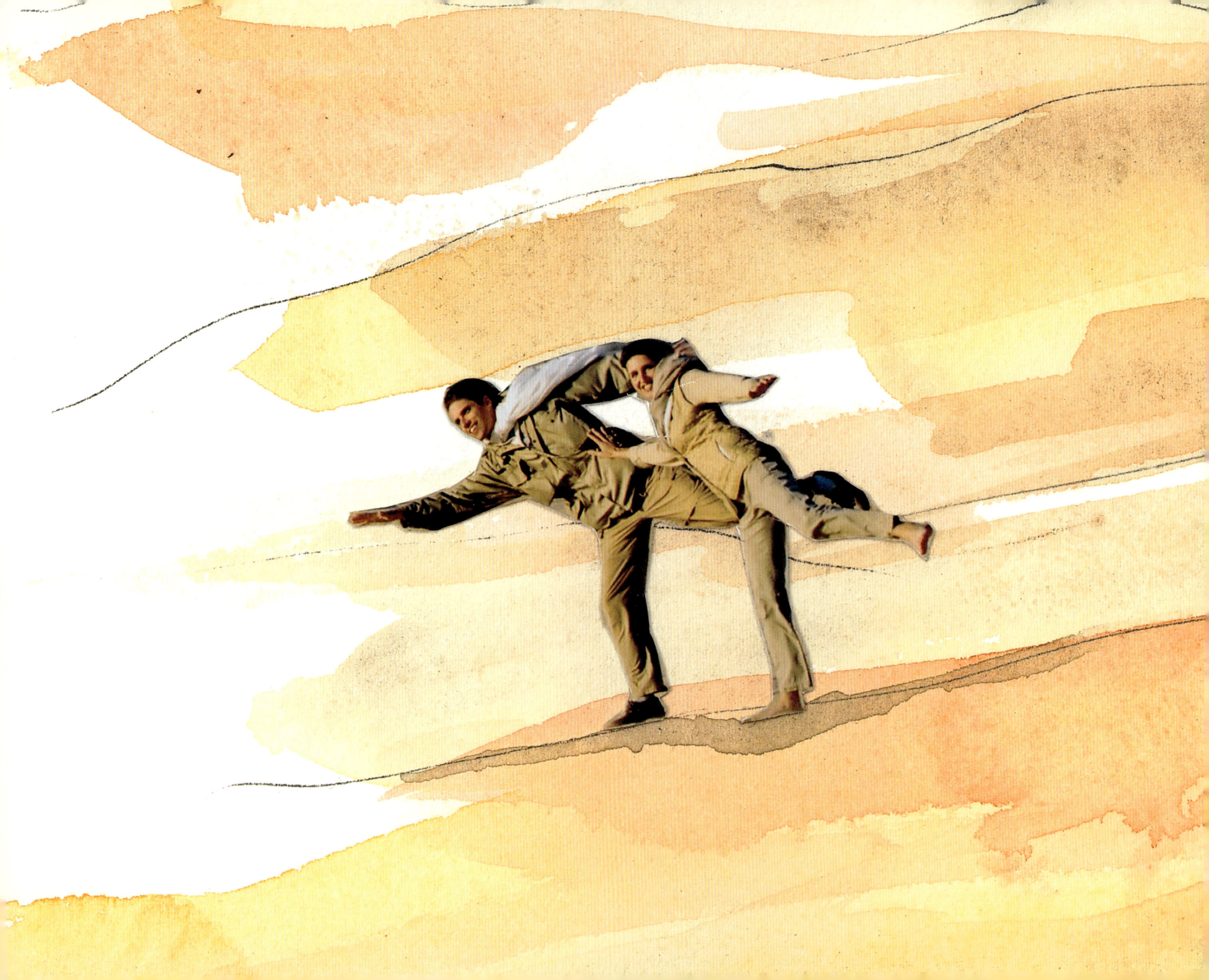

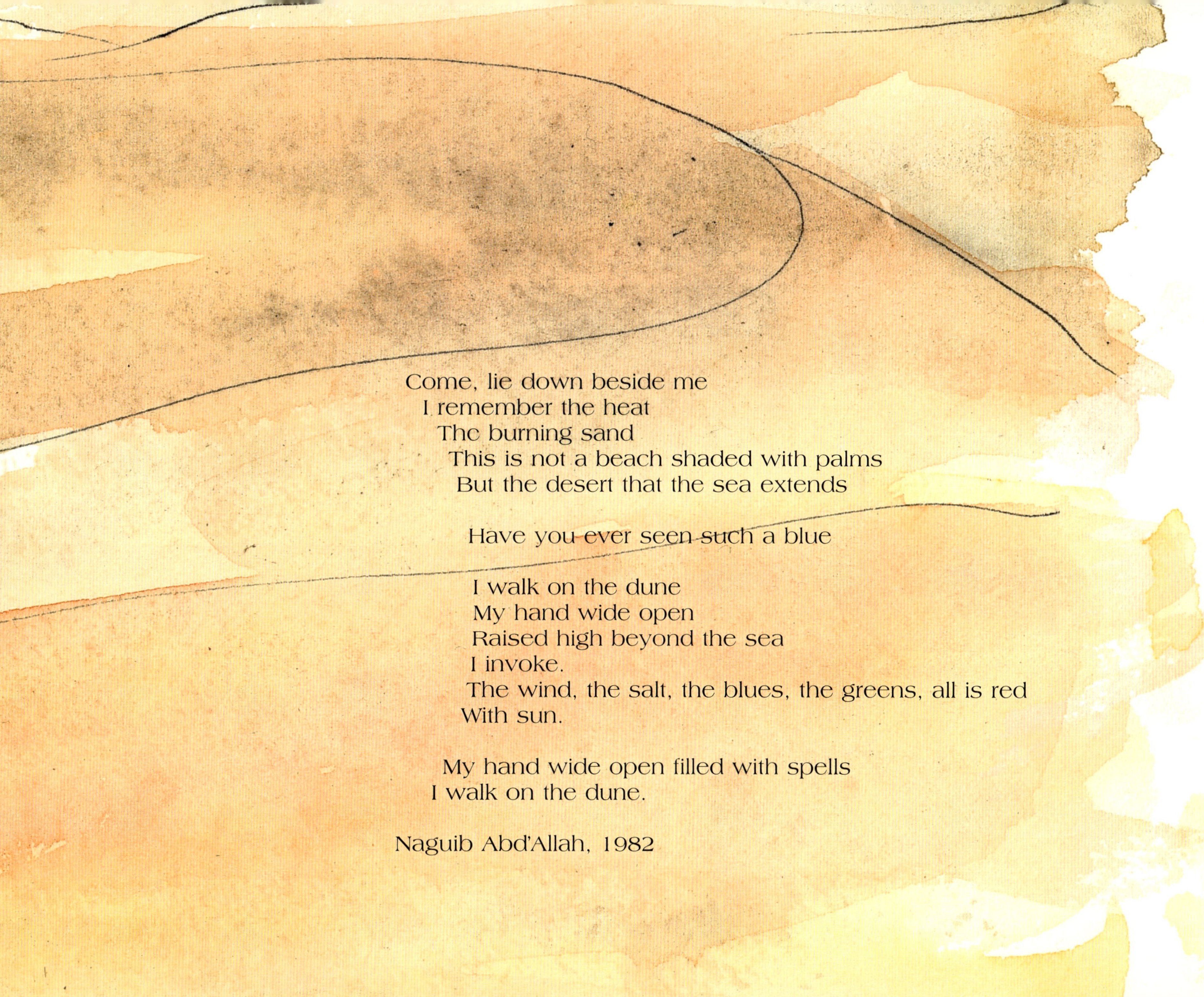

Come, lie down beside me
I remember the heat
The burning sand
This is not a beach shaded with palms
But the desert that the sea extends

Have you ever seen such a blue

I walk on the dune
My hand wide open
Raised high beyond the sea
I invoke.
The wind, the salt, the blues, the greens, all is red
With sun.

My hand wide open filled with spells
I walk on the dune.

Naguib Abd'Allah, 1982

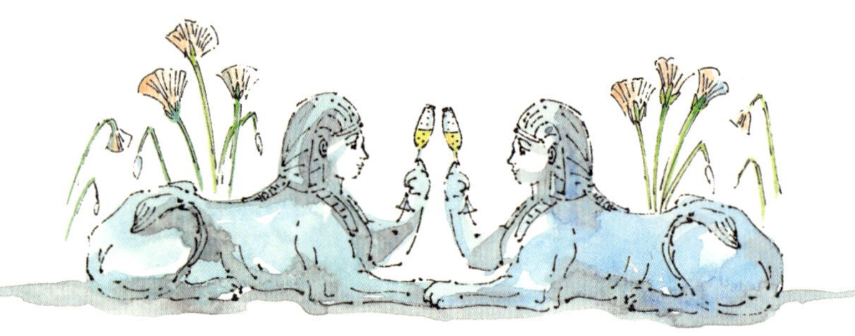

Thank you to the Egyptian friends who opened the doors of their country to me: Naguib Abd'Allah, Mounir Neamatalla, Jaqueline & Farouk Younes, Amr Khalil, and Zina & Karim Wissa

My deepest gratitude to Christiane Desroches Noblecourt for writing the preface.

Thanks to Estelle Arielle Bouchet for her invaluable help, as well as to Henrietta and Christopher Mac Call.

Many thanks to Jacques Martin Tardivat and Mahmoud Ibrahim for introducing me to Banque Misr.

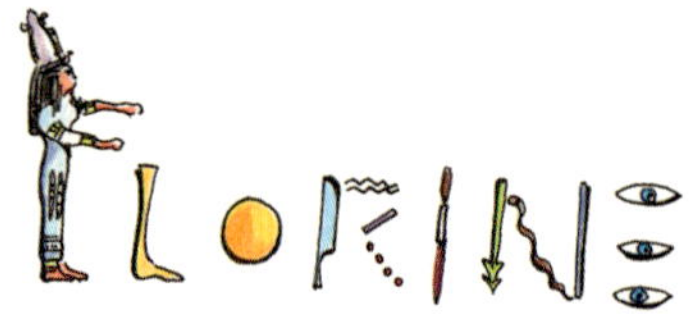

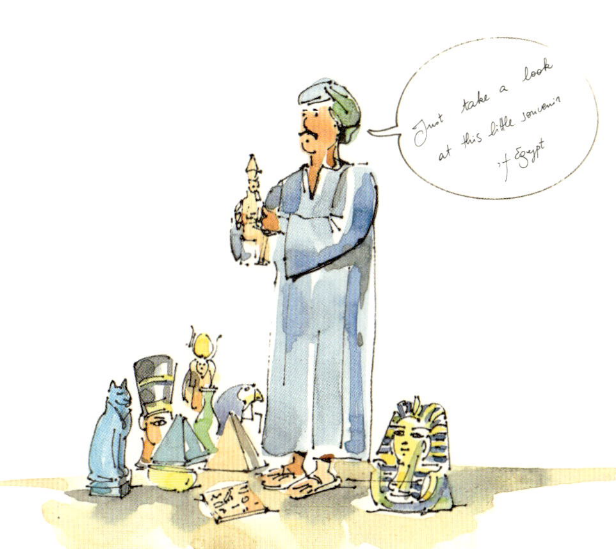

Just take a look
at this little souvenir
of Egypt

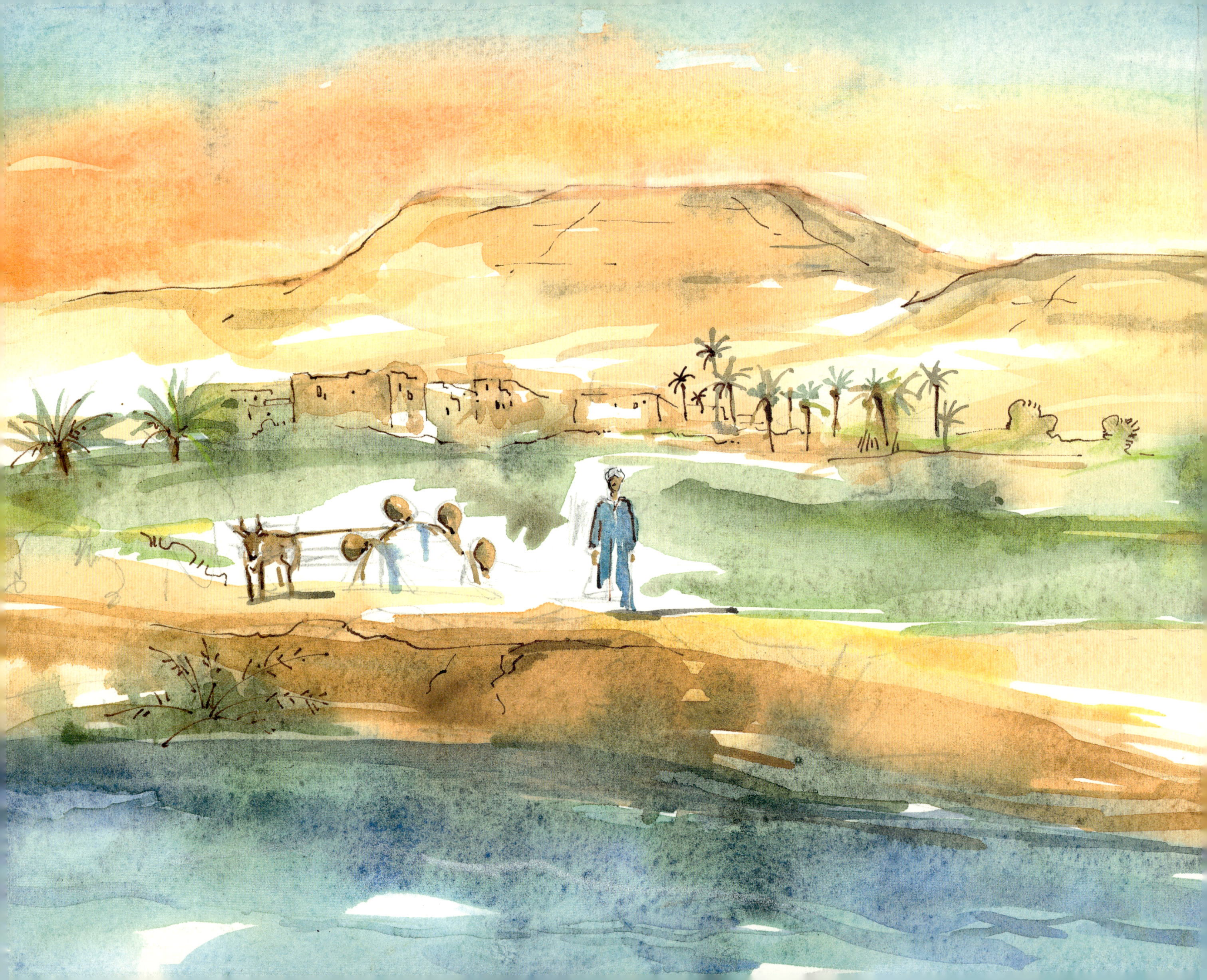